Dr Raj Persaud is a consultant psychiatrist working at London's Maudsley Hospital, the author of the critically acclaimed books *Staying Sane* and *From the Edge of the Couch*, and the presenter of various Radio 4 series including *All in the Mind*. Unusually for a psychiatrist he also holds a degree in psychology which he obtained with First Class Honours. He has received numerous academic awards and prizes for the innovative nature of his research, including the prestigious Royal College of Psychiatrists Research Medal and Prize, the Morris Markowe Prize and the Maudsley Hospital's own Denis Hill Prize, as well as the exclusive medical award the Osler Medal. In 2004 he was appointed Gresham Professor for Public Understanding of Psychiatry. In 2002 the *Independent on Sunday* conducted a poll amongst members of the Royal College of Psychiatrists and the Institute of Psychiatry to discover who were the top ten psychiatrists in the UK as rated by fellow clinicians. Dr Raj Persaud was the youngest doctor to make it into this esteemed list. He lives in London.

In 2004, the *Times* newspaper voted him one of the top twenty gurus in the world.

Critical Acclaim for Dr Raj Persaud

Simply Irresistible

'In his new book Dr Raj Persaud shows you not only how to increase your attractiveness but how, once you're in a relationship, you can improve your sex life and spot if your partner is unfaithful. Some of the most fascinating relationship tips you'll discover this year'
Daily Mail

'Revealed: the lost art of seduction. Today's wannabe lotharios have a host of advice on how to lure the object of their desire, but the real answers are timeless according to *Simply Irresistible*'
The Scotsman

'*Simply Irresistible* explores the laws of seduction by examining how best to behave on a date and the ways in which we can physically improve our chances of finding a partner'
Scotland on Sunday

The Motivated Mind

'The proof of the pudding is in the eating, and Raj's direct application of his motivational theories to three case-studies on our programme was an unqualified success. The plan works!'
Richard & Judy, Channel 4

'Not where you want to be in life but frustrated by fluffy self-help books? *The Motivated Mind* could be the read you need. Dr Raj Persaud has produced a fascinating, intellectual essay on the secrets behind success and fulfilment. This book helps you gain real understanding of how your mind works and how, unwittingly, you may be sabotaging your happiness'
Health and Fitness

SIMPLY IRRESISTIBLE

The Psychology of Seduction

How to Catch and Keep
Your Perfect Partner

RAJ PERSAUD

BANTAM BOOKS

LONDON • TORONTO • SYDNEY • AUCKLAND • JOHANNESBURG

TRANSWORLD PUBLISHERS
61-63 Uxbridge Road, London W5 5SA
A Random House Group Company
www.rbooks.co.uk

SIMPLY IRRESISTIBLE
A BANTAM BOOK: 9780553817775

First published in Great Britain
in 2006 by Bantam Press
a division of Transworld Publishers
Bantam edition published 2008

Addresses for Random House Group Ltd companies outside the UK
can be found at: www.randomhouse.co.uk
The Random House Group Ltd Reg. No. 954009

The Random House Group Limited makes every effort to ensure that the
papers used in our books are made from trees that have been legally
sourced from well-managed and credibly certified forests. Our paper
procurement policy can be found on www.randomhouse.co.uk

Typeset in 11/14pt Sabon by
Falcon Oast Graphic Art Ltd.

Printed in the UK by CPI Cox & Wyman, Reading, RG1 8EX.

2 4 6 8 10 9 7 5 3 1

This is for Asha, our delightful daughter,
who inspired the title of this book.

Love one another and you will be happy.
It's as simple and as difficult as that.

Michael Leunig

CONTENTS

Acknowledgements   13

Introduction: Help! I Need Somebody   17

1   The Sinner Takes It All
    Understanding the basic rules of attraction   31

2   All You Bleed Is Love?
    How the science of psychology can help
    your relationships   50

3   Don't You Want Me?
    Dating with confidence   70

4   The Aim of the Game
    How to flirt   101

5   Take a Chance On Me
    Hey there, risk taker – spend a little time
    with me?   128

6   Knowing Me, Knowing Who?
    Detecting deception in relationships, and
    knowing how and when to trust   146

7   Then I Saw Her Face
    Is your face your fortune?   164

8   Body Talk
    What is the perfect body, and why?   178

9   Let's Talk About Sex
    Quick and dirty   197

10 Don't Take Your Love to Town
    Sleeping around   212

11 Love Is a Stranger in an Open Bar
    How to know who is right for you   244

12 Will You Still Need Me When I'm
    Sixty-four?
    Making it last   266

13 If You Can't Give Me Love, Honey,
    That Ain't Enough
    Breakdown, divorce and separation   284

14 Conclusion: Simply the Best?   305

Notes   315
Index   337

ACKNOWLEDGEMENTS

Economists have calculated what a good marriage is worth: it's approximately £100,000 a year. This is what it would cost if you went out to purchase on the free market all the services a loyal spouse provides, such as companionship, catering, psychotherapy, nursing, sexual and childcare services. It's a robust exercise to ask your partner to guess what monetary value he or she would put on your relationship, for the answer can be quite revealing, if not a bit disturbing – not least if your estimation is at marked variance with theirs!

I was inspired to write this book because I strongly believe those economists are seriously off beam. I think a great marriage is, quite simply, invaluable. As I argued in my first book, *Staying Sane*, choose your life partner carefully because it's the one key decision that will have more bearing on the future of your mental health than practically any other you will make in your life. Recent research evidence suggests that an unhappy marriage raises your chances of developing clinical depression by a factor approaching thirty.

I am extremely lucky in that the person who agreed to marry me, my wonderful wife Francesca, continues to make me feel more blessed with every passing day of our marriage. I wrote this book because I would wish this kind of good fortune for everyone else. I have seen at first hand how transformative an experience meeting the right person can be.

Thanks must go to my agent Maggie Pearlstine and her assistant Jamie Crawford who continue to be invaluable partners in all my book projects, as is my editor Brenda Kimber at Transworld.

Vanessa Cameron, the chief executive of the Royal College of Psychiatrists; my clinical director at the Maudsley Hospital, Dr Frank Holloway, as well as the medical director, Dr David Roy; Steve Davidson, our local directorate manager; Steve Bell, the chief executive of the Maudsley Hospital; Dr George Szmukler, the Dean of the Institute of Psychiatry; and Professor Robin Murray continue to support my efforts to disseminate psychiatric knowledge, and I am grateful to them all.

I am particularly indebted to all at Gresham College in the City of London. When, in 2004, my professorship was established there, the college became the first educational institution in the world to provide a platform for the public understanding of psychiatry.

Finally, I continue to be beholden to my NHS secretary Sheila Banks and all at the Bethlem Royal Hospital where my in-patient ward is based – the second oldest public hospital in the UK and the institution from which the word Bedlam is derived. Sadly, Bedlam characterizes the state of many people's affiliations. I hope this book will make a small contribution to improving the way in which those unaware of current psychological research approach and handle their relationships.

INTRODUCTION:
HELP! I NEED SOMEBODY

> To laugh often and love much ... to appreciate beauty,
> to find the best in others, to give one's self ... this is to
> have succeeded.
>
> Ralph Waldo Emerson

SCIENTISTS HAVE A REPUTATION FOR BEING WHITE-COATED
bespectacled nerds or geeks who need to get out more, so
why turn to science, in particular the science of
psychology, to try to improve our relationships – or, even
more prosaically, in order to get a date?

Well, one recent contribution of science to the understanding of love is getting a handle on how attraction
actually works. Is it the mysterious poetic process as
traditionally viewed by the arts, or does it actually obey
certain laws? If it does conform to rules, can we use them
to enhance our attraction to the opposite sex and even
develop better, more fulfilling relationships? Neuroscientists have begun to study those parts of our lives
which have so far resisted easy explanation – love, lust
and attraction – using new technologies such as brain

scanners, undreamed of only a few years ago. We now know what is actually going on in a brain when a person sees an attractive member of the opposite (or indeed same) sex.

I put science to the test in this respect by agreeing to take part in a speed-dating experiment for a BBC programme. In speed-dating you meet a large number of people but only for a short time, in this case just three minutes. Then a whistle is blown and the men move tables to sit with a new woman. The couples have another three minutes in which to get to know each other before the whistle blows again and the men have to move on. At the end of the evening each person fills out a form, ticking boxes to provide a record of who they met and the level of their interest in them – mere friendship, or something more intense?

Making a positive impression in just three minutes is quite a tough proposition, but given that a large number of people get to rate your attractiveness to them, particularly in comparison with a large number of others, it seemed to the BBC to provide a perfect opportunity to test some of the theories of attraction I was proposing. Initially I was less keen on the idea, anxious about the potential impact on the ego of the brutal feedback one might experience. I have been happily married to my lovely wife Francesca for over eleven years and would normally have no interest whatsoever in any kind of dating, speedy or slow – though it is remarkable how many married men I meet are fiercely jealous that I have been speed-dating! My nervousness about the upcoming 'experiment' was compounded by the fact that the number of women who ticked, or didn't tick, the box indicating a romantic interest in me was going to be broadcast nationally to an audience of millions. The potential for personal humiliation seemed enormous (did I mention that already?). Adding further to my nerves was the fact that I spent my entire adolescence completely unable to secure a date, despite colossal effort. My wife hates it whenever I declare this as it implies she has married a 'loser' – to use her word.

However, not having been particularly successful with the opposite sex provided an added twist to the experiment: could my knowledge and use of the latest attraction research salvage my dating record from the dismal depths? The producer of the programme was certainly looking forward to the experiment, which was being covertly recorded, though I was still a bag of nerves. The other participants on the genuine speed-dating event that night had been told the BBC were recording it but hadn't been briefed that an experiment was being conducted or precisely who was the guinea pig.

We used a subtle disguise to try to prevent participants recognizing me from my television appearances and it did not appear that anyone 'clocked' me.

I had a chat with some of the male speed-daters who were having a drink at the bar to steady their nerves and asked them if they were going to be using any tactics or strategies. They gave me a blank look and insisted that they were going to be 'just themselves' and had no plans to use any particular 'devices'. I had to hold myself back from responding, 'Have you ever wondered *why* you are single? It's because you are being too much like your normal self. Time to try some tactics!'

I met nine women that evening and used some techniques derived from the latest research on seduction and attraction, which I will be exploring later in this book. The plan was that the BBC producer would collect the women's ratings of me from the organizers later that evening and I could ring the next day to find out my 'score'. The next morning at one minute past nine I rang in and the producer answered the phone on the *fifth ring* (not that I was anxious about the result or anything). I asked her how it had gone and she replied that she thought the recording was going to make a great programme. 'Forget that!' I said agitatedly. 'How many women ticked the box for future romance?' It turned out that nine out of the nine women I had met the previous night wanted to meet me again for possible intimacy. That I 'scored' 100 per cent, particularly given the baseline I started from, is a strong vindication, I believe, of the power of the latest findings about the psychology of attraction. It's just such a pity I did all this research *after* I got married . . .

One key reason why men and women are not as good at seducing each other as they might like to be is that there are important gender differences in the way the sexes think and view the world. This means it's difficult for most of us to get into the minds of the opposite sex, or your adversary as it were, in order to work out what they are thinking, and thus what they are looking for and what they would respond most positively to. Theory of Mind, or the branch of psychology devoted to the skill of being able to read the minds of others in order to be more able to manipulate or seduce them, is a topic I explored in depth in my previous book *The Motivated Mind*, so I won't go over that territory again here. Suffice it to say that men and women continue to find each other rather mysterious, and this explains the plethora of misunderstandings between them.

One key gender difference psychology has uncovered recently is that women value high status in men, but men put less store on this and place greater emphasis on physical appearance. One theory for this is that women have a menopause, which means there is a definite period later in their lives when they are no longer fertile, and fertility drops off dramatically during a period prior to that. Men don't experience quite the same profound change in fertility later in life, though it too declines. Older men can father children long after women are too old to bear them. According to evolutionary theory it follows that in order to maximize the chances of passing on their genes men should be particularly responsive to physical cues for youthfulness in women, and this is what modern psychology indeed finds. We will explore in greater detail which specific female features mean what to the 'neolithic' male brain as there are many myths clustered around this subject.

When it comes to what women prefer, it is useful to recall that hundreds of thousands of years ago women, being the physically weaker sex and often being burdened with pregnancy, needed protection from marauding males for whom a favourite Saturday afternoon activity was raping and pillaging. This meant women favoured men who could look after them, i.e. those who were physically strong enough to beat off any adversaries or of sufficiently high status – a tribe chieftain, or close to that position – to deter the unwanted advances of the lower orders. It is intriguing to note that the male body shape women say they prefer appears to be less focused on overall weight and instead emphasizes shape. In particular, women seem keen on the V-shaped torso that delineates a large chest and a thin waist, which is often accompanied by large pectoral muscles. It is also fascinating to observe that pectoral muscles are mainly useful for throwing punches. Hence, whether they fully know it or not, women are unconsciously drawn to men who are useful in a brawl.

Fascinating though such findings might be, you could argue that people have been attracted to each other for millennia otherwise the human race wouldn't have survived and thrived as it has done, so why do we need psychology and science to help us find a mate and be happy with them? Shouldn't we just leave it to nature to resolve these issues and not tinker with things using techniques borrowed from research?

The reason I contend that we need to understand the science of attraction more than ever today is that we now live in very different circumstances. As recently as a few hundred years ago most people were born into a community of roughly 150 souls and would live there all their lives. The number of eligible members of the opposite sex for you to unite with would have been a mere handful. The most attractive member of a community, to be frank, didn't have to be that striking to secure your attentions. Today we are much more geographically mobile; we encounter many more people so our choice is theoretically much greater. Yet we have much less time in which to meet others and really get to know them before making a decision about their appeal or compatibility. Furthermore, the media bombards us with images of gorgeous members of the opposite sex including super-models and handsome actors with whom we find ourselves consciously or unconsciously compared. It's tougher out there in the dating market place, so to speak, because expectations have been raised dramatically by these eye-catching images. Some of us as a result seek to use the most striking tactic of all in order to enhance desirability – cosmetic surgery.

Also, back in that community of a few hundred people you would already know pretty much everything there was to know about your prospective partner because you grew up with them. You knew their parents, their family and all their bad habits before having to make a decision on whether they were right for you. Contrast that with today, when you have to make a judgement on who is to be your lifetime partner with much less information. Some indication of how much things have changed in recent times is the spate of 'meet the parents' type movies: if meeting the parents really is such a big deal, this indicates how little we actually know of our lovers' backgrounds before we make some key decisions about them. How modest our knowledge is of each other's family today; a few centuries ago the families of prospective partners would not have been the strangers they are today.

I believe we need all the help we can get to lasso the best possible mate, otherwise we are going to get trampled by the herd. Not only that, I also believe that after you have secured your perfect partner, which the science of attraction can help you to do, you need to be aware of what the research tells us about gender differences and relationship dynamics, which will make us better informed in terms of techniques for keeping partners tied to us. Never before have distracting temptations been so great. It's never been tougher to keep a relationship going. Moreover, because longevity has continually increased over the centuries most marriages will now last longer than relationships were ever designed to do. They began simply as a means of propagating genes. So I will argue that we need not just to learn how to seduce more effectively, but how to continue the seduction as long as the relationship continues and keep ourselves happy and fulfilled in our affiliations. We also need to 'seduce' relatives, friends and colleagues if we are to remain popular and get what we want in terms of our wider social goals.

Life, in a fundamental sense, *is* a seduction.

As I proved during my encounter with speed-dating, I believe it is possible to achieve a 100 per cent success rate when it comes to attracting the opposite sex. In other words, attraction obeys laws which are almost as rigid as the rules of physics, but instead these are psychological laws. If you want to become more attractive to the opposite sex, you have to become good at psychology.

To kick things off, here's one psychological tip on how to get anyone to fall in love with you: identify your target person's favourite emotion, then simply go out of your way to supply that emotion in quantities that person has never experienced before. Let's take an example that is rather close to home: how would you seduce a psychiatrist? Well, psychiatrists like to feel insightful, so if you met a psychiatrist and kept subtly responding to them in a way that led them to believe they were incredibly insightful it's highly likely that psychiatrist would develop a deep bond with you. Particularly if they always felt much more insightful in your company than in anyone else's. You don't have to be so crass as to keep complimenting them on how insightful they are; you could more subtly respond to them in such a way that they got a strong sense their insights were amazing and constantly welcome.

I made this point once on a TV programme with a popular male presenter, who immediately responded with, 'But, Raj, I am always saying how insightful you are. Does that mean we are going to fall in love?'

'No,' I observed drily, 'but I do quite like your company.'

The first thing we need to do before we launch into this book is establish what type of person you are when it comes to relationships. Are you someone who prefers to remain single for long periods? Or perhaps you like dating, but nothing too serious? Maybe you're someone who prefers long-term relationships, or someone who is strictly monogamous and looking for the one big relationship in your life.

The reason why it might be useful to conduct this personality test, which is adapted from the kind used in psychological research, is that the key to finding the right person for you starts with something that appears as simple as knowing yourself. However, self knowledge is not quite as straightforward as it might first appear.

Quite often the reason we make bad choices is not the

fault of our partner, but because we think we are a certain kind of personality when in fact the reality is quite different. Knowing yourself is the first step to finding the right person for you.

ARE YOU BETTER OFF SINGLE, DATING, COMMITTED OR MARRIED TO SOMEONE?

Single, Dating, Committed or Married Scale

Each statement is followed by two possible responses: agree or disagree. Read each statement carefully and decide which response best describes how you feel. Then tick the corresponding box. Please reply to every statement. If you are not completely sure which answer is more accurate, tick the one you feel is most appropriate. Do not read the scoring explanation before filling out the questionnaire. Do not spend too long on each statement. It is important that you answer each question as honestly as possible.

		AGREE	DISAGREE
1	Breaking off relationships that make me unhappy is easy	A	B
2	After fights with friends, I need to make amends quickly	B	A
3	People leaving me is not a danger I worry about	A	B
4	After an argument I feel lonely	B	A

		AGREE	DISAGREE
5	Losing close friends is not like losing a part of yourself	A	B
6	Anger in those close to me worries me, in case they leave me	B	A
7	When I get very angry with others it is usually justified	A	B
8	My problems are better solved through discussing them with others	B	A
9	Other people trying to be friendly distracts me from my goals	A	B
10	I often wonder about signs of rejection of me in others	B	A

Score

Add up your score by totalling the number of As and Bs in each box you have ticked.

8 or more Bs: You are the marrying type. You are not going to be at all content leading the single life and your mood will be at its best and your emotional life most stable when you are in a close relationship where you feel utterly secure about your and the other person's commitment. Ultimately this means married life is what you yearn for most. If you are someone still casually dating, you will be prone to low moods characterized by strong feelings associated with the fear of abandonment and helplessness.

You often get secretly angry with others for not showing the same commitment to relationships that you are prepared to; in fact, you often go out of your way to perform extraordinary acts of generosity to those you like. You may not realize, however, that these acts simply mean you are trying to deepen a relationship, and if they are not reciprocated it is because you have not yet found a person who wants to commit to you in the intense way you desire. One danger you should be aware of is that your search for devotion is partly driven by the idea that you need someone else to make you feel complete, and therefore to compensate for your own weaknesses.

Between 6 and 7 Bs: You definitely need to be in a committed relationship. Even if you may not yet feel quite ready for the responsibility of the full commitment required by marriage which higher scorers need, you will find yourself feeling occasionally weak, lonely, depleted and unloved when in a relationship where there is absolutely no prospect of full commitment. In other words, if you are not in a fully committed relationship you often feel something is missing in your life, and you may not realize that it may be there is a part of you which increasingly yearns for something more serious in your life than simply the fun of male or female company. You tend to feel helpless when not in a relationship, but then when you are in relationships which are not secure you constantly fear being abandoned. When threatened with the loss of a relationship you can sometimes respond by clinging desperately to others, or you urgently search for a substitute, which may take the form of an addiction of some kind. If not in a committed relationship, you may not realize that your tendency not to contemplate leaving a relationship which you know isn't right for you until another suitable mate comes on the scene means that basically you leapfrog from relationship to relationship. So although on the surface you appear independent, in fact you fear the reality of true independence, which means tolerating a gap between relationships. Yours is actually quite dependent behaviour. You should try to rely on others needing you a little more and your needing them a little less.

Between 3 and 5 Bs: You are best suited for dating without full commitment. You have a much stronger sense of your self-esteem, regardless of whether or not you are in a relationship, than those scoring higher on Bs, and this explains your ability to avoid being exploited in relationships by others, unlike those with higher scores. If someone begins to take advantage of you, you can walk away without as much pain as those who are more dependent. Having said that, you are vulnerable to strong feelings of dependency arising under conditions of stress, when you may find you cannot cope without clinging to those whom you may not have bothered to contact when things were going well. This see-saw approach to relationships is probably a little irritating to those around you, so you have to decide not only how much you need others, but also how much they might need you, and you should try to be available for others as much as they are for you. More independent people like yourself are not bothered so much by the threat of a relationship breakdown; instead, your low moods are more accounted for by achievement issues – feelings of inferiority, guilt, worthlessness, and a sense that you have failed to live up to expectations and standards in your career or ambitions.

Between 0 and 2 Bs: You prefer the single life. You tend to feel stifled very easily in even quite casual relationships, and your tendency to find those you are dating irritating or boring means you are not at all ready yet for any kind of serious commitment in your life – or you have yet to find the right person. In fact, your restlessness when in a relationship means you may in fact be happiest at the moment when single and independent of obligations to others who you feel often get in the way of what you really want to do. You probably had parents whose love appeared to be conditional on achievement. This explains why you are scoring highly for feelings of independence from others. While this makes you less prone to low moods due to feelings of dependency, your independence is characterized by self-criticism, a sense of failure to live up to standards and concerns about approval and recognition. In other words, your independence from others also cuts you off from the emotional side of relationships. Perhaps you fear dependency on others too much, leaving you to rely on your accomplishments as the only way to engage with others. You have to ask yourself, do you really just want an audience or would you prefer a genuine relationship?

I

THE SINNER TAKES IT ALL

Understanding the basic rules of attraction

True, we love life, not because we are used to living, but
because we are used to loving. There is always some madness in love, but there is also always some reason in
madness.

Friedrich Nietzsche

IN SOME ARABIC COUNTRIES DURING THE MIDDLE AGES THERE
was a disease known as love. The symptoms were really
rather severe: the sufferer lost appetite, couldn't sleep, lost
interest in life, had difficulty concentrating and shed
weight. The doctor would establish the diagnosis by listing the names of all the eligible members of the opposite
sex who lived in the village while taking the patient's
pulse. If the patient's pulse quickened at the sound of any
one name, the illness was confirmed. The treatment was
marriage.

In my experience as a consultant psychiatrist working
in the NHS at the Maudsley Hospital and as Professor of
Public Understanding of Psychiatry lecturing at Gresham

College, it has seemed obvious to me that relationships, attraction, sex and seduction in both clinical and 'normal' populations are some of the most potent issues in our lives. Much human unhappiness and ecstasy turns on these predicaments. As one patient put it to me succinctly, 'I don't need Prozac, doctor, I need a boyfriend!'

Scientific psychology and psychiatry have understood the importance of sex and love in human affairs yet found them difficult to study rigorously, but this has changed in recent years, with a burgeoning number of research studies of good quality genuinely illuminating this tumultuous part of life. This book is an attempt to present some of that research and explore its practical implications outside the laboratory in general, and in terms of your love life specifically. I hope it will demonstrate how scientific psychology can guide you on a date if you want to increase your attractiveness, how it can help you determine who is right for you for a longer-term relationship, and how it can advise on keeping a deeper relationship going for decades.

The reason why psychology and psychiatry have been neglected in books and the wider media as a steer in affairs of the heart is twofold. Firstly, academic research in these fields remains, perhaps understandably, obscure to the typical journalist or author with only a casual acquaintance of the university departments engaged in such work. Secondly, the neurological and behavioural sciences suffer from an unfortunate reputation for producing reams of data which merely reinforce common sense. This book, in contrast, will focus on the science that genuinely helps us by suggesting surprising ways of thinking about sex, love, attraction and romance. Prepare to be challenged and even irritated by what the research posits about what governs your heart. Whether you agree with the findings or not, I hope these studies will give you food for thought and provoke a more creative or at least different approach to this part of your life which may still prove helpful.

We should be cautious about rejecting scientific explanations in this arena because the fact of the matter remains that what we casually observe of our and others' love lives leads to much incredulity and perplexity, as so much of this part of life appears not to make sense at all. This in itself means we should consider what psychology has to say about affairs of the heart because at the very least it attempts to provide a coherent account of an area which defies easy explanation.

Let's begin our exploration of the subject by considering beauty. Given that they are widely regarded as two of the most desirable members of the opposite sex in the world, the recent news that the marriage of Hollywood film stars Brad Pitt and Jennifer Aniston has foundered raises the question of just how striking you have to be to keep a partner interested in you. The breakdown of other celebrity marriages between equally beautiful people – Cindy Crawford and Richard Gere, Jemima and Imran Khan, Richard Burton and Elizabeth Taylor – might lead most observers to wonder how much physical allure really predicts whose relationship is going to last the course.

Recent psychological research suggests that we shouldn't be surprised by this litany of broken marriages among the super-attractive. Indeed, it predicts that the ultra-desirable could be doomed to more difficulty than the rest of us mere mortals when it comes to staying together. This is not for the conventionally offered reason that couples in the media spotlight tend to find it too stressful. If that were the case, how do we explain the longevity of marriages involving prime ministers and presidents, which, while they may suffer their strains (Hillary and Bill Clinton), tend not to break down with the same frequency as those of the much prettier? More likely explanations for why beautiful people appear less likely to experience enduring marital happiness than the rest of us can be found in recent psychological research on the nature and impact of intense physical attractiveness.

The first surprising finding is that although Brad Pitt and Jennifer Aniston might appear outstandingly physically desirable to us, this may not be how they appear to each other. The key point here is that all ratings of attraction arise out of a comparison process. How attractive you rate someone rests largely on the general standard of attractiveness you tend to encounter routinely. A recent study by evolutionary psychologist Satoshi Kanazawa at the London School of Economics found that middle-aged men who spend their working days mingling with women who are much younger and at peak fertility (late teens, early twenties) than their more middle-aged wives back home tend to have much higher divorce rates than might otherwise be predicted. The study focused on professions like teaching. When the men returned home after a long day at work having seen nothing but younger women, their more middle-aged wives suffered from this comparison process and ended up appearing less desirable.

So, if you spend all day surrounded by nothing but stunning people, as you will if you work in a film studio or on the catwalk, then even the very gorgeous may not be handsome enough to retain your interest. Your standards are likely to become stratospheric. Also, if you are beautiful yourself, you are going to get exposed to much more temptation than the rest of us as many of those around you succumb to your charms and hit on you. So for the super-beautiful to stay married successfully they have to be more resolved to resist enticement than the rest of us.

The key issue of the psychological impact on your personality of being someone with stunning looks still needs to be fully comprehended. Recent research published in the *Journal of Sex Research* by psychologist Devendra Singh at the University of Texas found that the more attractive tend to flirt more with others, even when already in a relationship. This might not be conducive to long-term relationship stability, but it is a strategy they might use to keep partners jealous and therefore possessive. It could be that attractive people are used to finding it so easy to pull that they haven't learned how to do the necessary deeper emotional work to keep a relationship going in the longer term.

This point about the individual's own desirability is vital. Denise Previti and Paul Amato at Pennsylvania State University found that up to one in four marriages in the general population stay together only because partners *couldn't find a better alternative*. It would seem that a significant proportion of us only stay married not because we are still strongly attracted to our spouses, but more because there are significant barriers to leaving. Staying together for the sake of the children was the most commonly mentioned barrier, being cited by 31 per cent of all respondents; other barriers included a lack of financial resources and religious beliefs. Now, suppose you have no financial barriers to leaving a relationship. You are wealthy, you feel you can purchase the best child-care money can buy, and you're completely confident you will find another gorgeous partner because of your own desirability. Given these circumstances, how many of us would really stay married to our current partners? This is the conundrum faced by the gorgeous celebrity.

New psychological research has also established that there exists in the marriage market what could be called, for want of a better term, a kind of league table. We are all aware that some of us are more desirable than others when you add up all our characteristics. Some of us are 'Premier League' while others are 'Vauxhall Conference'. The point is that Premier League people tend to cluster together and to prefer matches with each other, and the same applies all the way down the league structure. In other words, we tend to go for those who we feel are in our league – who are roughly of the same attractiveness as us. There wouldn't be much point if we were 'Vauxhall Conference' in trying to pull a 'Premiership' individual because of the high likelihood of personal rejection. Even if a relationship begins, we know we are likely to be sidelined the minute a better package comes along. In terms of this league-table view of attraction, we can all think of celebrity couples whose careers have moved in opposite directions, i.e. one has become more desirable to the opposite sex while the other's stock has declined. Relegation is the logical end point.

All of this research, then, suggests that the gorgeous celebrity is actually unlikely to find long-term happiness in a relationship unless they address these psychological issues – that within a relationship their beauty is actually a burden. It's enough to make you pity the pretty, except that psychologists have long demonstrated that we tend to perceive the physically attractive as not just easy on the eye, but more intelligent and competent as well, even to the extent of thinking that they would be more capable than the rest of us ugly folk when faced with such seemingly unrelated and specific tasks as piloting a plane. This irrational tendency to assume that beautiful people possess a host of other desirable qualities explains why a more attractive defendant is likely to be handed a more lenient sentence, or even to be let off by a jury. Both genders perceive physically attractive men and women to be more intelligent and good. In addition, children as young as five and six years old hold the perception that better-looking teachers are more intelligent, and as it is unlikely that children so young are burdened by personal cognitive biases introduced by suffering from physical attraction or falling in love themselves, it would appear that something rather profound is going on in our assessment of the attractive.

Now evolutionary psychologists Satoshi Kanazawa from the London School of Economics and Jody Kovar from the University of Pennsylvania have published new research which argues that the beautiful really *are* more intelligent. So perhaps there is more than a kernel of truth to this widespread public perception.

Their argument, in a paper entitled 'Why Beautiful People Are More Intelligent', rests on some inescapable general genetic and evolutionary principles. Basically, women generally prefer more intelligent men, as has been repeatedly confirmed by attractiveness research. Meanwhile, most men place physical attractiveness as their highest valued feature in women. So it follows that if there are genes for attractiveness and intelligence, over time these two characteristics will tend to cluster in the products of liaisons between the more attractive and the highly intelligent. What also follows is the unpalatable fact that in a competitive market, the less desirable and therefore less intelligent and less physically attractive are left to mate with each other.

Before the appalled turn the page in disgust at such a politically incorrect theory, it might be useful to consider the science at play here, particularly since another recently published major study confirms the theory. Kanazawa and Kovar start by pointing out that physical attractiveness is not as superficial a quality as is commonly understood, and is definitely not merely in the eye of the beholder. Infants as young as two and three months gaze longer at a face adults have judged to be more attractive, and twelve-month-olds play significantly longer with facially attractive dolls. Because one year is not nearly enough time for infants to have learned and internalized the cultural values of beauty through socialization and media exposure, this suggests that standards of beauty might be innate.

Cross-culturally, there is considerable agreement in the judgement of beauty among the host of racial and national groups so far studied, including those as widely separated as the Ache of Paraguay and the Chinese (see chapters 7 and 8 for more on this topic). In none of this research does the degree of exposure to Western media have any influence on people's perception of beauty. The consensus seems to rest on one essential point: attractiveness appears to be rooted in how symmetrical your face and body are. Attractive faces are basically more symmetrical than unattractive faces. Interestingly, the symmetry of your body and face appears to be associated with how genetically fit you are, and with how many adverse conditions you suffered in the womb and while growing up. Bodies' resistance to parasites and other pathogens has been shown to be related to how symmetrical they are, so beauty appears to be an indicator of genetic and developmental health. Beauty is now seen by evolutionary biologists as a kind of 'health certification' guaranteeing that if you mate with such a person you are mingling your genes with higher-quality genetic material.

How symmetrical a face is can now be measured from a scanned photograph. A computer program measures the sizes of and distances between various facial parts, then assigns a single score for physical attractiveness, which correlates highly with scores of prettiness assigned by human judges. Beauty therefore appears to be an *objective* and *quantitative* attribute of individuals – a bit like height and weight.

While it might be disconcerting for women to know that their looks can be reduced to a single number, spare a thought for men, who have long known that women are primarily interested in their status, occupational prestige and intelligence. These too are eminently reducible to a series of stark figures. In the 1990s, Daniel Hamermesh and Jeff Biddle, economists at the University of Texas and Michigan State University, published a study in the *American Economic Review* entitled 'Beauty and the Labor Market' which found that relative to average-looking women, below-average-looking women are married to men with significantly less education. The available evidence thus indicates that there is a pattern to mating which is far from merely random between high-status, higher-intelligence men and physically attractive women.

Kanazawa and Kovar cite five previous studies that have found an association between physical attractiveness and intelligence, including a recent comprehensive meta-analysis (a pooling of all the available data from a wide variety of studies investigating the same question). The authors of the meta-analysis were so convinced that physical attractiveness is a strong sign of superior intelligence that they concluded the maxim 'beauty is skin deep' was a 'myth'.

But as the concept of intelligence is deeply contro-versial, evolutionary theorists have looked for a real world measure of success that should correlate with IQ. Irene Frieze and a team of researchers at the University of Pittsburgh found during a study of MBA graduates that the more physically attractive men had significantly higher starting salaries, and their advantage increased over time. For women, attractiveness had no effect on starting salaries, but better-looking women earned significantly more later in their careers. In their sample, men earned US$2,600 more on average for each unit of attractiveness (on a five-point scale), and women earned US$2,150 more. In a recent paper entitled 'Beauty, Productivity, and Discrimination: Lawyers' Looks and Lucre' in the *Journal of Labour Economics*, Biddle and Hamermesh found that better-looking attorneys earned more than others five years after graduation from law school, and their advantage increased over time. Once again, the effect of physical attractiveness on income seemed, perhaps puzzlingly, stronger for men than for women. Then again, if you go with Kanazawa and Kovar's theory that beauty is a sign of something more fundamental than just good looks and is a marker for superior intellectual ability and general genetic fitness, it would be precisely the kind of error based on the myth that 'beauty is skin deep' to assume that women should necessarily benefit from beauty more than men. Indeed, if men are benefiting from physical good looks more than women, it would be evidence that something beyond mere subjective perception of the beautiful is involved in their success.

Perhaps part of the unconscious reason men want to mate with beautiful women is that they know such a liaison will produce prettier sons as well as daughters who will in turn benefit from this genetic heritage. Along these lines, Geoffrey Miller, an evolutionary psychologist at the University of New Mexico in Albuquerque, directly measured the intelligence and body symmetry of seventy-eight male undergraduate volunteers. Electronic callipers were used to measure the right and left sides of ten body features on each participant, ranging from foot width and ear width to little finger length, to the nearest 0.01 mm. Intelligence was found to be strongly correlated with body symmetry. Miller argued that his astounding finding means that intelligence is as good a marker for generally 'good' genes as physical attractiveness is.

But if Miller's and Kanazawa and Kovar's arguments hold water, that intellectual capacity and physical attractiveness are clustering in individuals over time, men should begin going for intelligent women, and women should be as drawn to physically attractive men as to bright ones. And there is indeed a little evidence that the traditional contrast in gender preferences – of women for high-status, bright men, and men for pretty women – is beginning to change.

In a recent interactive *Tomorrow's World* Mega Lab experiment on BBC TV which I helped to devise, the viewing public was presented with two pictures of members of the opposite sex who definitely varied in terms of physical attractiveness – one was obviously prettier or more handsome than the other. Beneath each picture was a kind of lonely hearts column I had composed in which the person in the photograph was inviting the viewer of the programme to accompany them on a romantic weekend away in the Caribbean. The wording was more or less the same, but there were subtle differences which should have been so minor as to operate below conscious awareness. In one script, for instance, the person invited you to swim in the shimmering blue sea; in the other you were invited to swim in the shimmering azure sea. The viewers were then asked to choose the person they would prefer to go away with. Complex vocabulary was used as a proxy for education or intelligence.

The surprising finding was that women went more for looks in their choice of men, while the men prioritized intelligence in their choice of women. Just the use of a few words like 'azure' significantly swung the audience towards the lesser physically attractive person, indicating that the public generally were voting for intelligence over looks, yet amazingly this was more marked in the voting of the men. Are women now tending to favour looks over brains because they are more financially independent and therefore have less need of the higher-status, high-IQ man to look after them?

However, Kanazawa and Kovar caution us against making the mistake of using attractiveness as a measure of intelligence, and vice versa. They point out that their finding is only of an association, which while statistically significant, is an imperfect one. They urge you to assess intelligence and physical attractiveness in prospective mates separately, as there is still likely to be considerable variation within individuals on these two characteristics. Certainly you should never choose the pilot of your plane on the basis of their looks alone.

What was, I think, particularly intriguing about my *Tomorrow's World* experiment was that changing the wording of the lonely hearts ad did swing viewers significantly away from the more physically attractive person, despite the subtlety of the manipulation. In other words, no matter what hand of cards nature has dealt you in terms of physical appearance, there is still a lot to play for in terms of allowing psychology and science to inform your behaviour, attitudes and speech in order to maximize your appeal to the opposite sex.

DO YOU THINK YOU ARE ATTRACTIVE?

Attractiveness Scale

Each statement is followed by two possible responses: agree or disagree. Read each statement carefully and decide which response best describes how you feel. Then tick the corresponding box. Please reply to every statement. If you are not completely sure which answer is more accurate, tick the one you feel is most appropriate. Do not read the scoring explanation before filling out the questionnaire. Do not spend too long on each statement. It is important that you answer each question as honestly as possible.

		AGREE	DISAGREE
1	If someone is popular it will not make me attracted to them	A	B
2	Most of my energy goes on controlling my weight	B	A
3	My parents are, or were, attractive people	A	B
4	I am frequently jealous of how others look so good	B	A

AGREE   DISAGREE

5   I buy things with little regard to the
     impression they create   A   B

6   A small gain in weight is unacceptable   B   A

7   As the years go by I will become more
     popular   A   B

8   Staying hungry is good for you   B   A

9   I would not mind trying on bathing
     suits in a shop   A   B

10   Anything that upsets my diet upsets me   B   A

11   My weight will stay low in the future   A   B

12   Rejection by others is just as
     humiliating as ever   B   A

13   If I could change my life, I would not
     start with my body   A   B

14   I should get more Valentine cards than
     I do   B   A

15   I do not mind lying on a beach full of
     attractive people in bathing suits   A   B

16   I hate having my photograph taken   B   A

AGREE DISAGREE

17   I do not avoid sex because of how I
     feel about my body

     | A | B |

18   I hate film stars who seem to undress
     all the time

     | B | A |

19   I would be more popular if I had
     more time for socializing

     | A | B |

20   I get shy with very attractive
     members of the opposite sex

     | B | A |

Score

Add up your score by totalling the number of As and Bs in each box you have ticked.

16 or more Bs: You do not consider yourself very attractive at all. Hence you are a bit overwhelmed when in the presence of very attractive members of the opposite sex. You tend to go for people you consider more thoughtful or non-threatening in not wearing clothes that are too revealing. Your low opinion of yourself means you will tend to put up with too many problems in your partner as you will be pessimistic about forming a new relationship if the current one ends. You need to find and stay with people who appreciate your qualities, who will then boost your self-esteem. At the moment the way you love will tend to be feverish, obsessive and jealous. As you are scoring high on having a poor body image your life is probably being made a misery by your preoccupation with a better appearance. You probably have a fixed idea of what your appearance should be, and believe that you will be happy once you achieve this. The grave danger for you is that your prolonged concern with appearance will eventually lead to eating disorders or excessive working out, and you will become trapped in a cycle of using fad products for changing your appearance. You may even consider plastic surgery. You are either currently embroiled in a web of relationships which constantly undermine your confidence by providing negative feedback about yourself, or something unpleasant has happened recently which is undermining your confidence. Your morale will climb as you spend more time with those who believe in you and focus on those parts of your life where you are good at what you do, while only gradually expanding your horizons into new projects, in which you will eventually succeed given good enough morale.

Between 12 and 15 Bs: You consider yourself to be below average in attractiveness, but still better-looking than others you know. You tend to go for conventional members of the opposite sex as opposed to the wildly trendy or extrovert. When socializing you are quite sensitive to cues that members of the opposite sex may be becoming disinterested in you, like yawning or looking at their watch. This kind of negative feedback confirms your impression that you are not naturally attractive. You tend to try to compensate by overusing humour or compliments. While the techniques you use to bolster your attractiveness to others do work in the short term, in the long run you need to be able to fall back on a more natural confidence in yourself. You will tend to fall in love less often than lower scorers, but when you do it is more intense, partly because of the much-needed affirmation it provides. While your body image is about average, compared to those scoring lower on the scale, it does appear that it significantly influences your mood or self-confidence. Losing several pounds is followed by elation, pride and self-assurance; gaining weight results in depression, some self-loathing and even the curtailment of social plans. While your morale is good, it could be enhanced substantially if you had higher self-esteem, and this means you are often pessimistic about yourself and your abilities. Your occasional low zest for life at times turns into a self-fulfilling prophecy, leading you sometimes not to take risks and therefore not to explore your full potential. Don't forget that although those who appear more attractive may seem to have more fun than you, in fact all they really have is more belief in themselves.

Between 7 and 11 Bs: You think you are about average to possibly above average in attractiveness, hence you don't mind rejection that much and are more interested in finding someone who is right for you specifically, regardless of what others find attractive. You are practical, realistic and compatibility-seeking in affairs of the heart. How you feel about yourself is quite dependent on your mood. At times of increased confidence you need to capitalize and socialize more than you might otherwise do, increasing your chances of attracting the right person. Your body image is not as poor as higher scorers, but it is still lower than average on many occasions. At those times when you feel more confident about your ability to attract others, you tend to become interested in relationships that are playful, with the emphasis more on pleasure than commitment. If things are not working out you will tend to get restless at an early stage and consider moving on rather than staying to try and resolve problems.

Between 0 and 6 Bs: You have an extremely positive view of your body and of your personality. You are at only a negligible risk of developing problems linked to feelings of low attractiveness, such as an eating disorder. While you may on occasion like to change your appearance, you have many other more important goals in your life, like your career and your relationships, from which your self-esteem is more strongly derived, much more so than from the way you look. Your relative freedom from dieting leaves you the confidence to be able to enjoy life – something dieters fail to learn. They believe that enjoyment and confidence only come with thinness, but in fact it's the other way round: you can only gain control of your life and body if you are in the relaxed state that self-confidence brings. You are interested in exploring the physical side of a relationship at an early stage and place great store on this side of things. You tend to get impatient with those who are clearly not as confident as you. Beware the fact that you are quite competitive in terms of attractiveness and there are many other important attributes, like honesty and commitment.

2

ALL YOU BLEED IS LOVE?

How the science of psychology can help your relationships

Marriage is like a hot bath. Once you get used to it, it's not so hot.

Anonymous

BEFORE WE LAUNCH INTO A CONSIDERATION OF HOW psychology can help us in our relationships, we need to know what it can tell us about the mechanics of love. Many argue that love is something about which the arts are much better at communicating insights, in the form, say, of a Shakespearean sonnet or a Rachmaninov piano sonata. But now neuroscience promises to solve some of the greatest mysteries at the subject's heart in a way the arts or previous attempts by other forms of investigation were simply incapable of.

Andreas Bartels and Semir Zeki from the Wellcome Department of Neuroimaging at University College London have attempted to unravel for the first time whether there really are different forms of love, like the love between a parent and a child, or the emotion shared by lovers, or whether all forms of intense attachments are basic variations on the same theme. The tender intimacy and selflessness of a mother's love might be celebrated by inspiring music, literature and art, but the evolutionary biologist has a more prosaic formulation: lifelong commitment and altruism merely serve to help a parent's genetic material survive through to future generations. Similarly, the passion shared by two lovers fulfils a surprisingly similar function: it facilitates mating and parenting, and hence is again merely the selfish gene in action. If we didn't love, then the species would simply never be perpetuated, so maybe that is love's actual function.

But if all love boils down to, according to science, is a genetic prerogative being pursued through hard wiring in our brains, then the neurological basis of love, like the brain activity and hormonal responses which underpin love, should theoretically share similar biological underpinnings.

We obviously need more than sexual lust to perpetuate the species because we require love to keep parents together to help look after kids; we also need love between generations to ensure that the young are cared for during vulnerable periods. Indeed, love is essential for our species' survival because it involves self-sacrifice. It helps us to put others before ourselves and this is what actually keeps us going as a species. From a genetic or biological standpoint, love certainly does make the world go round.

To investigate this question, Bartels and Zeki, who have

a long-running programme investigating love using the very latest magnetic resonance imaging (MRI) techniques, measured brain activity in twenty-two mothers who viewed pictures of their own infants and compared this to the responses prompted by viewing pictures of other infants with whom they had been acquainted for the same period. In addition they compared this activity to that in the brains of volunteers viewing their partner, a best friend and an adult acquaintance. This allowed the scientists to determine brain activation related to maternal and romantic love while at the same time controlling for the effects of familiarity and merely friendly feelings.

The results were recently published in the journal *Neuroreport*, and the first intriguing finding was that there is a lot of overlap between the brain areas activated during feelings of romantic love for a partner and those involved in maternal love for one's own children. The neurones implicated are the same as those we know become active whenever an extremely rewarding activity is being undertaken, such as consuming a favourite food or drink, taking drugs like cocaine, or when we are given monetary rewards. So love is indeed like a drug.

However, a first surprising result was that it's not just that certain shared areas of the brain are reliably activated in both romantic and maternal love, but also that particular locations are *deactivated*. And it's the deactivation which is perhaps most revealing about love. Among other areas, parts of the pre-frontal cortex – the bit of the brain towards the front of the head – seem to get switched off when we are in love and when we love our children, as do areas linked with the experience of negative emotions as well as planning. These deactivated parts of the brain form a network that is implicated in the assessment of trustworthiness of others and, basically, critical social assessment. In other words, strong emotional ties to another person not only inhibit negative emotions but also affect the brain networks involved in making social judgements about that person. The results, conclude Bartels and Zeki, suggest that attachment involves a push-and-pull mechanism: you are pulled along by the strong sense of reward you feel when you love, but you are also pushed by a tendency not to objectively see faults in the other person which might threaten love, or put the brakes on it, thus preventing you from rushing headlong into a relationship.

This is a profound finding in the history of our attempt to understand this most complex and powerful human emotion. It means neuroscience can finally explain a puzzle that has flummoxed artists from Shakespeare to Sinatra: why can't we see the faults in our partners or children which others can clearly perceive, and who as a result find our affection mysterious? It also explains why we take so long to see the flaws in those we idealize through love, which of course means we can end up choosing the wrong person to commit to. Such short-comings become apparent only after our initial ardour has cooled, when the parts of the brain we use to think critically and dispassionately and to arrive at rational judgements about others physically begin to switch on again.

Another key finding from the Bartels and Zeki study is that there are important differences in the brain areas involved in parental as opposed to romantic love, so the two are not exactly the same. For example, in romantic love a part of the brain towards the base called the hypothalamus is specifically activated, and this area is implicated in the production of hormones which mediate sexual arousal, such as testosterone. The hypothalamus does not activate when we love our children.

Another difference was that the part of the brain involved in face processing and recognition appeared to be more active in maternal than in romantic love. The authors of the study speculate that the rapid rates with which the facial features of babies and young children change and the importance of reading children's facial expressions require a constant updating of the face-recognition machinery, leading to heightened activity in this part of the brain. The fact that this face-recognition area is not so active in romantic love perhaps suggests that we are meant to be monogamous, or at least not to sleep around so much that our brains might find it difficult to recognize who we wake up with in the morning.

Also in romantic love, some parts of the brain possibly implicated in what is termed 'Theory of Mind' seem to be more active compared to maternal love. 'Theory of Mind' is about the notion that for us to interact effectively we have to develop a good insight into what is going on in other people's minds so that we don't offend them and can work out how to please them. This finding suggests that an important part of the reward process we experience when we are romantically in love comes from understanding that another is in love with us. It is intriguing that this brain area doesn't seem to be so important in parental love; it suggests that knowing our children don't reciprocate our feelings for them doesn't stop us from loving them.

So, neuroscience is telling us that our brains literally dumb down as we rush into sex, encouraging us to produce children whom we also continue to care for no matter how little they reciprocate. It would seem that one of love's mysteries has at last been cracked by science. Had we used our brains to their full capacity all the time and failed to deactivate clear thinking and critical judgement for the purposes of attraction and seduction, our species might never have got off the ground. The research suggests that we need to become more aware of the way our genes and biological wiring may be driving us to promulgate our genes at the expense of our personal happiness, by forcing us to mate in the short term with those who might make poor long-term partners.

This brain research is also confirming something that psychologists have suspected for several decades: there may be more than one kind of love. So, just as it's vital to discover what kind of person you are in order to attract the right kind of mate, it's equally essential to know more about the kind of love you are drawn to, or prefer, in order to get a better sense of the best kind of relationship for you.

Love style personality tests have only relatively recently been pioneered in psychology, and an adaptation of these tests follows.

ARE YOU A CRAZY OR A SENSIBLE LOVER?

In terms of types of experience of love, there is the kind known as 'companionate', characterized as affectionate, friendly and reasonable, and the kind known as 'passionate' – puppy love, a crush – characterized by obsessiveness, lovesickness and infatuation, and frequently accompanied by outrageous behaviour. While for many passionate love simply characterizes the beginning of a relationship, and then gradually evolves into companionate love, for many others it appears that passionate or companionate love are ways of loving they are stuck with.

Love Style Scale

Each statement is followed by two possible responses: agree or disagree. Read each statement carefully and decide which response best describes how you feel. Then tick the corresponding box. Please reply to every statement. If you are not completely sure which answer is more accurate, tick the one you feel is most appropriate. Do not read the scoring explanation before filling out the questionnaire. Do not spend too long on each statement. It is important that you answer each question as honestly as possible.

		AGREE	DISAGREE
1	I spend little time now imagining and anticipating dates	A	B
2	Losing my lover means life could never again be worthwhile	B	A

AGREE   DISAGREE

3   Things I find out about my lover's past
usually impress me   [A]   [B]

4   I love finding out gossip about my
partner from others   [B]   [A]

5   Romantic stories and films are usually
very unrealistic   [A]   [B]

6   I am looking for someone who is
perfect in every major respect   [B]   [A]

7   I have never been accused of throwing
myself at someone   [A]   [B]

8   I want to be loved much more by my
partner than I am already   [B]   [A]

9   I find it easy to work out what my
lover is thinking   [A]   [B]

10 I persistently look out for signs that my
partner loves me   [B]   [A]

11 Once the relationship is established I
usually feel secure   [A]   [B]

12 Past things I did because of love I
now find embarrassing   [B]   [A]

AGREE DISAGREE

13 Thoughts of my lover do not distract
me from my work   A   B

14 Thinking hard about past
relationships makes me tearful   B   A

15 Other people could love my partner as
well as me   A   B

16 Once we are together nothing else can
ever go wrong again   B   A

17 Some people understand parts of me
better than my partner   A   B

18 I cannot bear to play waiting games
when it comes to lovers B   A

19 I relax and am most at ease when with
my partner   A   B

20 I have never experienced more
euphoria than when in love   B   A

Score

Add up your score by totalling the number of As and Bs
in each box you have ticked.

16 or more Bs: You are scoring very high for being fundamentally a passionate and therefore impetuous lover. This
means that your best relationships are a real roller-coaster

ride of emotions ranging from ecstasy to misery. The history of past relationships is dominated by dramatic acts of passion which have led some people to consider you a little crazy. Once the fantasizing and yearning about love is over and you commence a relationship, you often become too dependent on your mate, but also eventually terribly bored by them. When too dependent you are often so anxious not to upset them that you dare not risk true intimacy with them and reveal your true fears, irritations and anxieties. This stands in contrast to your ability to be physically intimate, which you find easier than lower scorers, but which you may be doing for the wrong reasons, because you believe your lover wants it rather than because it is something you desire for yourself. All this is due to your fear that they will leave the relationship if you upset them. One explanation for your addiction to excitement in relationships is you felt insecure as a child in terms of your attachment to your mother, hence you tend easily to become anxious about the stability of current relationships. You tend therefore to be susceptible to the drama of passionate love in adulthood, because you see true love as existing only in the form of drama rather than as the more sedate companionate love of lower scorers.

Between 11 and 15 Bs: You are scoring around average to just above average for preferring passionate love to companionate love and this means you are not quite as prone to outrageous behaviour in the pursuit of a lover as higher scorers, but there are things you have done which you keep from best friends because they are so embarrassing. You do tend over time to become less satisfied in relationships because your mate is not as perfect as you first thought they might be; however, you are beginning to learn to enjoy people as they are and have begun, albeit reluctantly, to let go of the idea that you are entitled to a partner who is much better than the one you have. Your passion is not in spite of the pain you experience in love, but because of it. In other words, when not in a relationship your passion is fuelled by a sprinkling of hope and a large dollop of loneliness, jealousy and terror. You need to learn that love can be more boring and still more wholesome. Because you tend to favour passion and drama you are a little too sold on the appearance of things and often choose lovers who will impress your friends. Instead, you need to insist on someone who really cares for you as a priority in your considerations, rather than some of the other characteristics you have been looking for so far.

Between 5 and 10 Bs: You are scoring around average to just above average for preferring companionate love to passionate love, and this means you tend towards excessive behaviour in the pursuit of love only when a little intoxicated or egged on by others. You are able, unlike higher scorers, to see even when your lover and you are united that the future is not going to be perfect bliss. This realism means your actions are not so much governed by fantasy; instead, your relationships are characterized by steadily growing affection, as the more you get to know each other, the less disappointed you are – the very opposite of higher scorers. It may be that one reason for relationship incompatibilities in the past is that you simply had a very different love style to your lovers, who may simply have been a little too irrational and impetuous for you. The kind of love you are looking for is companionate because this reflects your earliest childhood experiences of secure attachment to your parents. At no point did you ever feel anxiety over their love for you, hence you are accustomed to a love style devoid of anxiety, unlike higher scorers. However, you may need to make an effort to bring more uncertainty into your relationship to ensure things don't begin to get too boring after a while.

Between 0 and 4 Bs: You are scoring very high for being a companionate lover and this is partly because you see passionate love as immature and hence undesirable, the product of personal inadequacy which leads to exploitative and destructive behaviour. Some of these feelings of disdain for passion may be because you were also once like this but have now settled down; alternatively, you feel that more dispassionate love is based on true caring for the other. However, your lack of impulsiveness means you sometimes find it difficult to be spontaneous and creative when it comes to ways of expressing your love, but this doesn't bother you too much because you find it easier than higher scorers to accept yourself as you are. You have discovered or intuitively knew all along that your affection for each other actually increases when you frankly admit your irritations with each other. You hope to combine the delights of passionate love with the security of companionate love, but as you are too self-confident to suffer the highs and lows of truly passionate love, you may have to resign yourself to the fact that deep passion is something which now belongs to your more insecure adolescence. One of the reasons you may have grown up more than the more impetuous higher scorers is that over time your self-esteem has come less and less from relationships and more from other activities in your life, perhaps your career.

As psychology advances its understanding of the mind and the brain, and of love and attraction particularly, it provides tools for those among us who would rather not leave seduction so much to chance. For example, a favourite ritual on Valentine's Day is the romantic candlelit dinner, but why exactly is romance so strongly associated with abnormally low lighting conditions? One theory is that in low light your pupils dilate to help you see better, and we actually confuse the dilated pupils of our date peering at us through the candlelight with romantic interest, because dilated pupils are also a feature of arousal. Another theory is that low light renders those who are self-conscious about their appearance more relaxed or that the dark reminds us unconsciously, but romantically, of the bedroom.

However, psychologists established as far back as 1965 in a classic study of pupil size and attraction that men found women's faces to be more alluring when the pupils were rendered larger – a finding that has been reliably replicated since.

But just before you take your own low-wattage bulbs to your favourite restaurant, the latest research using evolutionary theory by psychologists Selina Tombs and Irwin Silverman of York University in Toronto, published in the journal *Evolution and Human Behaviour*, has found that while men prefer dilated pupils in women, most women prefer only *moderately* dilated pupils in a man. Women are more selective than men perhaps because a liaison always involves the risk of pregnancy, with much greater emotional and physical costs than for a man, so they are more cautious about who they consider for a relationship. Men, on the other hand, have been programmed by natural selection to respond without much equivocation to female sexual arousal and attention. Evolutionary theory therefore predicts that an obviously enthusiastic woman is much more attractive to a man than vice versa.

If men are willing to mate without as much emotional investment, a woman's interests are probably better served by moderate levels of male arousal at the beginning of a relationship, argue Tombs and Silverman. Before the modern age of women's rights and equality, overzealous sexual attention on the part of men may have presaged rape, over-possessiveness, and excessive sexual jealousy and/or promiscuity, all of which operate to the detriment of women's interests. Thus, Tombs and Silverman suggest, women have been programmed by natural selection over many generations to prefer 'steady moderation' in the sexual attentions and arousal of prospective suitors. So during that romantic meal, men should sit somewhere where the light is slightly better to ensure their pupils aren't too big and they aren't signalling too much zeal.

This need for moderation in male ardour to maximize attractiveness has also been confirmed by new research into the best vocal strategies to adopt during dating. Sandy Pentland and colleagues at the Affective Computing Lab at the Massachusetts Institute of Technology analysed conversations during speed-dating sessions and discovered that they could predict with 80 per cent accuracy which people were going to be attracted to each other simply from the way they spoke to each other. If men used frequent encouraging interjections in a conversation that lasted less than a second, typically words or phrases such as 'OK', 'I see' and 'Go on', women were more likely to report attraction at the end of the date. The key here is not for the man to talk too much, which is an indicator of neediness. If women varied the pitch of their voice more, they elicited more attraction from men. Perhaps pitch variability is a signal of emotional involvement from a woman, while short, encouraging interjections indicate a man who listens well and who might therefore be more predisposed towards 'steady moderation'.

Many will be sceptical of such modern psychological theories that boil down romance to a basic drive to pass on our genes to the next generation, but these theories offer some ingenious explanations for otherwise mysterious aspects of love. For if we don't use evolutionary psychology, how then do we explain why women wear blusher or rouge on their cheeks? The use of red ochre as a cosmetic has been confirmed by archaeological digs dating back long before the dawn of civilization, so perhaps there is a good evolutionary reason for this.

One intriguing theory is that as there is slight dilation of the female's blood vessels during ovulation, and there is therefore a slightly redder blush to her skin during this time, adding red to the face makes a prospective male believe that she is ovulating. From the man's standpoint this is a good time to try to seduce a woman in order to maximize his chances of passing on his genes to the next generation. A slight variation on this is that back in the caves, if some women were ovulating and therefore getting all the male attention, it made sense for the others to add red to the skin in order to confuse the men as to who was really ovulating and who wasn't, therefore ensuring you weren't shut out from the mating game at particular times of the month.

If the modern wearing of cosmetics can be explained by evolutionary theory, could the fact that we evolved in more dangerous times have a much greater impact on our mating psychology than we realize? For example, the search for safety as opposed to taking risks should theoretically lead us to be attracted to those who are more similar as opposed to dissimilar to us, and this has been dramatically confirmed by recent research which confirms that we prefer for romance those whose faces structurally resemble our own. But it doesn't stop there. Other similarities, with names for example, seem to promote attraction.

IMPLICIT EGOTISM

These findings reflect a new theory in psychology which powerfully explains our unconscious preferences in life and is termed 'implicit egotism'. Implicit egotism refers to the idea that people's positive associations about themselves spill over into their evaluations of objects associated with the self.

This new theory basically started life when psychologist Mauricio Carvallo and colleagues at the State University of New York had participants sample two cups of tea. Unbeknown to the subjects, the first three letters in the name of one of the two teas were engineered to match the first three letters in participants' first names (e.g., a person named Sandra might receive a tea named Sanya and a tea with a name totally unrelated to her name). When asked to choose a tea to take home as a gift, participants preferred the tea that contained their name letters. During debriefing after the experiment was over, the vast majority reported that the names of the teas had played no role in their choice. This is why the phenomenon is called *implicit* egotism: it acts below the level of conscious awareness and is therefore more difficult to guard against as a persuasion or manipulation tactic.

One explanation of the power of implicit egotism is that it constitutes a non-conscious safety signal that enhances people's connections to objects and to other people who resemble the self. In short, the least self-threatening person most people know is themselves. People who resemble the self may, by association, be deemed non-threatening as well.

Most situations where people are introduced to a potential mate are inherently threatening and therefore anxious experiences. Among other things, this anxiety may be the result of a concern with creating a certain impression on others, or the fear of rejection. The idea that threat or anxiety is a key component of the implicit egotism effect has now been tested in a study recently published in the *Journal of Personality and Social Psychology* by psychologist John Jones and colleagues from the State University of New York, where subjects rated their liking for various personal ads. In one condition a group of participants were asked before evaluating the ads to write three lines on their own greatest personal drawback or weakness as a potential dating partner. Being assigned to this condition was designed to make those participants more worried about their own desirability before coming to decide which personal ads they were attracted to. Sure enough, under such 'self-concept threat' there was a much stronger attraction to those personal ads where names had been manipulated covertly simply to include more letters of the names of the evaluator. Harry therefore rated Harriet as more attractive.

So if you want to extract the maximum bang for your buck (so to speak) from the implicit egotism theory you need to introduce some self-concept threat into your date on 14 February, and psychologists have conducted experiments that prove the effectiveness of doing just that. In one of the most famous demonstrations in social psychology, back in 1969, John Stapert and Gerald Clore at the University of Illinois set up a series of 'dates' during which colleagues planted by the experimenter spent the entire time agreeing or disagreeing with a subject who was unaware of the true purpose of the experiment, or that the date was a plant. The subjects either found themselves in a nightmare date where everything they said was vehemently contradicted, or had a more pleasant experience where the 'date' agreed throughout the evening with any proposition the subject asserted. It will come as no surprise that when asked to rate the attractiveness of the 'date', the subjects found those who had agreed with them more attractive than the constant contradictors. Then the experimenter threw in a third condition. In this date, the plant started the evening disagreeing and then halfway through switched to agreeing. In this final condition of initial disagreement followed by sudden agreement, the experimenter's plant was found most attractive of all – much more attractive than if they had merely agreed throughout the date.

This experiment may be famous within the cloisters of academic psychology, but it has remained stubbornly obscure to the outside world. Yet the theories which explain this dramatic counterintuitive effect could be used with some practical benefit on Valentine's Day. One theory is that the experience of sudden agreement after much disagreement makes you feel that you have had an impact on your date, and this is found to be attractive. Another theory is that finding yourself in such a situation of constant disagreement is extremely threatening and it raises your anxiety levels; the switch to agreement produces dramatic relief, the positive emotion of which you may at least in part mistake for attraction. All of which chimes nicely with the new attraction theory of Mauricio Carvallo and colleagues based on implicit egotism: a sense of threat and anxiety is created at first with the disagreement, which predisposes us to find any similarity or agreement much more attractive afterwards. Indeed, Stapert and Clore manipulated their experiment so that the plant timed the switch to agreement to later and later in the date, and found, surprisingly, more and more attraction the later the switch! The more stress or the more 'self-concept threat' during the initial part of the date, the more attraction at the end.

It could be that you don't even have to go as far as generating 'self-concept threat' – any stress will do. This will take the pressure off those concerned at timing the 'switch' to ensure that it happens *before* their date has stormed out of the door. Cindy Meston and colleagues at the University of Texas, in a recent paper entitled 'Love at First Fright' published in the journal *Archives of Sexual Behaviour*, confirmed that attraction to a stranger increased after a ride on a scary roller-coaster. Maybe stress adds to attraction because of the 'any port in a storm' theory that our standards drop dramatically in a crisis. When the lift or the train grinds to a halt, even strangers start talking to each other.

If these new theories are true, they go a long way to explaining why so much effort spent on relaxing and charming Valentine's dates won't actually generate the romantic excitement anticipated. They lend credence to the idea that forces beneath conscious awareness are indeed a vital part of attraction much ignored as a tactic by the innocent, unaware of how manipulative romance can get in the hands of the machiavellian evolutionary psychologist.

3

DON'T YOU WANT ME?

Dating with confidence

Marriage is like a bank account. You put it in, you take it out, you lose interest.

Irwin Corey

THERE IS AN INTRIGUING PHENOMENON KNOWN IN psychology as the 'spotlight effect' to which we have all fallen victim whenever we have pushed ourselves from the murk of anonymity into the spotlight of social encounters. Whenever we commit a social faux pas in a crowded room – getting the dress code completely wrong; turning up to a dinner party without a gift for the host – we certainly feel we are under the social spotlight, and squirm accordingly. The sensation of being scrutinized, our every move and expression dissected, can be overwhelming.

Getting a date frequently boils down to issues of confidence – not least, perhaps, admitting to yourself in the first place that you would rather like a date and prefer not to stay single – so there's good news for all you spotlight effect sufferers out there. Thomas Gilovich of

Cornell University, Victoria Medvec of Northwestern and Kenneth Savitsky of Williams College in the USA recently published the results of psychology experiments that demonstrate for the first time that people habitually *overestimate* the extent to which their actions and appearance are noted by others. It seems we believe the social spotlight shines more brightly upon us than it really does.

In one experiment, a student was required to don an embarrassing T-shirt (one sporting a large image of Barry Manilow – a popular singer but of low prestige among college students) before entering a room in which a group of their peers were assembled. The scientists noted in their paper that 'all participants nonetheless donned the shirt, although none looked particularly thrilled about doing so'. The wearer of the T-shirt was later asked to estimate the number of fellow students in the crowded room who definitely discerned the face on the shirt, and this was compared with the actual number who had noticed. In fact, the students were so consumed with their own embarrassment over wearing the attire that they were unable to accurately gauge how conspicuous it was to others. The T-shirt wearers overestimated how many others spotted the garment on average by a factor of two.

The psychologists contend that the systematic exaggeration of how much we are noticed in similar situations derives from this sensation of being 'in the spotlight', which nurtures an inability to see ourselves as we truly appear to others. The theory predicts that we will similarly overestimate how much others notice changes in our behaviour and appearance over time. An example of this phenomenon, argue Gilovich and colleagues, is the widespread narcissistic fear of having a 'bad hair day'. Clearly, the apprehension is not simply that hair can be disobedient and rogue wisps may pop up, they point out, it is more that others will notice such aberrations. But, as the experiments suggest, this concern may be 'overblown'. The variability an individual perceives in his or her own appearance is in fact likely to be altogether lost on most observers. To others, one's apparently bad hair days may be indistinguishable from the good.

In one study, Gilovich, Medvec and Savitsky approached students on unannounced occasions throughout a semester and asked them to rate how they thought they appeared to everyone else on that particular day, relative to how they appeared on most other days. Did they think others would see them as having a good day or a bad day in terms of physical appearance? As suggested by the theory, participants predicted substantially more variability – 24 per cent more – in others' ratings of them than was actually the case.

The explanation for these results, suggest these psychologists, is that most of us stand out in our own minds. We are usually focused on events happening to us, their significance to our lives, and how they appear to others. Each of us is the centre of our own universe. But because we are focused so inwardly, it can be difficult to arrive at an accurate assessment of how much, or how little, our looks or behaviour are noted by others. There is frequently a disparity between the way we view our performance (and think others will view it) and the way it is actually seen by others. Whether making a brilliant point during a boardroom discussion or executing the perfect shot on a tennis court, Gilovich and colleagues remind us, we often find that the efforts we view as remarkable and unforgettable go disregarded or under-appreciated by others. Why, then, should the same not apply to actions that embarrass rather than impress? They too may have less impact on our audience than we might realize, Gilovich and colleagues suggest. An 'obvious' social gaffe on a first date or an awkward stumble as you mount the podium to start your speech may seem ignominious and memorable to us, but they often pass unnoticed, or at least unremarked upon, by others.

Obviously people appreciate that others may see things differently, so they try to adjust from the baseline of their own experience. The ability to do this marks our development from childhood to adulthood, for young children assume everyone else sees things exactly as they do. Adults can take another's perspective in a way children can't, but this adult adjustment still tends to be insufficient. Guessing how you appear to others is still overly influenced by how you appear to yourself, and we still end up believing more eyes are on us than is actually the case.

But Savitsky and colleagues caution that we do not in fact always overestimate how much our appearance and behaviour are noticed by others. They argue that this occurs only when we are self-conscious of our own actions or appearance; only then are we particularly likely to overestimate our prominence in the eyes of others. When the psychologists repeated the T-shirt experiment but allowed the wearer more time to get used to sporting Barry Manilow, they became less embarrassed and got more accurate in guessing how many others noticed the apparel. It seems that when we are less focused on ourselves, perhaps when our behaviour has become more routine and automatic, or when we have acclimatized to some aspect of our appearance, we may be less likely to feel as if we are in the spotlight.

These researchers argue that this implies that something of a reverse spotlight effect might occur, when people are barely or not at all conscious of their own behaviour despite their actions being quite noticeable to others. Then we are likely to *underestimate* how prominent our actions and appearance are in the eyes of others. Smokers, for example, point out Gilovich and colleagues, frequently underrate how intrusive and disturbing their habit is to others because, having practised the habit so often, they often indulge in it inattentively. Likewise, those who douse themselves regularly with what seems like gallons of after-shave may – because they themselves have grown used to the reek – underestimate how obviously it is sensed by others.

Just as people fear that others will notice their social blunders, they may also worry about others forming a negative impression of them as a result. In fact, people may be slower to judge harshly after a social faux pas than one suspects. In another series of experiments, Savitsky and colleagues investigated what happens when an individual is the only guest at a party without a gift to offer the host; in another social blunder, an individual 'draws a blank' and cannot remember the name of an acquaintance. The guests who committed the gaffes tended to overestimate their impact; they believed their behaviour would bother the hosts more than it actually did, and that a more negative impression of them would be formed than was actually the case. The subjects of the name-forgetting experiment believed the faux pas would bother the friend and hurt his or her feelings more than it actually did. It seems, then, that not only do we over-estimate the extent to which others notice our appearance and behaviour, we also exaggerate the extent to which others frown upon us when we breach accepted rules of etiquette.

But perhaps the most important implications of this research are for the type of regrets we are likely to experience. Our biggest regrets in life tend to centre on opportunities we have failed to seize, argue Gilovich and colleagues, rather than things we have done. Regrets of omission often result from a reluctance to grasp a chance because of a fear of failure and the social approbation it might bring. Individuals do not reach out to others for fear of rejection; people do not join a party, or take part in a dance, or join in an organization's football game, or innumerable other social spectacles, because of the fear that they will look inadequate.

This present research suggests that most of our social dreads may be misplaced or overstated. Others are much less likely to detect or dredge up our failings than we usually imagine. Indeed, it was these psychologists' earlier work on regret, and the observation of the many regrets of inaction that stemmed from a concern with how failure would look to others, that led to the research on the 'spotlight effect'. The lesson of this, then, is that we might all have fewer regrets if we properly understood how much attention our actions actually draw from others.

The fact is, we are all too obsessed with ourselves, about how we come over to others, to notice what everyone else is up to. Paradoxically, this precisely explains why everyone else isn't noticing us as much as we think they are. Gilovich and colleagues conclude their paper with the thought that we might take a modest step towards more fulfilling lives if we took stock of Abraham Lincoln's comment that 'people will little note, nor long remember' what we say or do.

TEN STEPS TO IMPROVED SOCIAL CONFIDENCE

(1) *Being shy is not a handicap – it's a bonus*. In fact, shyness in a person is usually an extremely attractive personality trait. The shy are often found more appealing than those who are socially assertive, so don't see your shyness as a handicap to social intercourse. Instead, see it as a part of you with which many other people will identify (almost 50 per cent of people rate themselves as shy). Your shyness can be a part of you that connects you with others rather than distances you from them, if you have the right attitude to it.

(2) *Before you leap in to talk to someone, do a bit of reconnaissance*. Starting off a conversation with someone you don't know well, or have only just met, is particularly difficult for the shy, so take a tip from the more socially assertive who,

before they leap in, check the situation out as much as possible. You need to focus outwardly on what is going on around you rather than inwardly on how inadequate you are feeling, and in particular observe others closely to pick up as much as you can about how they are feeling and what their interests are. Great conversationalists kick off by making comments that are connected in some way to the person they are talking to. To overcome shyness you need to take an active and acute interest in what is going on around you, then adapt yourself to it.

(3) *Timing is everything when joining a conversation.* A terrible moment for the shy is at a party when you are at the periphery of a group who are animatedly discussing something and you are trying to join in. The mistake the shy make is to leap in and interrupt a free-flowing conversation in order to gain entry into the group. This is a big mistake: everyone feels irritated at your having disrupted the flow. Instead, have the patience to wait until a natural lull occurs before inserting an open-ended question that lets others participate; then, once you have got the conversation moving again, back off and give others a chance to talk. The most boring people are those who feel a need to dominate, to be the constant centre of attention.

(4) *Don't keep comparing yourself with the wittiest person you know*. Psychological research has found that one reason the less socially confident feel inadequate is that whenever they are at a social gathering, they tend to pay most attention to the most socially outstanding person there – the life and soul of the party – with whom they compare themselves unfavourably. Such a comparison will only heighten self-consciousness and inhibit social performance. Instead, start making a conscious effort to note how many people at a social gathering are not holding groups in idolized rapture, and you will begin to appreciate that you don't have to be an outstanding wit to find such situations worthwhile and enjoyable.

(5) *Don't start meeting people by only going to places where the very assertive are to be found*. New technology means it is easier than ever before for shy people to meet each other, for example via the Internet or on the phone via chat-lines. Such ways of connecting with people, before an actual 'in the flesh' meeting, provide the opportunity to practise social skills in an arena where there is less pressure and less assertiveness needed than in a crowded bar or nightclub.

(6) *Don't see awkwardness as defining all your interactions with others*. Another way of

looking at shyness is that you are simply slow to warm up socially – you merely need more time to adjust to new or stressful situations. So give yourself that time rather than simply abandoning the party or social encounter early.

(7) *If you don't think people are worth getting to know, you won't overcome your shyness.* Psychologists have recently identified a new group of shy people called the cynically shy, who, because they feel rejected by others, tend to feel resentful about making the effort to socialize because people are not worth it. They tend to adopt a superior stance, looking down on others, as a result. This is in the long run unhelpful and will merely compound your isolation. If you are finding it difficult to connect with those you meet, spread your net wider and make more of an active effort to meet those who share your interests. Everyone has within their lives some achievement which makes them worth looking up to, not down on, and if you can make an effort to find out what this is, you will be everyone's hero.

(8) *Not everything you say to others has to be immediately absorbing.* Shy people tend to have mistaken perfectionistic expectations about socializing, to believe that everything they say has to come out smoothly and wittily like some kind of seamlessly scripted sitcom. In reality,

times when conversation is a bit boring, or you commit faux pas, are entirely part of social life, and unless you learn not to feel mortified when these things inevitably happen you won't overcome your shyness.

(9) *Don't arrive late at parties – get there early.* Because the shy tend towards fearing social encounters, they often arrive later than usual at gatherings. They also reason that it should be easier to mingle when the party is in full swing, plus they hate the idea of standing out by arriving too early. Yet if you are shy, trying to break into groups of people already vigorously chatting when you arrive is more difficult. So get there early instead, precisely because there are so few people around. At such a time they will be grateful to talk to anyone; they are much less likely to have time for you when all their usual friends arrive.

(10) *Fight the modern plague of 'cocooning' by being constantly open to more small talk with relative strangers.* Increasingly we sit on trains buried in our books, tapping on laptops or talking into our mobile phones, and this means we are forever cocooning ourselves from interacting with others on a casual basis via small talk. Also, our tendency to rush from one appointment to the next contributes to this gradual social deskilling. Aim to enter into small talk in at least one casual social encounter every day as part of

your programme to overcome shyness, and soon you will find you have more new friends than you know what to do with. (See chapter 4 for further discussion of small talk.)

ARE YOU CONFIDENT?

Confidence Scale

Each statement is followed by two possible responses: agree or disagree. Read each statement carefully and decide which response best describes how you feel. Then tick the corresponding box. Please reply to every statement. If you are not completely sure which answer is more accurate, tick the one you feel is most appropriate. Do not read the scoring explanation before filling out the questionnaire. Do not spend too long on each statement. It is important that you answer each question as honestly as possible.

		AGREE	DISAGREE
1	Hard work explains success more than natural talent	A	B
2	Others can easily see my faults	B	A
3	I am no different in many ways from most others	A	B
4	I am deeply ashamed about some things I have done	B	A

		AGREE	DISAGREE
5	I impress others easily	A	B
6	Criticism from others makes me angry	B	A
7	I usually do the best I can	A	B
8	I do not like to complain about poor service	B	A
9	Others are less perceptive about me than I am	A	B
10	When I make mistakes they tend to be big ones	B	A
11	In my life the future is very exciting	A	B
12	I dislike many of the people I see daily	B	A
13	I am a lot of fun to be with	A	B
14	I have no one in whom I confide totally	B	A
15	These are the best years of my life	A	B
16	I would change my past if I could	B	A

AGREE   DISAGREE

17   People who have met me, remember
     me

A		B

18   I wish I could be more like other
     people

B		A

19   I find it easy to make new friends

A		B

20   Friends do not usually come to me
     for emotional support

B		A

Score

Add up your score by totalling the number of As and Bs in each box you have ticked.

16 or more Bs: You are scoring very low on confidence, hence your life is often racked by feelings of embarrassment, mortification and humiliation. The fear of such humiliation leads to multiple avoidances in your life, from not applying for new positions to avoiding opportunities to socialize. You tend to think authority figures in your life are constantly scrutinizing you in a disapproving way. What you may not realize is that these strong feelings of inferiority explain your melancholy, and that also explains why others' attempts to cheer you up are so often unsuccessful: when others are positive about you it has little impact because you are so negative about yourself. Listen to others a little more – they are more accurate about you than you can be about yourself.

Between 10 and 15 Bs: While you are not racked with the

constant feelings of low confidence of higher scorers, you are scoring above average in feelings of low confidence. This means that whenever things go wrong you are much more likely to believe it's all your fault and to respond with deep feelings of disgrace. This lack of confidence partly explains your tendency to shyness. You need to remember that your bias to be much harder on yourself than others means you are a poor judge of exactly how bad things really are. In fact, you are probably nicer to be with than you realize. However, as long as there is such a wide gap between your fantasy of how you would like to be and how you find yourself, low confidence will persist.

Between 5 and 9 Bs: Although you are scoring around average to above average for feelings of confidence, you are not so confident about your superiority over others as not to feel ridiculed on occasion, which deeply irritates you. It is your feelings of inferiority which make you reluctant to share some of your deepest feelings with others, as you fear scorn, or that others will not understand. In fact, growing confidence will follow gradually from more risk taking. You are still overly influenced by others' opinions and therefore tend not to voice and stick to your own point of view when you are going a bit out on a limb. Only when you can accept rejection without loss of self-esteem can you rate yourself as having moved up to the highest level of confidence and joined the lower scorers on this scale.

Between 0 and 4 Bs: You are scoring very low in feelings of inferiority, which explains your confidence in most social situations and your tendency to take risks, for example your enjoyment of flirting and positively asserting yourself, even when with strangers. What you may not realize is that most people are not as free of feelings of inferiority as you are, so you need to be a little more sensitive of others' deep and strong feelings of vulnerability. Your freedom from the embarrassment most others feel when an awkward event has occurred tends to make you too unapologetic for your social mistakes, compounding errors and perhaps making you more unpopular with strangers than is helpful to you.

THE IMPORTANCE OF FRIENDS

More confidence means that you are more likely to approach and initiate conversations with relative or complete strangers, which might lead on to something interesting in terms of a relationship. But don't just rely on casual encounters. One search strategy which is most neglected in my experience yet most fruitful is using a network of friends to supply you with possibilities. Friends of friends are a great way of broadening your romantic chances: they represent an upping perhaps by tenfold in terms of eyes and ears beyond your own on the lookout for a nice person for you. Moreover, friends know you and therefore have some sense of who might be suitable; certainly they will screen out the dangerous or unscrupulous (if they are good friends, that is).

But often the dateless are also relatively friendless, and this might be no accident. So if you are complaining about how come you never meet people you would like to date, take one step back from the issue and pose the question of whether you have enough friends as the key tools to help you find such a person. And remember, the challenge of meeting and making new friends is a good preparation for the kind of social skills needed for taking things one step further, beyond friendship and into romance. Friends are a vital part of all socializing and are often the crucial entrée into the world of romance.

Many people find that they can't seem to crack the problem of moving opposite-sex relationships in more romantic directions. This inevitably raises the issue of male/female friendship and the sexual tension that may or may not be lurking beneath the surface.

This is not to knock the importance of friendships with the opposite sex, which are absolutely vital for several reasons. However, I frequently advise women to be suspicious of very attractive men who seem to have no female friends – i.e. relationships with the opposite sex where the connection was not sexualized at some point. This usually means that these men are unable to 'do' female friendship, which is not only an ominous pointer for the future in terms of infidelity but also means there won't be much friendship in the relationship – a vital ingredient in any long-term romantic relationship.

Opposite-sex friends are crucial for advice on your own relationship – from tips on how best to present oneself and how to dress (particularly important for men), to getting a good insight into what your date might be thinking in various scenarios. Opposite-sex friends also help to broaden your circle and introduce you to other friends who might become dates in the future.

A branch of mathematics known as network theory suggests that the mistake most people make is to concentrate on the contacts of their best friends when looking for prospective dates. Precisely because you know your closest friends best they are likely to share most of their friends with you already. They are going to be a poor source of new potential dates. Instead, concentrate on those you know least well – their network of potential contacts is much wider in terms of those you don't already know.

So, work on your friendships and deepen your network as the best way of finally meeting the right person romantically for you.

TEN STEPS TO BETTER FRIENDSHIPS

(1) A vital ingredient that is too often missing in relationships, and which explains why so many people don't have the friendships they want, is time. People who give more time to others have more friends – it's as simple as that. Research has found that the typical seventeen-year-old (who has generally a lot of time on his or her hands) has on average nineteen friends, but this number drops to twelve for the average twenty-eight-year-old, though it rises again to sixteen for the average forty-five-year-old.

(2) When people are asked to focus only on the relationships that are most satisfying, intimate and close, however, the number of true friends drops dramatically from the higher numbers used to quantify acquaintances and falls to around six on average. What separates a true

close friend from an acquaintance seems to be loyalty and the ability to keep confidences. Practically, this is recognized as refraining from public criticism of a friend. So although we all enjoy a good gossip, true friends don't slander each other. Although you may find betraying another friend's confidences makes you temporarily the centre of attention, it will lose the respect and trust of those who were considering making you a good friend.

(3)   The fact that friends choose to spend time with you is in itself a compliment and a boost to self-esteem. It is this effect of good friendship that is vital, so to be seen as a good friend you should learn how to make people feel good about themselves with praise and compliments. Perhaps the biggest compliment of all is to be interested in and affected by other people's lives.

(4)   But good friends are not just interested in us, they also support us by and large in our viewpoints and our endeavours. They may not agree with everything we do, but our closest friends will tend to uphold our position when we turn to them for support in the face of a hostile world. Because good friends will tend to share our core attitudes, places to find good friends include organizations or activities that reflect our own approach to life.

(5)   While reciprocation is the unstated rule of

friendship, it is also true that if you never dare to ask a favour of a friend, then in a sense they are not really good friends. Helping friends without obvious expectation of an immediate return is an essential ingredient of friendship. Those who don't ever ask for help don't build the kind of interdependence close friendship requires, so fiercely independent people don't tend to have too many friends.

(6) All friendships exist because of communication. If you don't communicate, your friendship will wither. In particular, good friendship involves not holding back from saying what you feel in the way you might in a more formal relationship. You should therefore care less about 'impression management' with a good friend. Those who cannot properly self-disclose have difficulty building intimate friendships.

(7) Self-disclosing involves trusting, and usually friendships progress through deepening levels of self-disclosure. You notice the other person has revealed something personal about themselves, and you then feel able to reciprocate similarly. If there is an imbalance in who is doing the self-disclosing then a proper friendship cannot develop. Try to mirror the amount of self-disclosing the other person is achieving and take it slightly further in terms of what you reveal about yourself, but without jumping too far ahead of them.

(8)   Friends are lost most often when they move away and contact becomes more difficult because of geographical distance. A simple way to maintain friendships when this happens is to try to set aside at least one special day every year for a reunion. Your friend will get into the habit of keeping those days clear for you as well.

(9)   Friendship also involves patience with those who are unable to reciprocate quite as you would like all the time. But know when a friend is truly incapable of returning the affection and attention you desire, and invest your valuable time elsewhere rather than grow resentful over a friendship that is not working. In particular, realize that we all change with time and friends can grow apart because of an alteration in life direction. Hanging on to friendships that are no longer appropriate reveals an anxiety over how to form new friendships.

(10) Never give up on friends you have not heard from for a long time. Nothing is lost by sending a card to re-ignite a friendship. If you see yourself as a good friend you will have the confidence to realize that others won't want to lose the opportunity to rekindle a friendship with you. As friendship is one of the greatest gifts we can bestow, try to be generous with it.

GETTING OUT OF YOUR COMFORT ZONE

One of the most fascinating discoveries in the fields of psychology and psychiatry is that our understanding of ourselves is often grossly unreliable. Most dubious of all are the explanations we come up with for our motivations – why we chose this lover or that job. Although we should surely know ourselves better than anyone else, we frequently misunderstand ourselves because our choices, which determine our destiny, are often actually directed at preventing us from finding out the truth about ourselves.

One aspect of this is the idea of a 'comfort zone' or 'solace space'. This is the life-space defined by people or situations which make us feel comfortable. We gravitate towards them, not so much because of their attraction, but more because we are repelled by discomfort.

The key to understanding the powerful but subtle forces at work here is realizing that much of our behaviour is designed with a hidden purpose – so hidden that we often forget it's there. In addition to the goals we have everyday – getting to work, doing the shopping – we have more clandestine aspirations which are actually determining our behaviour. Basically, in any encounter with another person we try to behave in ways that reflect our desire to be viewed as reasonable, competent, attractive and moral people. Actually, almost all our behaviour in the presence of others is designed to generate a positive view of ourselves, so severe discomfort occurs when our ability to project a positive image is undermined. For example, those who avoid parties and clubs, despite the desire to meet others, are simply avoiding the mortification which accompanies threats to their ability to project a positive identity.

If you stay in alone at home, no matter how isolated that appears, you are still in your comfort zone. The fear of going out is that being alone at a crowded party will be humiliating. Public social rejection undermines our self-esteem much more than being alone at home, although in fact staying in is also a form of social rejection, *but one we do to ourselves in secret*. It is better to be alone but unseen rather than alone and seen to be alone.

Take another example, the case of the couple who never discuss sex frankly; the status quo is preferred to the discomfort of admitting to inexperience. It is preferable to continue quietly being bad at something rather than have attention drawn to our inadequacies.

A good example of abhorring the leaving of a comfort zone occurred in the case of Susan, a patient referred to me by her GP, who thought she was suffering from depression and loneliness. Susan actually had little trouble meeting men, and they frequently asked her out for the evening. However, as the night wore on Susan would get increasingly anxious about how to handle the ending of the evening. She had a strong religious background, so physical closeness and sex were issues of deep trepidation for her. She and her date would usually return to her flat and they would talk fairly intensely well into the night. The man would then leave in the early morning and Susan would be left frustrated and upset that nothing more had happened. The early part of any date would go smoothly because she found it easy in simple conversation to present a positive image of herself to a man. This was deep comfort zone territory. But she felt that any first move on her part, no matter how subtle, presented an image of permissiveness. She also believed this would be doubly confirmed if this was then rejected.

Susan's greatest fear was to appear promiscuous, hence her comfort zone became those situations where there was no possibility of that ever being inferred from her behaviour. To discover your comfort zones, all you have to do is consider the image you like to present to the world, and then the image you try to avoid projecting. Susan had to learn that only when she could see physical advances as compatible with a positive feminine image would she be able to stop avoiding this aspect of her life.

Embarrassment also occurs when events beyond our control communicate undesired information about ourselves to others. Because we detest this possibility, we retreat deep into comfort zone territory and dare not try new situations where our lack of familiarity with new social rules may cause unwelcome leakage of personal information. We are never as competent or as self-assured as we like to appear, when outside our comfort zones.

So, embarrassment results from the flustered uncertainty that follows not knowing how to behave in unfamiliar situations. Since we are accustomed to most of the expectations of people we encounter, we have evolved over time a set of rules which dictate what to do and when to do it – something psychologists call a 'script'. This governs most of our day-to-day dealings with others. Hence the couple who never talk frankly about sex, or those who avoid new social encounters, do so because they do not feel they know what to say and when. They have no script on which to rely, precisely because these are confrontations with which they rarely contend.

The only way to evolve an adequate script is to expose oneself to exactly these situations more frequently. However, the necessary loss of poise which accompanies learning new scripts is something so aversive that we retreat into our comfort zone instead.

Angela was a highly competent junior surgeon referred by her GP when she began to suffer symptoms of stress at work. It transpired that she usually finished seeing her patients earlier than the other surgeons in her team and she was then being asked to take over their cases, which were still waiting to be seen. Angela seemed incapable of saying no to her colleagues, and it appeared that her inability to delegate or refuse extra work was responsible for symptoms of burn-out. Angela clearly had no 'refusal script'. She avoided the embarrassment of having to confront this difficult situation by resorting instead to the only script she had, which I labelled her 'doormat script'. She lacked a refusal script because saying no was incompatible with her own image of herself as an omnipotent surgeon, and saying no appeared (to her) to portray an incompetent female struggling in a world of competent men. In fact, Angela was surrounded by incompetent men who did not care what she thought of them, but as she cared too much about what they thought of her, the comfort zone they manufactured between them was one where she always said yes.

We can also become uncomfortable when we have done nothing objectively wrong: merely being the conspicuous object of others' attention can be embarrassing. So it is really an intense fear of negative appraisal by others which causes people to become self-conscious, and makes them stay within their comfort zones.

In fact, whenever we present ourselves to others we risk rejection of some kind. The form this rejection takes may be flagrant, but it is more frequently quite subtle, perhaps only a missed beat in the rhythm of conversation. Just how negative an experience this is can be seen by our anxiety whenever we have misplaced our 'scripts'. If you are already worried about what the boss thinks of you, for example, having to be with him or her in an unfamiliar situation outside the office is an even more anxiety-laden experience. This highlights another clue as to whether comfort zones rule your life: a continuous yearning to be liked by others will naturally lead to a fearful avoidance of situations where there is a risk of public failure and rejection.

Some people's comfort zones are extremely small, because they are habitually self-conscious – hence their refusal to enter into relationships without strong guarantees of uncritical acceptance. Their exaggeration of the risks in everyday situations produces a restricted lifestyle dependent on a need for certainty and security. This combination of persistent and pervasive feelings of tension and apprehension, a strong wish for relationships, yet an avoidance of situations where there is a risk of rejection or failure, are characteristics of an 'avoidant personality'. Such features have been found in 10 per cent of the general population.

Another interesting paradox of the comfort zone thus emerges: an individual's psychological strength lies not in avoiding negative judgements by others, but in a willingness to confront the risk of appraisal. Independence requires the ability to accept others' opposition to yourself, such as a rejection, without a lowered sense of personal worth. The independent person often does things which might end in rejection, but is not deterred, because they do not see rejection as a reflection of their particular value.

When we avoid discomfort zones we are actually just running away from ourselves. It is useful to analyse situations when we tend to be uncomfortable because it tells us a great deal about ourselves. In particular, it illuminates those gaps between how we would like to appear and how we think we actually are. It is surprising how many people avoid seeking professional help for their emotional problems precisely because talking about themselves takes them into the discomfort zone. Publicly owning up to our vulnerabilities is often just too discordant with the way we like to appear. For others, therapy plays a valuable role precisely because the professional insists on confronting and staying in discomfort zone territory – something the client would otherwise resist, and which friends are unlikely to persist with. Then again, many in therapy, particularly those in treatment for a long time, cleverly avoid confronting those areas of life which lie outside their comfort zone. For these people, therapy is an indulgence, precisely because it has become too comfortable. So beware: if you are feeling too comfortable about life, that may be because you are really not exploring it at all.

Are you an avoider? You are if you . . .

- Are easily hurt by criticism and disapproval
- Have few confidants other than relatives
- Are unwilling to become involved with people unless certain of being liked
- Avoid activities which involve much interpersonal contact
- Are reticent in social situations because you are afraid of saying something inappropriate or foolish
- Exaggerate the potential difficulties involved in doing something outside usual routines
- Fear showing signs of anxiety in front of others
- Hate looking incompetent
- Are terrified of not looking your best at all times

ARE HIGH LEVELS OF CONFIDENCE GOOD FOR RELATIONSHIPS?

But, if in social situations you never feel like the most confident person in the world, take heart. 'If you do not love yourself you will be unable to love others' is a popular sentiment that permeates self-help books and the current spate of popular primetime TV dating advice programmes such as *Would Like To Meet* and *Perfect Match*. But this view, that high self-esteem is good for you, has now been challenged by new research published recently in the prestigious *Journal of Personality and Social Psychology*.

There are several theories for why self-liking should promote relationships. Perhaps those who do not like themselves do not believe that others can love them, and thus avoid healthy relationships. Or perhaps if we do not love ourselves, we will naturally select bad relationships as part of an overall self-destructive strategy. Properly testing this received wisdom for the first time, Dr Keith Campbell and colleagues from the University of Georgia took the relatively unusual step of interviewing those in relationships with people possessing high self-esteem. They found that those who strongly like themselves might indeed be confident, exciting and charming on a first date, but their likeability rapidly fades over time, as their grandiosity becomes apparent. People awed at the outset gradually lost patience with the oneupmanship and constant demands for admiration.

It seems, then, that the dating TV programmes' and self-help books' advice does contain a small kernel of truth – people do view those with high self-esteem favourably on an initial encounter. But the impression tends towards being reversed over repeated interactions. At the first meeting, those who had high liking for themselves were indeed rated agreeable, competent, intelligent, confident and entertaining, but by the seventh interaction or date they were seen as arrogant, overestimating their abilities and tending to brag and be hostile.

Another recent study by Dr Campbell found that high self-esteem strongly predicted future infidelity, as those who like themselves a lot constantly wonder if they have found someone as good as they truly deserve, and keep a constant roving eye out for a better prospect (there's more on this topic in chapters 4 and 10). Indeed, very high self-esteem is linked with a corresponding tendency to harbour disdain for everyone else. But precisely because they look down on all others, those with high self-esteem find it easier to flirt and be playful at the start of relationships, as they don't really care about being rebuffed by those beneath their standards anyway.

In fact, it seems that this latest psychological research has taken us full circle back to a truth the ancient Greeks well understood. According to Greek legend, Narcissus kept searching for the perfect romantic partner. Eventually he fell in love with the only person who met his exacting standards, his own reflection in a river, but he fell into the water and drowned as he attempted to embrace his image. From this legend the term 'narcissism' is derived, which is defined as an addiction to self-esteem.

Indeed, modern society at large seems currently to be dangerously addicted to self-esteem, and some psychologists argue that we are living in an era of unprecedented narcissism. Dr Claudia Mueller and Dr Carol Dweck of Columbia University recently conducted a series of studies into school students which established that modern parents have a tendency to heap too much praise on their offspring, in desperate attempts to raise self-esteem. They noted a modern trend for parents to describe their children as 'gifted' or 'talented' but discovered that this in the long run did the offspring no favours. Mueller and Dweck demonstrated that excessively commending children for their intelligence after good academic performance in the end backfires, by rendering their self-esteem highly fragile. It left students extremely vulnerable to a self-esteem roller-coaster ride in the face of subsequent setbacks. Children who are praised for their effort rather than their personality react better to future failures, as there are no longer any dramatic implications for self-esteem. If you are praised for your hard work rather than your character, you tend to see a setback as merely a signal that you need to invest more effort in the future, rather than as a sign that you are no good.

The modern preoccupation with high self-esteem is particularly dangerous as such dizzying self-confidence makes it very difficult to develop insight and seek help. James Masterson, an eminent New York City psychiatrist who has been extensively referred to in the *New York Times* as a world authority on excessively high self-esteem, relates a recent story of a dozen narcissists who came to see him for treatment shortly after his theories had appeared in the press. He diagnosed each of them as suffering from narcissistic personality disorder, or of having too high a sense of self-esteem, but explained that he was unable to see any more patients and suggested they see another clinician in his practice. Not one of the twelve narcissists returned for treatment. Each of them apparently desired therapy but only if they worked with a famous psychiatrist, which would increase their stock in New York society. Therapy with just any old doctor was clearly beneath them! So, as I said, if you are shy, take heart. You might be a slow starter like the tortoise, but there's every chance you can still run a better race than the hare.

4

THE AIM OF THE GAME

How to flirt

Marriage resembles a pair of shears, so joined that they cannot be separated; often moving in opposite directions, yet always punishing anyone who comes between them.

Sydney Smith

IN MY DAILY PROFESSIONAL LIFE I SEE MANY PEOPLE WHO ARE beset with anxieties about being unable to attract the opposite sex in the manner they would like, and who are curious about how to flirt more effectively. Flirting is undoubtedly an important art in the psychology of attraction, and one measure of your flirting skills is to try your hand at this simple test, which I like to set for the people who come to my clinics.

Imagine walking into a bar and there is only one person there, at the bar itself, having a rather solitary drink. This person is one of the most attractive people in the world, and indeed is the object of your own fascination. I want you to visualize who this person might be. You are free to pick anyone, but it's key to the exercise that they are well known for being extremely attractive. The task I want to set you is to go over to the bar, order a drink and think what you might say casually to Brad Pitt, Michelle Pfeiffer; whoever you've chosen that might lead on to further conversation and, you never know, something even better. Before reading on, I should like you to consider what you might say and get it clear in your mind.

The task is framed in this way for several reasons. Your chosen person is alone in the bar so that there is no obvious competition and you will not be interrupted, so you've got a chance to start a conversation. You have, of course, to say something which is likely to pique their interest in further interaction with you, so I've asked you to pick someone famous and attractive because such people are used to being 'chatted up'. In fact, they've probably heard every line in the book, as they say, so this makes your task even tougher. But it's an excellent test of your flirting skills, because the key to flirting is another F – flattery (I don't know what you were thinking . . .). So, how do you flatter someone who is used to flattery?

In this case, let's talk about what you definitely should *not* try. What you absolutely shouldn't do is what everyone tends to do. Don't say to George Clooney at the bar, 'I really loved you in *ER*.' The reason you should never say this is that a famous actor like George Clooney has heard it a hundred times before. Indeed, he's heard it so often that it's positively irritating to hear it being said yet again. So the first step of flattery is to get inside the mind of the person you are trying to flatter and get a sense of what they might *want* to hear.

What would probably be of genuine interest to George

or Brad or Michelle is if your conversational gambit went something like this: you pick an obscure piece of work they have done, perhaps a film they made at the beginning of their careers, and you make a comment about how impressive it was because it highlighted an aspect of their personality or talent which is not so widely known. You might instead pick something about them that you know but which is not widely known by the rest of the public. The key to why this kind of flattery is going to be more effective than 'I loved you in *ER*' is that it naturally demonstrates a much more specific interest in George Clooney, Brad Pitt or Michelle Pfeiffer than the usual platitudes about widely known aspects of their lives. You are signifying a genuine and deep interest in this celebrity as a person, and this is not something they will be used to.

So when it comes to flattery, and therefore flirting, do the unexpected – it's more interesting. And do something that marks you out as an individual with a specific and deep interest in that particular person. This is vital, otherwise flirting appears like an 'act' you've tried on loads of times with many others – which is extremely unflattering to its recipient.

One can then think more widely of what to do in terms of engaging such a person. You might leave the bar, then return and ask for help of some kind. Some of my more psychopathic clients have even used the tactic of returning to a bar having let the air out of a tyre of a car parked outside in order to claim it's their own car with a flat. Asking for help is not a bad way of flirting, and indeed is in itself a kind of flattery. Another good line to think about using is 'Are you having fun?' This is a useful approach as both positive and negative responses can lead to further conversational opportunities which are all about putting the 'target' person, their feelings and their preferences at the heart of the discourse. The usefulness of the 'are you having fun' approach is that it draws attention to your own interest in 'fun' – a key ingredient to attractiveness is to be someone with whom more fun is possible than with others.

One of the problems with flirting, however, is its ambiguity. Aspects of 'game playing' often lead to a sense in which flirting is conducted in a manipulative and rather dark manner – to knock the other person off balance and develop power over them.

Psychologists Keith Campbell, Craig Foster and Eli Finkel from the University of Georgia, the United States Air Force Academy and Carnegie Mellon University respectively have recently conducted a series of studies exploring the personality types of those who are extremely good at flirting – with some very unflattering results. These psychologists argue that expert flirters tend to be narcissists. They point out that relationships are good for narcissists because they can provide positive attention and sexual satisfaction, but they are bad in that they demand emotional intimacy and restrict attention and sexual satisfaction from other partners. The ideal solution, therefore, is for narcissists to find a way to receive the benefits of a relationship without having to endure the costs – to have their cake and eat it, so to speak. Conveniently, the feelings of the partner do not need to figure prominently in a narcissist's solution.

Campbell and colleagues argue that the ideal

narcissistic solution is to begin and maintain a relationship with a partner using charm, extroversion and
confidence, which gives them access to positive attention,
esteem and sexual resources. They would be careful to
keep this relationship from becoming too intimate or
emotionally close lest they lose control. They would also
covertly seek out other potential romantic partners, which
makes for an easier transition to another relationship if
the current one ends.

Campbell and colleagues point out that this strategy
clearly corresponds to a specific love style: ludus, or game
playing. By adopting a game-playing approach to love,
narcissists get what they want from a relationship while
avoiding the things they do not want. Game playing when
it comes to love is an ideal strategy for an individual who
(a) has an inflated view of himself or herself; (b) is less
interested in his or her partner's needs; (c) strives to maintain his or her own esteem, status and opportunities for
infidelity while avoiding excessive emotional intimacy; and
(d) has a confident, outgoing and extroverted personality.
But it's a bad strategy for long-term commitment. Game
playing is not a good approach to use if one wants a lasting relationship.

Of course, not everyone is a game player, and flirting is
a useful technique, but the danger if you encounter someone who is very good at it is that this person is potentially
using it not just on you but on others as well. Remember,
narcissists keep their love interests off balance and are
constantly searching for other partners. Self-love as con-
ceptualized by narcissism is not a boon for loving others.
The big mistake we all make when we find ourselves the

target of extremely effective flirting is to assume the game is being played purely for our benefit, when in fact it is being done for theirs. The best kind of flirting in terms of psychological health is that which arises out of a genuine interest in the other person and is not an attempt to hoodwink them or keep the upper hand. But note that highly skilled flirters may not be partaking of this set of values.

SMALL TALK

Highly skilled flirters know intuitively that the key to initiating a relationship is not to have 'a chat-up line' but instead to know how to engage in conversation those you have never met before. This requires 'small talk' skills.

Small talk is anything but small. It is in fact a deadly serious activity because it:

(1) Sets the emotional atmosphere in which more serious talk might occur.

(2) Serves to relax people so they do not find you threatening. When relaxed, people are more open to your ideas and to you as a person, making the task of getting people to like you easier.

(3) Subtly communicates important information about someone's present state of mind. From people's opening small talk you can learn things such as whether or not they have the time to talk about more serious things right now.

(4) Appears unimportant, so it frees people to take the opportunity to tell you if something is on their mind, which they might otherwise not share with you if you were talking about something more serious.

Hairdressers, taxi-drivers and bartenders are the street-smart experts when it comes to small talk. They find it useful because it can:

(1) Determine the size of tip they get – so why shouldn't you use small talk to improve your performance and profit from it?

(2) Cover embarrassing silences.

(3) Make the stressful business of dealing with different people more enjoyable.

(4) Help the transfer of more important information which could be of use in the future. You can learn so much from small talk that during the Second World War the governments checked the small talk of bartenders, hairdressers and taxi-drivers in an attempt to monitor rumours.

The ability to make small talk is a skill the experts have developed by:

(1) Monitoring the other person for signs of boredom, then changing the subject. Being good at

small talk means being exquisitely sensitive to the earliest sign of any lack of interest in what is being said. Small talk is more about keeping the other person engaged than it is about deeply meaningful content. If you find you are doing all the talking then something has gone wrong with the small talk.

(2) Having a broad range of subjects you are prepared to talk about. Small talk bores stick only to the one subject they are interested in; the small talk king can talk about literally anything.

(3) Finding ways of uncovering what the other person wants to talk about. Asking people what they do for a living is not about extracting their CV from them; it's more about getting clues about what they are interested in. The best small talk is about finding things you both have in common. Self-disclosure is therefore an important part of small talk. Revealing things about yourself helps the other person discover things they have in common with you which they may want to talk about, or instead simply provides them with an opportunity to ask questions about you.

(4) Asking open-ended questions, which are questions that cannot be answered by a simple yes or no. For example, you could say, 'What did you think of the film?', rather than saying, 'Wasn't that film terrible?'

(5) Asking questions that are very difficult to answer briefly. How did you get here? How did you come to be in that job? How do you think they do that?

(6) Praising people, which is another important part of small talk. People feel warm towards those who give them compliments and are more likely to want to stay and talk to them, naturally seeking more positive feedback. The classic small talk initiator is the compliment-and-question technique: you start by complimenting someone on some aspect of themselves, like their appearance, and then ask a follow-up question about themselves. For example, 'That's a lovely brooch you're wearing – wherever did you get it?'

(7) Having a sense of humour, which is crucial to small talk. Humour stops things from getting too serious, which usually causes discomfort in the early stages of any relationship.

(8) Avoiding self-consciousness, which tends to kill small talk. Whatever you do, don't think of yourself as doing small talk; think instead of yourself trying to get to know someone and at the same time making their time with you a little more pleasant. The best small talk occurs because of your concern for the other, not because you want to get something off your chest. If your small talk has a definite aim, like getting a bigger tip or

taking someone home for the evening, the goal usually becomes transparent and spoils the small talk for the other person. Small talk should not have too clear an aim – it's more about passing the time enjoyably. The rewards will spring naturally from that. This is often where the needy or desperate fall down: so keen are they to make a positive impression or to impress, they work too hard at it. It all matters too much to them and this robs them of that essential light touch. The best attitude to adopt is not to take yourself too seriously.

(9) Knowing when to shut up. Even small talk experts appreciate that not everyone is always willing to make small talk. Forcing small talk on those who would rather be left alone, no matter how good you might be at it, is just as poor a social skill as not being able to make small talk at all.

The best way of improving your small-talk skills is to take note when you are in the hands of an expert. Observe precisely what they talk about, and how they engage the other party. You will need to be especially vigilant because good small talk is so engaging you may not have time to notice you have been taking part in small talk at all!

ARE YOU A FLIRT AND/OR A CHARMER?

Flirting is often used to signal romantic interest, or to try to provoke it in others, without necessarily having any real intent to follow through should any interest begin to be shown by the other party. A good flirt may have no purpose other than to demonstrate their power over the other sex. But there is nothing genuinely entrancing about such a skill. The more interesting and alluring concept is the notion of charm – the ability to secure the interest of others because of some genuine personal investment in them.

Psychological research into seduction highlights some fascinating gender differences. For instance, men are more likely to use words to charm, while women prefer body language. Another intriguing difference is that once a woman is interested in a man, as long as he is available for romantic involvement, she is more likely to be able to seduce him than a man is able to provoke interest by charming a woman. Hence women find that signalling their availability is often the most powerful strategy for provoking male interest, while men have to resort to a gamut of alternative strategies to gain the same interest from women. And the ability to charm is also about sending precisely the right messages: research has also shown a chronic tendency for men to misunderstand women's messages, frequently misinterpreting mere friendliness as seduction.

Charm Scale

Each statement is followed by two possible responses: agree or disagree. Read each statement carefully and decide which response best describes how you feel. Then tick the corresponding box. Please reply to every statement. If you are not completely sure which answer is more accurate, tick the one you feel is most appropriate. Do not read the scoring explanation before filling out the questionnaire. Do not spend too long on each statement. It is important that you answer each question as honestly as possible.

		AGREE	DISAGREE
1	I give more compliments than I receive	A	B
2	None of my long-term opposite-sex friends secretly fancies me	B	A
3	I enjoy the time I spend buying gifts for others	A	B
4	Trying to look good is hard work and deceives nobody	B	A
5	If someone doesn't want romance we can still be friends	A	B
6	I cannot invest any more spare time to gain another's interest	B	A
7	I avoid telling the harsh truth if it's going to hurt feelings	A	B
8	Other people's interests usually bore me	B	A

AGREE DISAGREE

9   Being mysterious is better than being
     straightforward

     [A]   [B]

10   Impressing others would get me more
     romantic attention

     [B]   [A]

Score

Add up your score by totalling the number of As and Bs in each box you have ticked.

8 or more As: You are scoring extremely highly on charm, which means that you are aware consciously or unconsciously of most of the rules of charming the opposite sex, such as more people are laughed into bed than are impressed into bed. Your confidence in yourself adds to your charm as it allows you to be modest and not boorish in showing off, which is how many lower scorers think you charm someone of the opposite sex. The problem is, does your charm often prevent you from being assertive in some situations when others are not succumbing to your charm? You may rely too much on charm and neglect other important ways of communication, like frankness.

Between 5 and 7 As: You are scoring above average on charm, which means you use your empathy for others' feelings to good effect as they fall for your concern in them. However, you find it slightly more difficult to charm those from very different backgrounds to yourself as you tend to rely on what has worked in the past. You need to be slightly more open-minded when meeting new people about what motivates them before you can charm them as well. Another problem is you may often mistake flirting with charm. Sometimes you enjoy seeing others fall for you for reasons to do with reassuring yourself that you are attractive, rather than because of a genuine interest in them.

Between 3 and 4 As: You are scoring around average to below average on charm, and this may be because you see relationships as something spontaneous which either work or don't, and you neglect the fact that they often require effort to make them work. You may see passing compliments and feigning an interest in others' anecdotes as a charade, but you are neglecting the fact that once you work at being charming the rewards soon make the effort second nature. Charm can become a part of you, rather than something you adopted.

Between 0 and 2 As: You are scoring well below average on charm, and this is probably for two main reasons: either you already have personal resources which make you attractive to others without your needing to make the effort (you may be wealthy, fabulously good-looking or famous, or you may *believe* you are) so you have long dispensed with charm and concentrate more on deflecting attention; or you are not concerned with what others think of you, and you always put more personal goals first, such as your own ideals and ambitions.

THE BRUSH-OFF

Sometimes, oddly enough, the reason many are too afraid to engage in flirting is that they are worried about how to extricate themselves should things start to get too serious for their own liking. This is why flirting can be a fundamentally selfish behaviour if conducted in the wrong spirit. So if you are going to flirt, you are also going to have to build confidence in how to let people down gently if their interest in you is not reciprocated.

People want things from us all the time – our attention, our money, our love, our commitment, our possessions – and being able to hold on to these things and not give them to those you do not want to have them – in other words, being able to say no to others – is an extremely important life skill. But most people have difficulty with it. The reasons for this include the following:

(1) We feel guilty.

(2) We do not want others to feel bad because of us.

(3) We are worried about appearing nasty or uncaring.

(4) We do not want to alienate those whose help we might need at another time.

The problem with such concerns is that those who are trying to avoid the brush-off from us are usually aware of these natural feelings and use them against us; in other words, they try to make us feel guilty, or make us feel that by saying no we *are* uncaring and nasty, or that we have just been deeply offensive. However, for these techniques used against us to work on us we have to:

(1) Care what others think about us more than we care about ourselves.

(2) Put others' needs and feelings before our own.

(3) Believe we need to look after our relationship with the person trying to get us to say yes more than we need to look after ourselves.

(4) Fear what the other person is going to do in the future as a result of our brush-off.

You must always bear in mind that if you do not look after your interests, no one else will – this is the primary rule of the brush-off. Do not hope that by accommodating others they will accommodate you. People usually avoid saying no or giving the brush-off because to do so is vaguely unpleasant, and most of us would rather postpone unpleasantness to a later date. But if you do that you end up forever putting off the moment when you will say no and will end up saying yes. So remember, saying no or giving the brush-off will always be more unpleasant than saying yes, but in the long run it is the better decision. If the person in question is a friend, a family member or a business colleague, they may well be used to getting their own way with you – you have taught them by your acquiescence to dominate you. Saying no to such people will be met with great resistance to begin with and will be much more difficult than saying no to a virtual stranger, as a date will probably be. But if you persist, saying no gradually gets easier.

Remember, when you start to stand up for yourself and be true to your feelings:

(1) Do not criticize yourself for being assertive. If you feel the need to be self-critical, focus on the *way* you were assertive.

(2) You'll feel worse in the long run if you do nothing.

(3) It is more likely that you'll have difficulty giving the brush-off or saying no if caught off-guard by an unexpected request. The person asking usually knows this, which is why they may time a request to perfection. Do not acquiesce. Play for time and say you will give the request your consideration but you cannot give an answer right now.

(4) Be kind but firm in your brush-off.

(5) Repeat yourself over and over again if the other person tries different ways of persuading you, using a technique known as 'broken record': just say no over and over again without getting side-tracked into explaining why you are saying no or having to defend your decision. By doing this you will indicate to the other person that you are resolutely sticking to your guns.

(6) If saying no is just proving too much for you, say yes, but tie your acceptance to a favour you need

from the other person which will be difficult for them to comply with. Say, for instance, that you will go out with them on Saturday only if they agree to baby-sit for you on Sunday.

As with flirting, the best way to learn how to give others the brush-off is to watch others doing it well. And remember, as you hesitate to give the brush-off:

(1) Many people have difficulty saying no.

(2) White lies are acceptable to save someone's feelings.

(3) Be sensitive to the feelings of the person you are letting down.

(4) Use tact.

Those who find it difficult to mix with other people often suffer from personality issues which, unbeknown to them, are separating them from the rest of humanity. I refer to these as the Seven Deadly Emotions. If you are troubled on the inside you will feel less confident when you attempt to mingle or approach others. Furthermore, if you are not an entirely happy human being other people will sense that and will find it more difficult to be with you. Check that these are not issues that might need to be resolved before you can date with confidence.

Seven Deadly Emotions or Forbidden Feelings

We all have them – feelings that we dare not share with anyone else because they are so embarrassing, politically incorrect or downright nasty. Deep within the darkness of our heads is the only place we permit ourselves to wish that elderly relatives would hurry up and die, think the baby of our best friend is in fact repulsive and maddening, and inwardly sneer at our neighbours' bad taste.

It can be blindingly obvious to an objective observer why we are not as socially successful as we think we should be, and often this boils down to one of these seven personality problems. If we are hamstrung by being tied up in emotional knots on the inside over some or just one of these deadly emotions, then this makes us less pleasant to be with. Others will instinctively move away – even though they may not know why – because the Seven Deadly Emotions are coming between us and them.

So, here are the Seven Deadly Emotions to watch out for:

(1) Material Comparison

We like to think that we don't judge people by appearances, by where they live, or how desirable their car is. However, the truth is we make comparisons and judgements all the time and more often than not these are based on extremely superficial evidence.

This emotion is deadly because it's not just about status comparison but about the fact that we often derive a strong sense of superiority from comparing ourselves with others, even over the most trivial aspects of life.

If we could only see that self-respect and genuine emotional connection with others, both of which have little to do with the size of your jewellery collection, are in fact the true sources of genuine contentment. But because of our reluctance to commit to the hard emotional exertion required to build relationships and do things which might make us feel genuinely proud of ourselves, like charitable or voluntary work, we resort to materialism and thus also material comparison. Better instead to stop comparing (there will always be someone who has more than you) and start evaluating yourself on the really important things in life – like how genuinely helpful to others you are, whether your children would regard you as a good parent, your partner would value you as a true companion and your friends as a supportive confidant. The real liberation of acknowledging this forbidden feeling is not that you will stop judging others on superficial and useless qualities, but you might at last stop judging yourself.

(2) Disaster Voyeurism

Your neighbour has a crisis – her husband has left her and she is on your doorstep in floods of tears. You welcome her in and offer her a shoulder to cry on. Over the next few days and weeks you are there for her as she recounts the disaster that is her marriage. You are just being a good Samaritan, aren't you?

How then to explain that sneaky feeling of being cheated when she takes her husband back and the marriage seems to be on track again. She is now happy, but deep down you aren't. You liked nothing better than when she needed you and appreciated your concern. You loved it when she said she didn't know how she would have coped without you. When you took those crisis calls from her in the middle of that girls' night out, you just had to mention to everyone how much she needed you.

Psychologists will tell you that you were in reality feeding off her disaster in various emotional ways; you were getting a buzz from not just driving past the wreckage of her marriage, but being invited in to have a good poke around.

In fact, several different emotions are involved here but perhaps we should first recognize that other people's disasters make us feel more secure in ourselves. You might question your friend's intelligence ('How could she have been so stupid to trust him!') but actually, you enjoy how superior you now feel because you clearly aren't nearly so dumb. The other uncomfortable fact is that we all need to be needed and another person's crisis puts us in pole position to get some valuable attention from them.

But becoming a disaster voyeur is not good for us in the long run because in feeding off other people's misfortunes, we are in grave danger of becoming unhealthily addicted to their pathological need for us. This means that when their lives turn a corner and they recover, we don't find them so interesting and cannot therefore sustain healthy relationships with those who are less needy. You know you are a disaster voyeur if all your friends have problems and they spend most of their time with you discussing them rather than just having fun.

(3) The Grass is Always Greener

Why can't one of our children be a bit more like the neighbour's choirboy? Or why can't my husband be a bit fitter, like the nice man who delivers the milk? These are the dark questions which we secretly whisper in the dead of night.

Even after you have gone up the aisle, you are still plagued by those awful wedding-morning questions – am I making a dreadful mistake? These 'what if' questions – what if I met someone else who was different in this or that way, or what if our children could be less grumpy and selfish – are the kinds of questions we feel deeply guilty for even considering, but they are inevitable once we find ourselves in irreversible scenarios, like having children or moving in with someone.

Sometimes the 'what ifs' are a sign that we think our marriage needs some input, like counselling or even a divorce lawyer, but more often than not these 'what ifs' are simply a sign that you are ambitious and wish for more than you have.

It is vital to stem the tide of 'what ifs', however, if they are beginning to get in the way of your enjoying your children or your husband. Sometimes they signify your inability to express your dissatisfaction or frustration with those closest to you. You simply are not having the impact on those dearest to you and perhaps it's time to become more assertive and express yourself more forcefully about your desires and preferences. You may be surprised – maybe your husband if given the chance could become more like the nice man who delivers the milk.

(4) Friendly Foe

You go round to their place for barbecues, they borrow your hose, and from the outside it seems a perfectly routine and ordinary friendship. Deep inside, however, something much darker is stirring: secretly you might resent or even hate them and their shiny new car. The fact is, we often make friends and nurture relationships not because we actually like the other person but because they could be good for us. You have heard of marriages of convenience; in fact a lot of friendships are exactly like that. They are more convenient than anything else.

Come on now, would you *really* choose to turn up to your neighbour's birthday party if you weren't worried that if you didn't maintain good relations with them they could stop you using their drive? The problem with these friendships of convenience is that when the relationship stops being convenient, i.e. you realize you are no longer going to personally benefit from what they have to offer, the relationship rapidly withers and dies. How many neighbours have you actually kept up with after you or they moved?

There is nothing wrong with a friendship of convenience – it's only sensible to try and stay in your neighbours' good books. But the problem with this kind of friendship is that you have to be clear about your boundaries. If you aren't, you could soon find your valuable time and resources taken up because your neighbours think it's a genuine friendship, when you, in fact, were only being nice so you could borrow their hose.

Be nice to people by all means, but have a clear sense of who you actually like and who it's useful to stay onside with. Having a clear sense of the hierarchy of relationships in your life and their emotional depth is vital to avoid ending up neglecting genuine friends in order to have access to that hose.

(5) Anxious Avoidance

You see the letter from the bank manager drop on to the doormat and you immediately try to push away the cold hand that has grabbed for your heart. What you should do is open the letter, find out exactly how bad the financial crisis is and call the bank to start sorting it all out. But what you do instead is hide the letter and hope that if you ignore it for long enough the problem will go away of its own accord.

The treatment for this – perhaps the most lethal of the Seven Deadly Emotions – is to first acknowledge what is really going on. Ignoring the bank is not a sensible rational strategy; that tactic is driven by fear, and only once you confront the reality of the fear can you start dealing with it. Do this gradually. Don't hide the letter from the bank manager. You may not have the courage to open it immediately, but if you put it in a prominent place that you can't avoid your anxiety will soon abate to the extent that you can face up to actually opening it. Perhaps then open it but don't read it. Take one step at a time. Phased or gradual exposure to the threat is the correct treatment for anxious avoidance.

(6) Taking a Gamble

You are in a rush and you simply haven't got time to buckle up that darned difficult seatbelt for your three-year-old struggling in the child seat of the car. So you take a gamble that it's going to be OK and you won't have an accident in the five minutes it takes to get to the supermarket. Mostly you get away with it, which is why the emotion – a secret satisfaction that the gamble pays off – sustains you in persisting with these dangerous short-cuts. After a while, as this emotion runs unchecked through your life, you develop a feeling of superiority over all the other mugs who bother with seatbelts for their kids. After all, what have they got to show for it? They take ages to set off on the school run and you're there ahead of them. The lure of the short-cut is deeply seductive until, of course, like Nick Leeson – the arch grand wizard of taking a gamble – you get found out spectacularly when the gamble doesn't work in your favour. The key here is to focus on how terrible things could be for everyone if the gamble doesn't pay off and things go wrong – not *how likely* they are to go wrong – which is what all short-cutters prefer to dwell on.

(7) Embarrassment

Thousands of men and women each year die of this deadly emotion – embarrassment. It's the embarrassment of being examined for cervical or prostate cancer that leads these victims to avoid the doctor rather than go for routine checks. Colon cancer also kills through embarrassment. People develop symptoms, such as blood in their bowel motions or needing to go to the loo more often than usual, and are simply too embarrassed to discuss these symptoms with their doctor, so they leave them until it's all too late. Yes, it's embarrassing to have a doctor stick a tube up your bottom in order to check for colonic cancer, but the strength of this emotion is such that we prefer to avoid experiencing it and die early, and often unnecessarily, instead. There is an intriguing link here with a separate but related area of life – career satisfaction.

One key finding from research into the psychology that separates self-made millionaires from the rest of us is that they experience less embarrassment – they aren't embarrassed to ask for help or for a loan or for their product or service to be introduced even though it has never been heard of before. It's vital, if you are to break out of the rut that can be your life, that you don't care too much what others think of you. If you do you will be too embarrassed to dare to be a bit different, to look foolish and ask for things that most others don't ask for because they are too afraid of sticking out from the crowd. Don't let embarrassment ruin your life – or shorten it.

In the old days of psychiatry, all clinicians had to have their own therapy before being let loose on patients. The idea was that you had to resolve your own issues before you could be genuinely therapeutic when dealing with patients whose own pathology was likely to provoke and agitate the darker stirrings within you. For example, perhaps a seductive patient might lure you into bed if you hadn't become completely focused on issues of professional boundaries and your own vulnerability to temptation because of your own rocky marriage.

There is a sense in which something similar – but

perhaps on a much smaller scale – is necessary for all of us entering the fraught world of relationships. We need to think about our own issues and resolve them to some extent in order to be able to give emotionally and sustain the stress of dealing with others. If we appear to be experiencing 'all men are bastards' or 'all women are crazy' scenarios on a regular basis, then it's time to look within to see whether the real issue isn't hidden somewhere deep within us.

5

TAKE A CHANCE ON ME

Hey there, risk taker – spend a little time with me?

The loving are the daring.
Bayard Taylor

RECENT EVIDENCE SUGGESTS THAT THE BIGGER THE difference between the lengths of the second and fourth digits in the right hands of men, the more sexual partners they have had throughout their lifetime. The study was published by psychologist John T. Manning from the University of Central Lancashire in the UK, who pointed out that men tend to have much longer fourth digits in comparison to their second than women do because when your fingers are being formed in the womb their length is partly determined by how much testosterone you are exposed to at that time. Men have much higher levels of testosterone than women, so how much longer your fourth finger is compared to your second is a rough measure of what testosterone exposure was like for you as a foetus. Manning's study appears to confirm that pre-natal testosterone is having a crucial impact on the brain which will determine our behaviour and success in bed long afterwards.

It's another example of how science is helping us to understand the forces that underpin the enigma of attraction. James Roney, a psychologist at the University of Chicago, in a recently published separate study found that longer fourth finger length in men is significantly and strongly associated with women's ratings of men's physical attractiveness and 'levels of courtship-like behaviour' during a brief conversation. So it looks as if there is something about testosterone that is drawing women to men and explains why men with high levels of this hormone are more successful sexually with women. And now there is a new twist: could it be that high-testosterone men are getting more sex because of the *kind* of woman who is attracted to them?

Testosterone is a hormone with many effects on the body and brain, but it also increases bone growth and density; in particular, the squarer or heavier male jaw has been shown to be linked to high testosterone levels. Another facial feature likely to be influenced by the hormone is the development of more prominent bony eyebrow ridges, otherwise referred to as supra-orbital ridges, which results in squarer and smaller eye sockets relative to skull size. These eye and jaw features are routinely used for sex determination in forensic analyses, as they are such a reliable indicator of underlying testosterone levels.

Psychological theory of attraction suggests that women who show a preference for male faces with squarer and heavier jaws and more prominent eyebrow ridges are unconsciously signalling an interest in men with higher testosterone levels. Previously it was thought that higher testosterone was generally a more desirable biological feature in men, as it was associated with more symmetrical bodies and therefore perhaps physically fitter men. But now more recent research, conducted by a team of psychologists from the University of Durham, has confirmed that men producing more testosterone are not only less likely to marry and more likely to divorce if they do marry, but once married, they are more likely to split up from their partners because of extramarital sex.

Higher testosterone levels in men are associated with dominance, competitiveness and 'sensation-seeking' behaviour, which according to evolutionary theory might explain not only their attraction to women, because they would have been more likely in the distant past to bring back more meat to the cave, but also why long-term stable relationships may not be compatible with their restless personality. This new study, however, recently published in the academic journal *Evolution and Human Behaviour*, suggests that instead of women putting up with the unfortunate relationship side-effects of high-testosterone men, some of them are actively choosing this kind of man because they prefer a series of short-term mates rather than a longer-term relationship. High-testosterone men rate themselves as less interested in being a father and less energetic at 'relationship maintenance', yet it seems according to this new research that there are a significant group of women who actively prefer this kind of man.

The team of scientists led by David Waynforth took facial photographs of forty-five men, and details about jaw size and eyebrow ridge development were taken from these. Measurements included chin depth – the distance from the mouth to the chin – and jaw width – the widest point of the face; the bigger these measurements are, the higher the testosterone levels in the man and the more 'masculine' the face tends to be rated. Sixty women were presented with ten randomly chosen pairs of male faces and asked to select the more attractive. Women who preferred the more masculine or high-testosterone faces, as exemplified by squarer and heavier jaws plus more prominent eyebrow ridges, were significantly more likely to be women who were more interested in uncommitted sexual relations; who would engage in sex at an early point in a relationship; who would have sex with more than one partner at a time; and who would be involved in relationships characterized by less investment, commitment, love and dependency.

Given, according to evolutionary theory, that women at some point must desire to pass on their genes to future generations and would therefore prefer a man who is interested in 'settling down', why these women should prefer the more fickle high-testosterone man is the subject of much psychological speculation. And 47 per cent of the women who took part in this study preferred the high-testosterone male faces, so it's not an insignificant number. One theory is that as women become more financially and emotionally independent, they become less interested in being 'looked after' by a man and more interested in the excitement and other possible benefits of a relationship with a high-testosterone male. After all, high-testosterone men have a stronger sex drive than those with lower testosterone levels.

It does indeed seem that men who behave badly are often much more exciting for women to go out with, oddly enough precisely because you are never entirely sure where you stand with them. The roller-coaster ride of emotion, from plumbing the depths of watching them ogling someone else to the highs of their actually turning up on time for a date, means there is never a dull moment. These swings of emotion ensure that when he does finally give you some attention, you feel so much happier than if you'd had him eating out of your hand from the outset. Also, if you manage to pull the kind of man who has a reputation for playing the field, this seems to serve as a validation of your attractiveness compared to other women. A fatal mistake made by many women who are attracted to the wild and dangerous is that they believe they can tame them eventually with the force of their affection. But some women love this challenge. After all, what greater proof of the strength of your desire for each other that it was you rather than any other woman who finally managed to tame him? Not all women like men who behave badly, of course, so perhaps those who particularly want a brief fling are drawn to this kind of man as they know it won't be too difficult to dump him when the time comes. He won't get hurt – he is, after all, immune to pain.

One paradox at the heart of what we desire is that we want someone who is interested in us, yet we also want someone who is leading such a desirable life that their interest in us doesn't arise out of boredom. This notion of interest in us is fundamental. Repeatedly when I survey women in the audience during the talks I give on the psychology of attraction and ask them which male occupation is most desirable in a male partner, cosmetic surgeon seems to crop up an amazing number of times. In fact, I suspect that part of the deadly seduction of plastic surgeons specifically is their unique ability to provide a sympathetic male listening ear into which women can vent their deepest insecurities and fears about their appearance – and then they can do something practical about it. Women find that most other men are interminably bored by any expression of their concerns about their appearance. Well, here at last is one group of men who are masters of the art of displaying interest in a woman's anxieties about her looks. It is in fact part of their job.

Indeed, research confirms that people tend, in social encounters, to be willing to confide in doctors more than in any other profession, so the trust and discretion doctors command in general could be a part of the allure for women. Mills and Boon have realized this: the specialist romance novel publishers devote a whole series in their catalogue to books that feature trysts with doctors. They don't publish such a list devoted to any other profession. There is no 'Lawyer Lover' section in their catalogue, or even an 'Accountant Ardour' series. It is no accident that the men who play doctors in popular TV dramas such as *ER*, *Peak Practice*, *Chicago Hope* and *Casualty* usually end up as favourite heart-throbs. George Clooney may be good-looking, but how much of his allure is due to having reached public consciousness through his portrayal of a sexy doctor in *ER*?

So why do women so easily swoon at the sight of a stethoscope draped elegantly around a white-coated neck?

As we know, scientific research into the psychology of attraction has found that while men tend to place highest value on appearance in females, women primarily go for intelligence and status in men. Medicine appears to combine both features uniquely. It is one of the most difficult subjects to get into university to study, and one of the most demanding courses thereafter; plus, while doctors don't earn as much as high-flying City traders, as a profession medicine still commands the highest average salary. No doctor earns little money, or is ever unemployed. So there is the promise of stability and a degree of respect from the community if you secure yourself a doctor. In addition, unlike the City trader, doctors appear to be doing genuinely valuable work, and also seem interested in people and should be good listeners. There is also the promise that with all that anatomy training these men should understand a woman's body.

In fact, the reasons why doctors are so attractive to women should be of interest to men. You don't have to become a doctor to get a date, of course; you simply have to emulate some of their qualities.

WHO DO WOMEN PREFER – THE RECKLESS OR THE KIND?

From Hollywood films to car adverts, heroism is a celebrated male quality, and new research now confirms that heroism is for women one of the most attractive features in a man, which explains a host of previously puzzling aspects of sexual attraction – for example, why women so often fall for 'loveable rogues', and why men like to show off recklessly when there is an audience of women.

The persistence of heroism is a puzzle to evolutionary psychologists as often the heroic are the first to be killed in genuinely dangerous situations. For example, it was probably the bravest members of the New York emergency services who were first up the staircases of the Twin Towers on 11 September 2001, and who therefore lost their lives. The brave, who are likely to take repeated risks, are expected to be rare: in terms of lifetime survival chances, the more risks taken, the greater the likelihood of eventual disaster. There is a debate as to the difference between bravery and foolhardiness, yet clearly we need some people willing to take risks as many lives are saved by risk takers. Risk taking occurs even in a safe, comfortable, pampered society. It is especially found among young males, who show a striking gender bias in terms of willingness to engage in behaviour some might consider brave, but which is also extremely risky. For example, young men are more likely to have unprotected sex, drive dangerously at excessive speed, gamble, take risky financial decisions, and take part in dangerous outdoor sports.

Psychologists Susan Kelly and Robin Dunbar from Liverpool University have now come up with an intriguing explanation from their recently published research: it could be that young men are so risk prone because this is a reliable way of attracting women. After all, this is the period of their lives when both sexes' interest in each other is greatest. For their ground-breaking study, entitled 'Who Dares Wins', Kelly and Dunbar conducted experiments on attraction and found that women do prefer risk-prone brave males to risk-avoidant non-brave males, and also that men are aware of this preference. Bravery in a male was shown to be the strongest factor influencing female choice of short-term partners, long-term partners and male friends; kindness played a lesser role in their choices. When bravery is pitted against unselfishness, the surprising result is that women put much more store by courage than kindness. Kindness was deemed to be an important factor in friendships, but particularly for sexual relationships a man's tendency to take risks was preferred to his unselfishness.

One explanation for this intriguing finding is that women in our ancestral and more dangerous past would have needed to choose mates who were able to protect them from both animal and human predators, so the women would have logically favoured skilled and courageous men. Women could still be programmed by their genes and brains to favour a brave mate rather than a more timid 'stay-at-home'. In the environments in which we evolved, the provision of meat acquired by hunting was a male province, and hunting for game often involved some degree of personal risk, so choosing a brave man as a mate would have ensured a woman and her children were more likely to be fed as well as protected from the unwanted attentions of other males.

But Kelly and Dunbar were also interested in comparing unselfish courage with selfish bravery. After all, one could argue that there is a difference between the risk taking involved with the kind of man who goes in and rescues another person, thus placing his own life in danger, and someone who just drives fast because he enjoys it.

In order to see what kind of person women were most attracted to, Kelly and Dunbar studied how eight contrasting male personality profiles fared in evoking female approval. By way of example, let's meet Bill, Frank, Edward and Charles. Bill is a quiet but capable man. He's always ready to lend a hand, but is unobtrusive about it. He works as a mechanic during the day, which allows him the flexibility he needs as a key member of the local lifeboat crew. Bill would be classed as brave but kind, in contrast to someone brave but more selfish like Frank, who likes to be outdoors whenever he can. He is attracted by danger and spends many weekends and holidays rock-climbing. He has recently taken up free-fall parachuting. Similar to Frank is Edward, who is a bit of an action man. He is always on the go, and throws himself into his work. He used to be a steeplejack, but now works as a deep-sea diver. When not working he goes jet-skiing and plays tennis. In marked contrast to Edward and Frank, Charles enjoys looking after people. He works as a nurse at present, but is considering training to be a counsellor as he thinks the prospects might be better. He is learning to play the clarinet, but doesn't practise as much as he should as he worries about disturbing the neighbours.

The researchers found that of the eight possible choices, Edward and Frank, both brave but not kind, did much better than anyone else in terms of an approval rating by women for a short-term fling. When bravery is pitted against unselfishness, bravery across all types of relationships, short- or long-term, carries much more weight for women. Kelly and Dunbar also asked a group of men which of the male personality profiles they thought women would be most attracted to, and the men were able correctly to predict the female preference for bravery over kindness. This suggests that exhibitions of bravery could be part of the male mating strategy. In other words, one reason why men do heroic things in the first place is to attract female interest. A lot of brave behaviour could be much less unselfish than it at first appears.

There are, of course, disadvantages to selecting a mate who habitually takes risks. Brave, risk-prone men are likely to have a higher mortality rate than risk-avoidant men, so a woman choosing a risk-prone mate runs a risk herself – of being left alone with no support. This risk is reflected in Kelly and Dunbar's research, which found that for long-term relationships bravery had slightly less impact than it did for short-term flings in terms of female attraction to brave men. Unselfishness was also more valued in long-term relationships than in short-term flings. But whatever the scenario, short- or long-term relationships, brave men were still preferred to the non-brave, so it appears that for women the benefits outweigh the potential costs. This begins to explain the puzzling attraction so many women feel for the 'loveable rogue' even if he is obviously unfaithful. It could be that as the risk taker is seen as a good bet in terms of foraging successfully in a dangerous world, you might as well hang on to the risk taker you know than leave him for yet another risk taker where the long-term prognosis for fidelity is the same anyway.

Another intriguing finding from the research was that bravery was found to be most attractive when the man involved was 'professionally' brave (e.g. a fireman) as opposed to someone who was brave only fitfully (e.g. a volunteer for a lifeboat charity). It would seem that women prefer men who are consistently brave, and linked to this might be some element of dependability or professionalism. Casual bravery, it could perhaps be reasoned, is more likely to end in disaster. The other fascinating implication of Kelly and Dunbar's research is that they found risk taking attracts women only when it is on display in some way. Given that men are aware that women find risk taking attractive, it could be that much male bravado now becomes understandable in terms of 'showing off', rather like a male peacock displays its colourful feathers to attract a mate. Studies of primitive tribes where hunting is the main way of providing food has found that often male hunters like to share their kills around the village, more than would make sense if they wanted their own families to be well fed. It seems this very public sharing around of the fruits of the hunt is a way of advertising their skills and bravery to other possible female mates in the village.

Sigmund Freud famously asked in a fit of frustration, 'What do women want?' From research like Kelly and Dunbar's, increasingly the answer appears to be that women want it all: they want a man who is sensitive and kind in general but who is also macho in emergencies. This often presents a conflict for women as in the longer term they understand that kindness and sharing are extremely useful in a relationship, but they also realize that this kind of man is unlikely to rise to the top in a competitive world. The research evidence from all around the world is that women place much greater store on status and wealth in what they find attractive in men, than men do in women. So it seems that the ability to provide resources is a vital aspect of what women are looking for in a man. This also explains why ambition and industriousness are found by psychological researchers to be some of the most attractive male personality features for women.

The world we live in today until quite recently seemed much safer than the world in which humans evolved, so physical bravery did not seem such an obviously useful feature. Kelly and Dunbar are arguing that there hasn't been enough time to allow genes to adapt to the safer circumstances of modern life, so women continue to be influenced by their Stone Age genes which are still driving them to favour the physically strong risk taker. Now that the world is again perceived as a dangerous place, bravery seems set to remain a desired characteristic.

Advice for Women from the 'Who Dares Wins' Research

(1) Although risk-taking men may appear to be more attractive, because a man needs to take a few risks to succeed in life, ask yourself if his risk taking is reckless, or does he take risks with some consideration for the consequences? If he is basically just reckless, can you deal with the fall-out when he takes on one risk too far?

(2) If you find yourself getting bored in a relationship and are thinking of straying, maybe you should encourage your partner to take more risks. He may in fact be playing safe to protect you and hasn't realized he needs to take a few more risks to keep you interested.

(3) Remember that someone who becomes used to successfully taking risks in their job might come to believe they can take risks elsewhere in their lives and get away with them, perhaps by chancing an affair. If your partner is used to taking risks in his career you should be more vigilant about his fidelity.

Advice for Men from the 'Who Dares Wins' Research

(1) Kindness and unselfishness in men is valued by women, but risk taking and bravery may be even more attractive. You shouldn't dispense with altruism, but don't rely on it alone to attract her.

(2) Dates that involve some display of bravery, like a frightening roller-coaster ride or even a horror film, are more likely to impress, but only if you manage to stay calm yourself and don't turn to her for support when terrified. And yes, you should go down to check out that noise in the middle of the night, otherwise you may soon find yourself alone in the house.

(3) It would now seem that the racy car is part of the armoury you need to attract women, because it suggests a tendency to take risks. Think about what your lifestyle says about your bravery. Perhaps it's time to throw away the cardigans and give the SAS uniform a try instead.

(1) Why Does He Do That? – It's Because He's Stressed

If a woman gets together with her best female friends, and she is stressed, then her friends are likely to notice it, or the woman herself will want to talk about it. With men, however, owning up to being stressed and therefore vulnerable is not part of their competitive culture, so they often deal with stress in, what seems to women, surprising ways. For example, one recent survey from Leeds University investigated the favourite male pastime of going to a bar for a drink after work. When asked their reason for going, 9.5 per cent said they went to drink alcohol, 5.5 per cent said it was to meet women, but an overwhelming 85 per cent said they went in order to relieve stress.

So if you want to know why your man does something puzzling like watching the television when there is nothing worth watching, often the answer is because it's his way of dealing with stress. The key is for women to decide whether their men's approach to stress is effective. If it does seem to work, then it is best not to interfere, so long as it does not involve inherent dangers such as alcoholism or obesity.

The fact that men often like to brood about their problems rather than air them is often perceived by women as a distancing tactic, which makes them feel pushed away from the man's life. Women need to learn to tolerate men's preference for knocking about the cave ruminating. But they should also let the man know that she is available to be his sounding board, if and when he feels like talking.

(2) For a Man Winning Isn't Everything – It's the Only Thing

Men often don't read to the kids before bedtime or help with the washing up, and to women this is upsetting because it appears to them that men are either lazy or they just don't care. Instead, what is often the case is that men don't feel they do these tasks well – and often women will reinforce this impression by criticizing and generally poking fun at their attempts to help. Men particularly need to feel competent. They like to feel like winners. So, to get him to do something, a woman needs to shower a man with praise – no matter how disturbing his faltering efforts might appear. This advice counts for double in the bedroom!

(3) He Needs to Feel He's Important

The key social change over the last fifty years – and indeed it's nothing less than a revolution – is that women now, quite rightly, feel they can do anything.

They can be astronauts, run countries and fight in wars. Women's lib has rather left men feeling that they lag behind, and wondering what exactly they are needed for. Women often radiate a strong sense of independence, but the problem with this is that it can create in men a feeling that they don't play an important role in their partners' achievements or progress through life.

It's vital that a woman makes her man feel he has been an important part of the successes of her life. Marital therapists call this key issue 'impact': strong relationships are formed when each party feels that they have an influence – or impact – on the other.

(4) Don't Attack Him for Your Problems

One of the most intriguing findings from David Buss and Todd Shackelford's study at the University of Texas involved a concept they termed 'Mate Value Discrepancy'. MVD is not something we like to talk about in polite company, but, put simply, it's the scientific attempt to quantify what is going on when a very desirable person marries someone much less so. All couples probably vary a little in MVD, and some much more than others (the 'What's she doing with *him*?!' type couples).

In the research, the husband who was thought much more desirable than the wife was much less likely to indulge in an extramarital affair than his wife believed. However, when the wife was much more desirable than her husband, her chances of having an affair were much higher.

Put simply, a very attractive woman married to a less attractive man is to be trusted much less than when the attractiveness is distributed the other way round. Desirable men can actually be trusted more than women think they can.

This has an interesting but profound implication on relationships. Many women, because they don't think an attractive man can be trusted in the long term, opt for a slightly less obviously desirable man, because it makes them feel more secure. However, they then come to resent the fact that he is not what she really wanted. From my experience at my busy marital therapy clinics at the Maudsley Hospital, women are more acutely aware of MVD than are men. They often accuse men of putting desire before security, but they could actually learn a thing or two by not dismissing this tactic so readily.

6

KNOWING ME, KNOWING WHO?

Detecting deception in relationships, and knowing how and when to trust

You can't buy love, but you can pay heavily for it.

Henny Youngman

I WAS TAKING PART IN A LIVE TELEVISED PHONE-IN ON A nationally broadcast programme recently when a woman rang in to ask me whether in my opinion her partner was having an affair. He had returned from a business trip abroad and on unpacking his suitcase for him she had discovered several opened packets of condoms. To the audience watching at home and to me it was fairly obvious that this was very good evidence indeed that he was having an affair, but when she confronted him with her finding he had denied everything, using the rather pathetic excuse that he had been carrying the condoms for a colleague as a favour. She was inclined to believe this explanation, much to the disbelief of my audience.

There are powerful psychological reasons why many women in relationships tend not to see when their male partner is lying to them, despite the fact that the deception is blindingly obvious to those outside the relationship. If, for example, you feel you could never leave a man because of your fear of surviving alone outside the relationship, then you are not motivated to spot a deception even when it's right in front of you. Denial allows you to remain in the relationship without too much discomfort. So if you want to know whether or not your partner is lying to you, the clear message from psychology is this: have a clear sense, *before* you start looking closely at them and their behaviour, of what your plan is should you find out they are indeed lying.

This advice of mine to women wondering whether or not their partners are lying to them appears to have received some support from new research conducted by a team of psychologists led by Amanda Johnson and Julian Paul Keenan at Montclair University's Cognitive Neuroimaging Laboratory in New Jersey, who examined the issue of who is better at spotting deception in men, women already in a relationship or those who are still single. The research, just about to be published in the academic journal *Personality and Individual Differences*, focused particularly on the kind of lying in which many men indulge when in the presence of a female, particularly an unattached one they are trying to impress and seduce. This lying is termed by psychologists 'faking good' – in other words, exaggerating positive aspects of yourself. Claiming to drive a Ferrari when in fact your Fiat is parked outside is a good example. The finding was that women who were not in a relationship with a man were far superior to women in relationships when it came to correctly spotting men 'faking good'.

The Montclair team argues that the reason for this profound difference in women's ability to detect deception hinges on our biological evolutionary history. From the selfish gene standpoint it makes sense for single women to be more wary of men and to be better able to select a mate with a Ferrari than one with a Fiat (no disrespect intended to the latter, of course; I'm merely continuing the metaphor from the previous paragraph – and I think we can all agree that a Fiat, though a fine Italian car, is *not* a Ferrari). Only one error is needed for you to end up bearing the child of a Fiat driver. Once you have decided to commit, it's probably too late to do much about discovering the Fiat in the garage, as you have probably already mixed your genes with your partner. Being duped into a 'reproductive situation' (as the psychologists put it) entails great risks for females, so it makes sense that the antennae of non-mated women work better.

The research also found that women who were more aware of themselves and their own internal emotional and mental states – for instance, those who fully appreciate the extent of their dependency on a male partner – were more likely to spot men faking good. Again, this suggests that you need to know yourself well in order to know others.

Of course, women are not alone in this respect. The most recent psychological research also suggests that people are generally not as good at spotting deception as they would like to think they are. Indeed, studies show that people can detect lies in others at a rate of only 44 per cent. This is actually lower than the success rate you would get if you just tossed a coin and used that to determine whether or not someone was lying. Even professionals who are meant to have a lot of specific experience in this area, like police officers and customs officials, perform no better at lie detection than at the level of chance.

This is particularly surprising as in these vocations spotting liars is known as a 'high-stakes' situation. It matters crucially that the police, for instance, are able to spot deception, whereas it may not matter quite so much for a nurse. In one famous experiment on precisely the kind of high-stakes situation the police regularly face, officers were exposed to videotaped press conferences of people who were asking the general public for help in finding their missing relatives, or the murderers of their relatives. All these people had been found guilty of these crimes, but the police officers didn't know this. None of them performed any better at spotting deceit at these press conferences than could be expected by chance. Psychologist Professor Aldert Vrij from the University of Portsmouth, who conducted this experiment, found that the only professionals more adept at such formal psychological testing than the general public were officers who work for the US Secret Service. But this could be partly because these agents seem to adopt a powerful but simple strategy: they don't appear to trust *anyone*.

One explanation of why professionals are no better at detecting lies is that they are burdened with the same false beliefs about how liars behave. For example, one key non-verbal behaviour many assume is exhibited by liars is gaze aversion. One survey found that 75 per cent of professional lie detectors (police officers, customs officers and so on) believe that liars look away in an interview, although rigorous scientific research has established that this is not a reliable indicator of deception.

In fact, liars are having to manufacture reality, and this usually requires a lot more intellectual effort than simply reporting the truth. As well as watching their words, liars need to monitor closely how their story is coming over so as to know whether or not to modify their strategy. Truth-tellers are not so involved in monitoring the listener because disbelief is less of an issue for them – after all, they know they are telling the truth. As a result, liars usually watch the listener closely rather than look away. Someone who maintains more eye contact than usual is the person to be concerned about. Deceivers take longer to answer questions, too; they pause more, they aren't as fluent with their answers and, if they are very good liars, they tend to make fewer gestures to try and ensure that they don't 'leak' body language clues.

This last point is intriguing because most listeners tend to focus on the content of what is being said, not on the body language of the speaker. But as non-verbal behaviour such as gestures and posture are less easy to control, particularly if you are concentrating on making up a story, this is actually the area on which to focus your deceit-detection antennae. It's particularly useful to notice a change in body language as the sophisticated interviewer switches from a topic where it's known the interviewee is telling the truth to one where lying is possible, and back again.

Another useful tip from the scientific psychological research into deceit to remember when you're dating or in a relationship is that liars experience three main emotions during lying: fear of being caught, excitement at the opportunity of fooling someone ('duping delight') and guilt. If you are vigilant for these particular emotions, you are more likely to spot them in the form of 'micro' expressions – facial movements that appear for short periods of time and betray these emotions. These expressions are usually barely perceptible to most and intense concentration is needed to pick up on them, along with a certain amount of insight into what emotion a person might really be feeling or trying to cover up.

THEORY OF MIND

It is clear, then, that with enough knowledge and practice anyone can learn to dramatically improve their rate of reliably detecting deceit in others. So the puzzle remains: how come so many of us, even professional lie detectors, are so lamentably bad at spotting liars? Maybe we tend to collude with deception because there are strong emotional reasons to do so. Freud, as far back as 1938, argued that some truths are too painful to know, so we forget them, transform them, project them, sublimate them or distort them into a form we can bear. Examples of this range from Neville Chamberlain's believing Hitler's incredible protestations to spouses over-looking blatant infidelity, with which topic I began this chapter.

Inferring what is going on in others' minds is referred to as 'Theory of Mind', and this is a branch of psychology that has recently attracted greater interest because it is thought that many of the symptoms of disorders such as schizophrenia, Asperger's Syndrome and autism could be explained as 'Theory of Mind' deficits.

Because, according to the theory, intentional deception requires one to understand the mental state of another, it is also predicted that there is a positive relationship between self-awareness and the *ability* to deceive. Existing data appear to support this. For example, the ability to deceive in children emerges shortly after the development of self-awareness, as indicated by self-recognition, self-pronoun use and self-conscious emotions. Furthermore, populations where there are deficits of self-awareness (e.g. schizophrenics) don't appear to be good at lying or spotting deception. Intriguingly, the latest brain-scanning research found that both deception and self-awareness appear to be right-hemisphere-mediated.

The Montclair University group are about to publish new research on the link between high self-monitoring and deception ability. The study, published in the journal *Personality and Individual Differences* and entitled 'Me, Myself, and Lie: The Role of Self-awareness in Deception', used a group of people who had varied in their scores on a self-awareness test and asked them to lie on videotape. The tapes were then played to a general population of undergraduate students who had to determine when they were lying and when they were telling the truth. Individuals who scored highly in private self-awareness tended to be more conscious of their feelings, attitudes and motives, and being aware of one's own thoughts may be beneficial in that these can be used to enter the mind of another person and ultimately to deceive them. There is, then, a strong relationship between self-awareness and Theory of Mind, and these faculties appear to be correlated positively with deception.

HOW TO TRUST

A new notion of trust is now developing among theorists – that it involves the willingness to engage in risk-taking behaviour, and requires people to make themselves vulnerable to others.

Trust and its use and exploitation are at the heart of life, central to relationships, office politics and the like. We have all encountered examples of 'two-person-exchange environments', as experimental psychologists would put it: a sister lets her younger brother go first at a computer game with the understanding that she will get a longer turn later; a couple might go to a football match one evening with the understanding that next week they will attend the opera. In an example familiar from labour economics, a firm offers an employee a wage above the market level expecting that in exchange the worker will put in greater effort (thus achieving a co-operative outcome). Indeed, on the subject of the commercial market place, the surprising thing is how much trust there is out there, given recent economic uncertainty. This realization has led to the development of a new field, neuroeconomics, whose grand ambition is to understand human interactions starting from the level of the synapse. The latest neuroeconomic theory about trust is that actually we suffer from a fundamental biological drive to have faith in each other.

The reason economists are so surprised that there is such a high degree of trust prevalent in human interaction, argues Paul Zak, a neuroscientist at the Center for Neuroeconomic Studies at Claremont Graduate University in California, is because they haven't allowed for the fact that there is a neurological basis to trust. Zak believes his 'trust games' are revealing results that only make sense as an echo from our distant evolutionary past, because our brains are shaped by evolution to cope with social living. Previously, evolutionary psychologists tended to emphasize that our intelligence evolved in order to outwit rivals for sex, supper and status – in other words, our brains are largely machiavellian in nature. Yet Zak contends that our brains also possess strong social and co-operative adaptations, because we derive significant benefits from working together, not just competing relentlessly.

Zak, whose research was first reported in *New Scientist* in 2003, has produced an astonishing recent finding which is that how much we are willing to trust others is influenced by forces that operate below conscious control. Indeed, they may not be as amenable to rational direction as we might like to believe. For example, after looking at a wide variety of biological variables, like hormone levels, Zak found that it was levels of a particular hormone called oxytocin in our bodies which strongly predicts how much we are willing to trust others. A lot of the variables that predict high trust also predict higher general oxytocin levels across the world. For example, breast feeding tends to raise oxytocin levels in mothers and is a vital part of the bonding process between them and their infants; indeed, there is an association between how much breast feeding there is in a society and its levels of trust. In fact, there was such a robust link between oxytocin and how much we trust that it could almost be called the 'trust hormone'. Generally, the hormone's levels are high when we take part in rewarding activities such as eating, touching or warm baths. Intriguingly, the hormone is also strongly released in the body when we have sex, and particularly when we orgasm, leading some neuroscientists to nickname it the 'lust and trust hormone'.

A by-product of this research that will catch the attention of those involved in the dating game is that there is a strong neurological basis for the effectiveness of wining and dining a prospective partner. Stroking their arms during dinner may be more rewarding than you think. You might even suggest a warm bath before attempting to initiate intercourse. Of course, more machiavellian pursuers of sex and con artists have historically exploited this effect, the latter by often appearing to give something to the 'mark' spontaneously, thus displaying unexpected trust at the outset and setting the victim up for their later reciprocating trust to be mercilessly exploited.

If con artists, governments, advertisers, salesmen and sexual predators utilize our natural tendency to trust on a daily basis, although there are disadvantages to this, this means that on balance it was evolutionarily advantageous for our genes to trust rather than distrust. Trust can only have evolved as an adaptation to group living if it gave an individual an edge in terms of survival and reproduction. But if the need to trust is so fundamental, and if its exploitation by others who take our trust and abuse it produces advantages for them, there is clearly an evolutionary arms race between those who are out to deceive and those trying to detect deceit.

But just in case this result has made you completely paranoid about who to trust, remember, never taking the risk of trusting is as deficient a strategy as trusting everyone. The great first-century Roman statesman and philosopher Seneca recognized this: 'It's a vice to trust all,' he said, 'and equally a vice to trust none.' Indeed, giving people your unconditional trust appears to be one of the most rewarding aspects of relationships. Ronald Reagan once said about weapons inspections that you should 'trust then verify', but the problem with this strategy in terms of personal relationships is that the cost of constant verification often becomes prohibitive, so eventually you have to just trust. But never forget, trust is a gamble.

Yet imagine someone who had evolved the ability to tell lies and not to give away what they were up to because they had perfect control over their body language and vocal tremors. Such a person would be amazingly successful socially speaking, given their ability to exploit the rest of us. This thought leads to a quandary at the heart of evolutionary psychology: why, then, has perfect deception not evolved? Most of us have had a go at telling lies and indeed have sometimes been successful. (Come on now, be honest, have you always told your partner the absolute truth?) But often we are not perfect deceivers, and as a result we lack the confidence in our ability to spin our way out of trouble, so we stick to the straight and narrow probably more than we would really like to.

Paul Andrews, an evolutionary psychologist at the University of New Mexico, has now come up with an intriguing theory to explain our tendency to lie imperfectly. He mathematically modelled the best strategy in trust games – experimental scenarios where participants are asked to trust others, having been given some benefit while remaining uncertain as to whether it will be reciprocated or shared. The problem with perfect deception is that no one would want to enter a personal or business relationship with you if they felt totally unable to 'read' you. Absolute inscrutability is not an appealing prospect in relationships because you are then utterly vulnerable to your trust being abused. Instead, as we know that deceit is an inevitable part of human affairs, it is our confidence that we can spot deceit in others that leads us to entertain the possibility of giving over our trust, because we feel we can determine when to do so and when not to.

Actually, the truly perfect strategy in the game of life is to allow another player to believe they can read you by allowing deceit to be detected at times, but retaining the ability to put one over undetected when it really counts. It is in our interests to 'leak' our true intentions from time to time because that makes others believe they are in control of the trust in the relationship. The perfect machiavellian strategy is therefore to appear to be an imperfect liar while harbouring the perfect skill. Could this be the real reason why no perfect liar has yet been recruited into a study? It is, after all, not in the interests of a perfect liar to be detected as one.

TEN STEPS TO NOT BEING TAKEN IN

Increasingly we live in a society where you have to be on your guard, as more and more attempts are made to dupe, con or manipulate you. Liars or deceivers come in many shapes and sizes, from lovers and colleagues to salespeople and those offering 'get rich quick' schemes. Follow the ten key steps below to avoid being taken in by potential partners trying to exploit your good nature.

(1) *Know your vulnerabilities, because the insincere person does.* We are most susceptible to being manipulated when our vulnerabilities are being traded on: we might take on a scheme because it flatters us, for example; politicians get duped by bogus TV interview programmes because of the implicit compliment of the attention. So we get most easily deceived when a need of ours which doesn't normally get met is being fed. You are more likely to be taken in by the lies of someone trying to woo you when you are feeling lonely. To spot the deception, separate your neediness from the situation and examine what you are being told as if your own emotional needs were not involved.

(2) *When you are told what you want to hear, question it.* The reason we often don't investigate a situation further, which might allow us to uncover what is really going on, is that we are being told what we want to hear. When this happens, as asking deeper questions could end in our being told what we don't want to hear, we are motivated to stop asking questions. The

solution to this is to be more open to hearing what you may not want to hear, and given this new openness, be suspicious of anyone who is telling you precisely what you want to hear. It is possible that the attractive person you have only just met is interested in you alone and is not already attached, but are you just being told what you want to hear?

(3) *All deceptions are about short-cuts, so you are most vulnerable when you are in a hurry.* Deceivers often spin stories as a means of gaining a short-cut to getting what they want. Instead of working hard for money, for example, they prefer the short-cut of cheating their way to wealth. In a sense, this problem of the short-cut also explains why we get deceived. Waiting to find out more information or putting in the effort to gather more data are wearisome, so we tend to take a short-cut when it comes to judging whether something is true or not on the available information, which is usually not sufficient. If you are not aware of your own need to take short-cuts, you will get lied to successfully. Most people who end up being duped heavily in a romantic relationship are in too much of a hurry to be patient enough to find out more before committing themselves.

(4) *Just because you have uncovered deceptions in the past doesn't mean the same technique will*

work in the future. Often you will have discovered a deception by using a particular method: perhaps the body language of a salesman alerted you, or there was a verbal slip by a vendor during negotiations. However, beware relying on the same principle in the future. Different people lie in contrasting ways, so don't get fixated on using body language or verbal slips just because these have worked for you in the past. You may have discovered your partner's illicit affair from their mobile phone bill, but that doesn't mean they are going to slip up in that way again. Don't rely on a clean mobile phone bill as a guarantee of complete fidelity.

(5) *Come up with your own alternative explanations for what is going on.* One reason many people are successfully duped is that they cannot understand what alternative reason there might be for telling the false story. For example, many believe tales told about alien abduction because they cannot conceive of an alternative reason why this kind of story should be made up; therefore, to them these accounts must be true. However, a viable alternative explanation is that these people crave the attention their bizarre stories create. If you are not aware of alternative scenarios to the one being sold to you by the liar, you are vulnerable to accepting only their version of events.

(6) *To put liars off their guard, pretend that you believe them.* When deceivers suspect they are being interrogated by those who don't believe them, they are very cautious in what they say and make doubly sure they won't be caught out with an inconsistency. However, if a liar believes they are getting away with their story, and that their victim is entirely within their thrall, they are more likely to relax, and in that state they are more likely to make a slip. When detecting deceit it is often better to hide your suspicions and in so doing give the liar enough rope with which to hang themselves. Therefore, one technique is to show that you believe them totally, keeping your suspicions to yourself, thus lulling them into a false sense of security.

(7) *Beware your preconceptions.* Salesmen often dress smartly because we have a strange but deep preconception that someone who looks 'respectable' is unlikely to be lying to us. Yet obviously this preconception is so widespread it is exploited by liars. Hoax TV interviewers use the preconception that TV interviews are not normally hoaxes to exploit their victims. Become more aware of your preconceptions in order to ensure they are not used against you by liars.

(8) *Liars don't like the unexpected question.* Most liars have rehearsed the answers to the questions

they imagine they are going to be asked, but they are unlikely to have rehearsed all the possible questions they could be asked. So it is the unexpected question that is more likely to unseat them and cause anxiety. Don't always ask the usual questions; throw in a few unusual ones too. So, for example, if you wonder whether your spouse really was at that business meeting in Birmingham last Tuesday, you might ask them what the weather was like there. This might not be the kind of question they were expecting and, therefore, had prepared for.

(9) *Beware people you like.* Research on con artists indicates that they are more outgoing than the usual criminal, and they score high on the personality traits of being easy to get on with. The most successful liars are the most likeable ones, and this is because when we like someone we are disarmed, and find it more difficult to be suspicious of them. So be particularly cautious around someone who is trying to put a proposition to you who you find yourself liking.

(10) *Learn from your past mistakes.* Learning that you have been lied to is very painful and usually means you end up blaming the liar bitterly for your being duped. But there are valuable things you can learn about other people who have duped you, so don't put these past bad

experiences to the back of your mind too soon. As so many people lie in very different ways, it is also wise to focus on what this painful experience tells you about yourself, and when you are most vulnerable to being lied to.

7

THEN I SAW HER FACE

Is your face your fortune?

You'd be surprised how much it costs to look this cheap.
Dolly Parton

IF YOU WANT TO GET A DATE, OR CHOOSE SOMEONE WHO IS likely to stay committed to you for a long time, a new approach has been suggested by recent psychological research in Britain and the USA which could increase your chances of success: go for someone whose face resembles your own, because they are more likely to find you attractive.

Attraction to faces is a vital aspect of relationships. Scientific research confirms that the single best predictor of satisfaction with a 'blind date' is facial attractiveness for both men and women. But the problem before now has been to try and predict who would fancy who, given the individual variations in preferences for facial appearance. In an effort to address this, Dr Ian Penton-Voak, a psychologist at the University of Stirling in Scotland, conducted an experiment using computer graphic technology to transform photographic images of women's faces into their male equivalents. In other words, the images showed how these women would look if they had been born men. He then asked the women whose faces had been photographed to rate their attraction to a variety of pictures of male faces, including the one of their own face looking like a man. None of the fifty-two women involved in the experiment knew that one of the male faces they were being presented with was in fact their own digitally manipulated face. The startling finding, of course, was a strong tendency for women to be more attracted to men who look facially like themselves.

But it was Verlin Hinsz, a psychologist from North Dakota State University, who first discovered that couples tend to look more like each other facially than could be accounted for just by chance. He conducted experiments where photographs of individual members of engaged and married couples were compared with other random photographs of faces; information about who was in a relationship with whom was hidden from raters, who had to pair faces up in terms of resemblance. A key part of the experiment was that no two photographs were taken with the same background, to reduce possible clues that two individuals were partners. The faces of those who turned out to be in a relationship with each other were rated by independent observers as looking more like each other – again, more consistently than could be accounted for just by chance. The results provide strong support for the theory that people who are attracted to each other tend to resemble each other facially.

Yet another study found that the longer couples

successfully stayed together the more they appeared to resemble each other facially – which again suggests that a key to a viable long-term relationship is choosing someone who looks a lot like you.

One theory to explain these findings is referred to as the 'repeated exposure' hypothesis. It seems we spend an awful lot of time looking at our own faces – in mirrors every day, and at our mugshots on passports, travel cards and similar documentation. This means the face we probably see more than any one other is actually our own. Also, we were surrounded as we grew up by those who were facially similar to us because of genes, which means we become very familiar with facial characteristics close to our own. Perhaps through this repeated exposure to our own face and to the faces of others that are genetically similar we develop an attraction to faces that resemble ours. Even if you are endowed with a facial characteristic that is not commonly seen as desirable (e.g. a large nose, a receding chin, an overbite, etc.), after repeated exposure to this facial characteristic in the mirror and in family members you might become much more comfortable with such an attribute than others.

One other possible explanation comes from perhaps the most established psychological 'law' of physical attraction, known as the 'matching hypothesis'. This states that people tend to end up choosing those who match themselves in terms of desirable qualities. All other things being equal, we lean towards going for those in our own league in terms of physical attractiveness. If you are average looking, you will tend not to try and chat up someone as stunning as Brad Pitt or Michelle Pfeiffer. The key phrase here is 'all things being equal', as elderly billionaires seem to be able to pull young, attractive partners, because they have compensating qualities outside the arena of looks. However, Dr Hinsz took this 'matching' theory into account when he analysed his data on independent observers pairing up photographs of couples in terms of facial similarity, and he still found it was actual physical facial resemblance that more powerfully predicted who was with whom rather than levels of attractiveness. It was possible to distinguish between the two theories because, for example, often a female face resembling a male face would render the woman's face significantly less attractive than the man's.

All of this research raises the spooky possibility that when you fall in love with someone else, although you don't consciously realize it, you are really falling in love with the bit of them that reminds you of yourself.

PERSONAL TASTE, OR HARD WIRING?

A plethora of recently published scientific research has surprisingly suggested that our preference for certain facial features might actually have little to do with personal taste. I touched on this subject briefly in chapter 1 in a discussion of the importance of symmetry to the perception of beauty. The studies perhaps explain for the first time why some faces are universally found attractive. Psychologist Alan Slater and colleagues from the University of Exeter, for example, have reported that even babies between 14 and 15 hours from birth prefer to look at more attractive grown-up faces (as graded by adults). Since babies so young could surely not be influenced by social or cultural preferences, this is strong evidence that there is a universal standard for what kind of face we find attractive.

Evolution could have favoured the selection of mates who looked healthy. Perhaps a flawless countenance was a sign of better physical health, and therefore being sexually attracted to these faces would make sense in terms of passing on fitter genes to the next generation. In that scenario, we are indeed biologically programmed to find certain looks universally attractive.

This theory held sway for decades, until more recent research began to contradict it. Psychologists at the University of Massachusetts asked subjects to estimate, just from photographs of faces of adolescents, how healthy and how attractive they were. The researchers compared these ratings with the actual health records of the photographed people, followed up into middle and late adulthood. The recently published results have uncovered the fact that there is no association at all between having a beautiful face and genuine bodily health. In fact, the more alluring a face is, the greater the likelihood its owner is perceived to be physically healthier than he or she really is. It seems we are 'blinded by beauty', and are more likely to make an error when trying to assess another's true physical health. If anything, these findings suggest that evolution favoured facial attractiveness as a deception ploy: it helped cover up poor physical health, and assisted the selection of the mate despite his or her not being as fit as the less attractive.

It is possible to mount arguments for why primitive tribes might prefer heavier mates to thin ones, for example – and there is more discussion of body shape in the following chapter – but it is less easy to explain other widely found preferences in physical appearance. For example, what possible biological reason is there for the preference Western men seem to have for blonde women; and, as there is a clear tendency for women to accentuate the size of their eyes with make-up, why are large eyes attractive to men? Another new theory contradicts the idea that we choose our mates purely on the grounds of their physical fitness. Instead, it argues that we find certain faces more attractive because of an overspill of our genetic programming to react positively and lovingly to babies.

According to this argument, the more 'baby-faced' a person looks, the greater our attraction to them. After all, if babies' appearance did not elicit such a reflexive positive reaction from us, they would not be cared for properly and might not make it into adulthood to pass on genes to the next generation. Psychologists have repeatedly found from experiments that the more baby-faced a woman appears, the more attractive she is usually rated by others. A 'baby-faced' adult woman has a rounder and less angular face, larger and rounder eyes, higher eyebrows, a smaller nose, a higher forehead and a smaller chin. The tendency to associate large eyes with attractiveness is shown not only by lay persons, but also by novelists. The conspirators in Balzac's epic series of novels *The Human Comedy*, for example, typically have small eyes, and evil characters in Stendhal's *Le Rouge et*

Le Noir are described as having 'evil little grey eyes' and 'small dark eyes made to frighten the bravest of us'. The mysterious attractiveness of blondes is also perhaps now solved as babies' hair colour is lighter than that of adults, particularly in Caucasians, among whom babies are often blond and adults typically brunette.

A baby's wide-eyed look is due to the fact that its eyes are larger in proportion to its face than in an adult. The eyes grow very little from the point of birth, whereas the face continues to develop, rendering the eyes of an adult smaller in relation to the face. Babies also have fine eyebrows, and perhaps high eyebrows are another sign of youth because children typically look up at adults, thus raising their eyebrows. Adult women pluck their eyebrows and apply make-up to enlarge the appearance of their eyes – perhaps in order to become more baby-faced. As female infertility increases with age, perhaps men are attracted to baby-faced women because they look youthful, and therefore appear more likely to be fertile.

But Terri Pettijohn and Abraham Tesser, psychologists at the University of Georgia, have recently produced preliminary data which suggests that women with less baby-faced features and more mature faces – characterized by smaller eyes, thin cheeks and larger chins – should not despair. They wondered whether looking baby-faced was always going to be attractive to males regardless of wider environmental conditions, and hypothesized that when times are good, for example during an economic boom time, men, feeling correspondingly more flush, might presume they have the necessary resources to look after the baby-faced woman, whose appearance suggests helplessness and therefore a need to be cared for. The youthful look might also suggest fun and playfulness, which fits the prevailing mood at times of prosperity. But when the going gets tough, during an economic downturn for example, men might look for more support from women, and in particular prefer partners who appear less dependent.

The test of this hypothesis involved examining the annual polls of the top five most popular American actresses for each year between 1932 and 1995, which were then compared with measures of the state of the economy for those years. Precise computerized measurements were taken from photographs of each actress's facial features. Pettijohn and Tesser indeed found that during prosperous periods actresses with baby-faced features were more popular, but during hard times, actresses with maturer faces were favoured. For example, the worst years for the economy in the US were 1932 and 1933, and then the more mature-looking Marie Dressler and Janet Gaynor were the most popular actresses. During the more affluent years of the late 1940s and the 1950s, the baby-faced Ann Sheridan, Bette Davis, Judy Garland and Rita Hayworth were more fancied. It is also notable that the childlike Marilyn Monroe could be fairly described as the female face of the thriving sixties.

The conclusion drawn from this body of work is that what we find attractive in others depends on the wider context in which the romance is played out. Going back to the research that found that infants liked the same faces adults did, what babies find attractive might depend on whether you do the experiment when they are well fed or not. The same applies analogously for adults. It appears that if you want to know what others find attractive, you must first find out what they most need.

COULD YOUR FACE REALLY BE YOUR DESTINY?

Evolutionary theory predicts that individuals gain aspects of quality for their offspring by mating with attractive individuals, perhaps by obtaining good genes. That we may be biologically or genetically predetermined to find certain faces attractive has been robustly demonstrated by experimental work over the past fifteen years. One explanation for this is that we are drawn to attractive faces because you might indeed be able to judge a book by its cover, and the face could reveal something important about the brain encased behind it.

Dr Robin Hennessy and Dr John Waddington at the Royal College of Surgeons Research Unit in Dublin have recently pioneered a laser surface scanning technique that allows for the first time a 3D analysis of how facial shape might vary with brain structure. They and their team argue that in early fetal life brain and face development are intimately connected, and abnormalities in brain elaboration probably affect face development as well. Their recent research suggests strong links between the differences in size between male and female brains and the contrast in size in male and female faces.

Hennessy and Waddington point out that numerous developmental disturbances such as Down's Syndrome demonstrate a link between brain alteration and striking facial features. Their team demonstrated that other disorders linked to brain aberrations are also associated with facial alterations. For example, they have shown that those suffering from schizophrenia are more likely to have, among other facial differences, an overall narrowing and elongation of the mid and lower front of the face, with reduced mouth width.

Support for these theories comes from a study recently published by Professor Leslie Zebrowitz and psychologist colleagues at Brandeis University in the USA, who have now demonstrated that there is an association between facial attractiveness and the IQ of the possessor of the face. Furthermore, strangers were found to be able to correctly judge intelligence at levels significantly better than chance from brief exposures to a target's face. The research found that the widespread assumption in the population that more facially attractive people are more intelligent was indeed borne out to be true to a surprising extent.

Does this mean that your face really could be your destiny? Sociologists Dr Ulrich Mueller and Dr Allan Mazur of the University of Marburg in Germany recently analysed the final-year photographs of faces of a cohort of military officers, graduates of the class of 1950 of the elite United States Military Academy at West Point. Dominant facial appearance – as defined by strong jaws, broad cheekbones, thin lips and/or a prominent forehead – was a consistent and important predictor of rank attainment in the army over twenty years later. Exactly why remains a mystery. One theory is that dominance in facial features is a marker of higher testosterone levels in the body, and testosterone is known to be associated with competitiveness and aggression. Or it could be a self-fulfilling prophecy effect. Because some men appear dominant they get more respect and obedience from others which assists their rise through the ranks.

There was some support for the self-fulfilling prophecy effect in Professor Zebrowitz's work. His team found that past facial attractiveness predicted future intelligence scores better than past intelligence results did. In other words, how you looked predicted how intelligent you apparently became more accurately than your past intelligence did. Perhaps because the more attractive were treated as more intelligent they ended up having more stimulating and therefore intelligence-enhancing lives.

If dominant features in a male face significantly aid you in terms of promotion in the army, is it possible using similar research techniques to ascertain the facial features that would render us the most attractive?

Prior to puberty, the lower jaw of the male and female face are similar in length. At puberty, however, men undergo a rapid growth spurt in the lower jaw which is driven by testosterone and related hormones. The female jaw undergoes a similar process of growth, but it's much reduced because of lower levels of testosterone-like hormones. In order to signal the lower testosterone and higher female hormones conducive to female fertility, the shorter the lower jaw in women, the better. Indeed, a shorter than average lower jaw in women appears to account for most of the attractive female facial proportions (eye–chin, eye–nose, eye–mouth and mouth–chin). Recent research confirms that the most beautiful female faces have lower jaws that are shorter than two-thirds of average females. Like the jaw, female lips vary with age, and fullness appears to depend on female hormones such as oestrogen. As optimal female fertility appears to hinge on a combination of low testosterone-like hormones and high oestrogen, this supports the idea that the attractive female face will be found to have full lips and a short lower jaw.

But why, then, didn't evolution ensure that women over hundreds of generations had jaws that just got smaller and smaller, and lips that got larger and larger? Of course, functional requirements for chewing, vision and brain development probably account for major constraints on human facial structure. Different environments, too, will have selected for advantageous facial features. For example, a long nose with narrow nostrils is best suited for a cold, arid climate in order to add moisture and warm the cold air. Conversely, a short nose with wide nostrils is a better adaptation for a hot, steamy tropical climate.

But the very latest research on facial attractiveness, recently published by psychologists Dr Caroline Keating and Dr James Doyle based in New York, has found that the most attractive faces contain a mixture of features signalling warmth, power and dominance, with no one characteristic eclipsing the other.

A new and intriguing theory to explain this finding is based on the idea that the facial features a woman passes on to her offspring include an anti-cuckoldry mechanism, which ensures that she continues to secure parental investment from her male mate. An overly striking female face that varies too extremely from the average might make it more difficult for a man to discern his own features in their offspring. A face tending towards a balance of features allows more room for the man's characteristics to show through in the facial appearance of their children, thus reassuring him that they really are his, and he should hang around to assist in the preservation of his genes for the future.

Also, in separate recent work psychologists Dr Ian Penton-Voak and Dr David Perrett from St Andrews University in Scotland found that what kind of male face women were attracted to depended on where they were in their menstrual cycle: around the time of ovulation they were more attracted to hyper-masculine male faces, but during menstruation they preferred more feminine male faces. The evolutionary theory is that when they are most likely to conceive, women aim to mate with a man signalling the most dominant and aggressive characteristics, because as a survival strategy it is best for her offspring to have these tough genes. However, it might be best to have her children raised by a partner who is more nurturing, though unknowingly cuckolded. The New York psychologists Keating and Doyle's work on the idea of an ideal balance of facial features now makes sense, if we are being pulled in different directions in terms of facial attractiveness depending on our goals and circumstances.

The experimental data supporting this overall 'average is best' position is based on an image-processing technique whereby individual faces are photographed and the images are digitally combined then printed as a simulated photograph. This method has revealed that average faces are judged to be more physically attractive than the individual faces that make up the average. Furthermore, the attractiveness of a multi-face composite increases with the number of faces in the average. So the very latest scientific research ironically suggests that although the enhancement of facial beauty supports a multi-billion-dollar industry, and many spend a great deal of time and effort and incur much cost and pain in an endless attempt to improve their faces, they shouldn't try to look too obviously different from the average. Is it the same for body shape?

8

BODY TALK

What is the perfect body, and why?

A narcissist is someone better-looking than you are.

Gore Vidal

ONE SIGN IN TODAY'S WORLD OF OUR DISCONTENT WITH OUR bodies is the rising number of cosmetic surgery patients. But why exactly are so many people nowadays spending so much time down the gym, jogging around the park, at the cosmetic surgeon's or skipping lunch, desperately trying to acquire a different – and, so the perception goes, more attractive – body from their own?

Part of the answer lies in a study by psychologists Shawn Lynch and Debra Zellner, based in Philadelphia – the first ever in-depth investigation of men's views on the muscularity of their own bodies. A group of men selected from a choice of silhouettes those which came closest to the body contour they would prefer in an ideal world; they were also asked to choose what they thought would be the preferred male body shape among women. The surprising result was that in both instances younger men (under the age of twenty-three) picked dramatically more muscular body shapes than their present body shape. So younger men believe, erroneously, that a more muscular figure, especially in the upper body area, is what women find most attractive. But when women were asked what their ideal male body shape was, they indicated a male contour that was much less muscular.

Men aged over thirty picked body shapes very close to their own. Could it be that younger men produced such contrasting results because they have grown up in a media environment that has increasingly emphasized muscularity as determining male attractiveness?

This prevalence of body dissatisfaction among younger men could explain why Dr Devra Braun and colleagues at the Cornell University Hospital in New York have recently reported a rise of almost 10 per cent in male admissions to the eating disorders unit in the 1990s compared to the 1980s. There is now talk among specialists of a new kind of eating disorder emerging among young men which includes disordered dieting, the abuse of anabolic steroids and obsessive over-exercising with weights in order to build muscle mass.

Marc Mishkind, a psychologist at Yale, in trying to explain his own recent research finding that 95 per cent of college-aged men are dissatisfied with their bodies, has argued that male fashions over the last few years have changed significantly to accentuate a more muscular and trim body. Male dissatisfaction is highly focused on particular areas: chest, weight and waist. The degree of this dislike for their own figures is strongly associated with how far away their bodies are from the male ideal of the 'hypermesomorphic' or 'muscleman' type body. Mishkind believes this explains why more men are turning to body building and other lifestyle changes than ever before.

But why should this precise moment in history be associated with a strong surge in interest in attaining a muscular build? Research conducted only fifteen years ago found much less body dissatisfaction among men, which suggests that something recent has prompted a dramatic rise in this problem. Mishkind argues that previously men could be assured of their masculinity by virtue of their occupations, interests or personality dispositions, but now the advance of feminism means women are opting for the same roles and positions. The five traditional archetypes of masculinity are 'soldier', 'frontiersman', 'expert', 'breadwinner' and 'lord of the manor', points out Mishkind, but the frontiersman and lord are no longer viable roles for anyone, and the expert and breadwinner are not exclusively male. Men are left to grasp for the soldier archetype, which is perceived to require a strong, well-muscled, 'armoured' body. Thus, one of the only remaining ways for men to express and preserve traditional male characteristics could be to build muscle. War films and muscular movie heroes such as Arnold Schwarzenegger and Sylvester Stallone certainly became extremely popular as the era of women's liberation grew apace.

Mishkind also argues that the thin female body ideal represents the flip side of this phenomenon. The thin female body connotes such stereotypically feminine traits as smallness, weakness and fragility, which are the mirror opposites of the strength and power represented by the muscular male body.

Mishkind terms this the 'polarization' hypothesis. The muscular male and thin female body ideals, which are physically and symbolically opposite extremes, may be a reaction against sexual equality, an expression of a wish to preserve some semblance of traditional male–female differences. Research, as we know, confirms that younger men wildly overestimate how muscular a male body shape women prefer, and women overestimate the thinness of the preferred female shape of men, but the puzzling question remains: how come both sexes are getting it so wrong?

Light is shed on this conundrum by research conducted by Marilyn Zivian and psychologist colleagues at York University in Canada, who examined the weights of male models featured in *Playgirl* magazine and the female Miss America beauty pageant winners. The study, which has recently been published, found that Miss America beauty pageant winners fell in weight on average by six kilograms between the 1950s and the 1980s. Meanwhile, the weight of *Playgirl* magazine male models rose on average by twelve kilograms between 1986 and 1997, this increase in weight reflecting a rise in muscularity. The authors noted in a related study that almost all the female *Playboy* magazine centrefold models they measured between 1977 and 1996 were underweight according to medical guidelines, and a third met the weight criteria for anorexia nervosa.

In the light of the polarization hypothesis, it is particularly staggering to note that the difference in weight between the average male *Playgirl* model and the female *Playboy* model is now some thirty-eight times greater than the difference in average weight between ordinary men and women. The study's authors therefore concluded that not only are body sizes of men and women portrayed in the media differing hugely, the difference appears to be widening over time. A massive chasm is opening up between ordinary men and women and media images.

The work of psychologists Gregory Fouts and Kimberley Burggraf of Calgary University in Canada found more evidence of this alarming trend. They examined the body weights of fifty-two central female characters in twenty-eight different current prime-time television situation comedies, among them *Friends*, *Seinfeld*, *Roseanne* and *Frasier*. These TV programmes had 48 per cent more younger women, 8 per cent more women of below average weight, and 18 per cent fewer above-average-weight women than could be expected if they represented the general population of women. Previous research uncovered that the proportion of overweight women in prime-time TV programmes halved during the 1980s. As teenage girls watch an average of two TV situation comedies a day, the authors of this study argue that the impact of this distorted sample of female body shapes portrayed incessantly on TV will make viewers more dissatisfied with their own bodies. The study also found that the thinner the female character in a situation comedy, the more positive the comments she received from male characters about her body. The implicit message was that men prefer thinner women.

It seems the media is directly contributing to a misunderstanding of what each sex truly appreciates in the other by portraying men and women hankering after bodies which in real life they don't necessarily desire, if allowed to express a personal preference. It is perhaps because we are insecure about our bodies and uncertain about what the opposite sex really desires that we pay attention to what the media tells us the opposite sex likes. But the research is converging on the conclusion that the media may be particularly unreliable on this issue.

This could explain another recent remarkable finding, by psychologists Eric Stice and colleagues at the Arizona State University, which is that the more TV you watch and the more magazines you read, of whatever variety, the more likely you are to end up suffering from an eating disorder. This effect is most likely achieved through the relentless onslaught of unrealistic body images. Indeed, the British Medical Association recently launched a report that claimed it is the media's obsession with stick-thin supermodels that accounts for the rise in the number of young women who develop eating disorders.

But is the link really that simple? The theory is attractive because it appears superficially logical, and also the media are a current favourite whipping boy of doctors (perhaps because doctors are now a favourite whipping boy of the media). But before we accept this orgy of flagellation unquestioningly, the proposition that it is exposure to the media and their portrayal of unrealistic body shapes that is a causal factor for eating disorders requires proper scientific testing. Otherwise there is a danger we could devote useless energy to reforming the media while the real causes go unhindered.

Very few studies have compared body shape predilection in societies with differing levels of exposure to Western media, but Alexandra Brewis, a US anthropologist at the University of Georgia, recently studied Samoans living in the traditional, rural and isolated island of Samoa with Samoans living in urban Auckland in New Zealand. Exposure to thinness-depicting media is considerably greater in Auckland than in Samoa. Samoan women in Auckland and Samoa estimated that men would prefer a significantly smaller female body size than the one they currently possessed, with no differences in the estimates between the locations. This raises the issue of whether a preference for thinner women is not something implanted by the media, but runs deeper. Is the media in fact merely reflecting our preferences rather than stimulating them? For example, as women's fertility is usually better when they are younger, the biological theory is that this explains the consistent male preference for younger women, while as male status and economic resources rise with age, with little fall-off in fertility, the female preference is for older men. As thinness can be associated with youth, and obesity with age, it could be that a preference for thinner women simply reflects the desirability of youth.

The real issue, then, is what the desire for thinness is really about, what body shape means in a culture. This problem has been neglected by doctors, who seem to assume that the media can foist anything on a gullible public, who would merely follow blindly like the living dead.

Across all world cultures men have been found to prefer women who have thin waists and relatively wider hips – the famous hourglass shape. Such a waist-to-hip ratio (see the next section for more on this) has been found to predict improved female physical health, including less likelihood of becoming diabetic or infertile. But do men prefer these features because they are driven to by their genes, or because they have been persuaded by a Western media which seems currently obsessed with thin-waisted women? In order to test this, Douglas Yu of Imperial College London and Glenn Shepard from the University of California tried to find a group living in a remote area that has not yet had access to television, cinema or advertising – in other words, where the men would never have seen a woman with a thin waist draped over desirable products such as cars or beer, and so could not have been corrupted by Western values of attractiveness.

Their results were published recently in the prestigious science journal *Nature*. They did indeed find that a male preference for hourglass-shaped women in remote tribes increased the more exposure there was to Western culture. But they also managed to track down a tribe living in remote Peru which appeared to be the least Westernized found to date. The men in this tribe not only preferred women who would be regarded by modern Western standards as being overweight, but also appeared deeply concerned about the poor health of the women who had thinner waists. When shown pictures of slim women, the men from the Yomybato tribe thought they were probably suffering from diarrhoea or fever, and even perceived them as 'almost dead'.

Yu and Shepard argue that these reactions suggest that perhaps what we find physically attractive depends on the situation we find ourselves in. Plumpness is certainly associated with fertility and therefore desirability in many non-Western cultures; indeed, in some African societies young girls were sent to 'fattening houses' in order to make them more desirable. In a country where food is scarce, being 'overweight' is symbolic of wealth, ingenuity or security, and therefore desirable in a potential marriage partner. In regions subject to frequent famines, having fat deposits on your body ensures you will survive lean periods. As a society gets wealthier and scarcity is no longer a problem, the whole meaning and value of being overweight understandably changes. Now, it is remaining slim that requires resources and ingenuity. Indeed, studies in the food-abundant West have found that roughly one-third of women of lower socio-economic status are obese, compared with only approximately 15 per cent of women from the middle classes, while no more than around 5 per cent of the wealthiest classes are overweight. In other words, being thin in the West now indicates you have outstanding resources, combined with determination, to overcome the epidemic of obesity. You can probably afford fresh, healthy foods, membership of a gym and a tennis club, and your own personal trainer. Thinness now implies self-control and competence in this context.

Another recent study conducted by Professor Adrian Furnham at University College London comparing the body shape preferences of Ugandan and British students found that Ugandans were much more likely to see the overweight as healthy compared to the British, and given the contrasting economic conditions of the two societies, this in fact makes eminent sense.

There are, then, wider cultural forces at work here than

merely a group of editors who choose what images should front a magazine. It is the multiplicity of associations that need to be understood before the media is simplistically blamed. Nowadays, how you look sends complex messages, not just about your nutritional status, but the kind of person you are, your personality and your class.

BMI AND WHR

Evolutionary psychologists suggest that what we find physically attractive is linked to the fundamental desire to pass on our genes to future generations. In other words, we are influenced by our biology to desire healthy mates who will provide a good physical basis for the production and protection of future children. Even if you are no longer in the market to reproduce, this biological urge still theoretically determines what you find attractive, so it's vital to pay attention to it when trying to alter body shape and size to become more alluring.

Psychologist Martin Tovée and colleagues from the Department of Psychology at Newcastle University have recently been asking the question whether science can determine what is the most attractive female body size and shape. Since the wrong partner choice will obviously have a negative impact on an individual's potential for reproduction, so these psychologists argue, one might expect very strong evolutionary selective pressures for the development of mechanisms that accurately detect signs of health and fertility in potential partners.

In women, two potentially critical signs are shape and weight. As far as shape is concerned, scientific research has focused on the ratio of the width of the waist to the width of the hips – the waist-to-hip ratio, or WHR. A low WHR (i.e. a curvaceous body) is believed to correspond to the optimal fat distribution for high fertility, so, evolutionary psychologists argue, this shape should be highly attractive to men. This has been tested by asking subjects to rate line drawings of women for attractiveness, and the results suggest that the optimal WHR for attractiveness is 0.7 and that WHR is a more important predictor of attractiveness than the apparent weight of the female figure. This WHR figure means that women should ideally aim for a waist that is just over two thirds the measurement of their hips.

But how does that square with the widespread view that supermodels are much thinner than the typical female body? Supermodels have indeed been criticized for being bad role models for young women because of their stick-insect-like appearance, and have even been linked to the increase in eating disorders such as anorexia and bulimia.

In an attempt to resolve the puzzle over the attractiveness of supermodels in a study entitled 'Supermodels: Stick Insects or Hourglasses?', published in the medical journal *The Lancet*, Tovée and his colleagues recently compiled a database of 300 fashion models, 300 glamour models and 300 normal women. The information on the fashion models was drawn from model agencies and comprised the accurate biometric data (height, bust, waist and hip measurements) on the basis of which the models are hired. They obtained the statistics for 'glamour' models from *Playboy* magazine. The normal women, as a control group, were undergraduates and postgraduates with no clinical history of eating disorders who scored within the normal range on a battery of seven questionnaires on eating disorders. For comparison, they included two smaller samples of thirty anorexic women and thirty bulimic women recruited from Newcastle City Eating Disorder Service.

For each woman the team calculated the body mass index (or BMI), the waist-hip ratio, the waist-bust ratio, and the bust-hip ratio. These values gave a summary of variation in body shape. BMI is a measure of your weight taking into account your height: tall people should weigh more. To determine whether a person is overweight you need to divide their weight by their height: BMI is calculated as weight in kilograms divided by height in metres squared. Tables exist on the Internet and elsewhere to indicate what your BMI is from your height and weight.

Fashion models were indeed found to be significantly taller than all the other groups of women by, on average, eleven centimetres. Both fashion models and glamour models were rated significantly underweight on the basis of BMI, but were consistently heavier than anorexic women. Fashion models and glamour models had a waist-hip ratio close to the optimum of 0.7 – basically, the ratio at which a woman is most likely to be ovulating effectively – and tended to have an hourglass figure, as shown by the bust-hip ratio. Indeed, fashion and glamour models had similar measurements, although glamour models are usually regarded as more curvaceous than fashion models. The key difference may be height. A shorter hourglass figure will appear more curvaceous. The take-home message from this study is that supermodels are both tall and curvaceous, and dieting will not make you look like a *Vogue* covergirl. It could be that supermodels appear a lot thinner than they really are simply because they are so tall. Intriguingly, then, it might be that many women are vainly dieting in a bid to look like a supermodel when this project is doomed, because no matter how healthy or fit weight you achieve, shorter women are always going to look fatter than supermodels. However, another intriguing finding from the study was the narrow range of BMI that the supermodels and glamour models fell into, which was basically 18 (remember, your BMI is your weight in kilograms divided by your height in metres squared).

But which of these is the most important measure of attractiveness – BMI, or your body shape as measured by WHR? It is interesting that many women intuitively seem to place more store on weight (i.e. BMI) than shape, yet, as Tovée and colleagues point out, the eye does not have a set of bathroom scales and a tape measure, so when we take someone in visually, theoretically it's the WHR which should be more important in terms of visual impact. Tovée and colleagues found that if women increase their body weight, the effect on body shape tends to be localized. Specifically, fat is deposited around the chest, waist and hip/thigh regions. The waist turns out to be the most reliable guide to BMI or weight. This may be because changes in the width of the chest and hips are constrained by the underlying bone structure, whereas the waist has more freedom of movement to reflect a change in BMI or weight.

In another more recent study, Tovée and his team asked

forty male undergraduate subjects aged around twenty to rate frontal colour images of fifty real women to gauge which aspects of the female body were found most attractive. In particular, was it overall weight as adjusted for height (BMI) or was it body shape (WHR)? BMI, or basically your weight, emerged as the major factor in determining sexual attractiveness.

The psychologists argue that there are clear advantages to using BMI or weight as a basis for mate selection, for BMI is closely correlated with health and fertility. In a recent study, 115,195 women were followed over a period of sixteen years. The lowest mortality rate (all causes) was associated with BMIs close to 19. Although still representing the 'normal' range, women whose BMI fell between 19 and 24.9 had a 20 per cent increase in relative risk of mortality. At still higher values of BMI, relative risk of mortality accelerated considerably: 33 per cent for BMIs of 25 to 26.9; 60 per cent for BMIs of 27 to 28.9; and over 100 per cent for BMIs of 29 to 32. At the opposite end of the scale, a BMI below 19 has a negative impact on both health and reproductive potential. Fertility is particularly strongly affected, being reduced to zero at very low BMI, when women become amenorrhoeic or stop having periods.

The evidence suggests that the optimal BMI for health and fertility is struck at around a value of 18 to 19, which in Tovée's study is also the preferred BMI for attractiveness; even small increases or decreases either side of that narrow range radically reduce attractiveness ratings. There is evidence that body-fat distribution, as measured by WHR, plays a role in fertility, but the linkage of WHR with fertility is far weaker than that of BMI with fertility, and this is one of the reasons that WHR may be a poorer predictor of attractiveness. For example, Tovée and colleagues point out, there is a considerable overlap in the WHRs of populations of normal women and anorexic patients. The latter are not menstruating, so a woman who is basically infertile can have the same WHR as a woman with normal fertility.

Tovée and colleagues suggest there exists a hierarchy of signals used to determine the attractiveness of a potential partner. BMI or weight may be used as a 'screening measure' to select the most desirable (i.e. biologically and evolutionarily the healthiest and most fertile) women from a range of possible partners, and then secondary factors such as body shape, including WHR, may be used to distinguish between these attractive possibilities.

While most women are dissatisfied with the size and shape of their bodies, this discontent does not necessarily interfere with daily life, and it is important to remember that men are also victim to society's prejudices about bodies. In one study, job recruiters interviewed equally qualified men who varied only in height: 75 per cent of recruiters hired the 6'1" individual rather than the 5'5" man.

Other research finds that taller political candidates attract more votes than their shorter rivals, surely good evidence, if any more were needed, that we would all be better off if our society did not so overrate physique.

There are several important psychological implications in these findings. One is known anecdotally as the Napoleon Syndrome – the tendency for shorter men, such as Napoleon and Hitler, to compensate for their diminished stature by being more aggressive.

New research has demonstrated scientifically that indeed our physical appearance does dramatically influence our psychology. In particular we try hard to compensate for defects in our appearance, which reduce our attractiveness to others, with increased attention to relationships. We do this perhaps because at some level we are aware of the psychological evidence that the less physically attractive are perceived as not only being less healthy, but also less intelligent and less sexually inviting.

People who are overweight are sometimes thought to be lazy, gluttonous, slow and even unintelligent. Of course, none of these stereotypes or prejudices might be true: they are merely conclusions that people jump to. But psychologists now believe that people whose appearance is likely to produce negative first impressions are aware of this fact, and try to compensate by working harder at the things they *can* control. So, according to psychological research, physically less attractive people have been found to be more socially skilled than the more attractive.

However, it is possible that many may overcompensate in the social skills arena for deficits in the physical field. For example, 'baby-faced' (round face, large eyes, small nose bridge, small chin) young men have been found by psychological research to overcompensate for their belief that they will be perceived as submissive, naive and warm by in fact becoming more assertive and hostile than less baby-faced-looking men. Indeed, surveys have found that short, baby-faced young men were more likely to become juvenile delinquents.

This means that those who are overweight or generally unfit-looking could well have adapted to this psychologically by being overly fawning and unassertive in relationships in an attempt to compensate for their lack of physical attractiveness. In other words, looking unfit could have turned you into a psychological doormat for others to walk all over. This raises the interesting suggestion that one reason to work harder in the gym and get fit is because it may help you *dare* to express yourself with less fear of rejection. In other words, it could give you the social confidence to be more yourself, and less prone to seeking approval through spineless toadying. Hey, I didn't say it – it's in the research.

Another recent study examining the effect of body appearance on male psychology, conducted by psychiatrist Dr Aikarakudy Alias, who has been working on the relationship between body hair and intelligence for twenty-two years, informed the Eighth Congress of the Association of European Psychiatrists that hairy chests are more likely to be found among the most intelligent and highly educated than in the general population. According to this new research, excessive body hair could also mean higher intelligence.

Dr Alias's research, which focused on medical students in the United States, showed that 45 per cent of male doctors in training were 'very hairy', compared with less than 10 per cent of men overall. In a region of southern India, research among medical and engineering students and manual labourers found that both groups of students had more body hair on average than the manual workers. Further investigations showed that when academic ranking among students was examined, the hairier men got better grades. Taking this study one step further, Dr Alias studied 117 Mensa members (who have an IQ of at least 140) and found that this group tended to have thick body hair. In fact, some of the most intelligent men appeared to be those who had hair on their backs as well as on their chests.

Dr Alias, who, it is reported, kept his shirt firmly buttoned during his presentation at the Congress, cited Peter Sellers, Robin Williams, chess player Garry Kasparov and Charles Darwin as hairy intelligent men. In comparison, he noted that most 'boxers, such as Muhammad Ali and Mike Tyson, are not at all hairy'. Smooth-skinned people should not despair, however. While men who possess the proverbial 'fur-coat on their back' may tend to be more intelligent, there are also very intelligent men with little or no body hair. After all, apparently one of the greatest men who ever lived, Albert Einstein, had no body hair.

The issue of hair is a preoccupation for many, perhaps because it's the part of our appearance that is easiest to change. However, we live in fast-moving times in terms of medical technological advances, and more and more surgical procedures and medical interventions are allowing us to change our appearance – often radically. This means that more of us are confronting the question of whether to go under the surgeon's knife to improve our appearance.

The issue of cosmetic surgery goes to the heart of one of the deepest dilemmas in relationships between men and women – the issue of truth. The paradox is that both sexes list honesty as being one of the most valued characteristics in a potential mate. But when either sex is trying to seduce or impress the other, honesty is usually the first characteristic to be sacrificed. If truth is the first casualty of war, as Winston Churchill remarked, then in the battle of the sexes truth went missing in action right at the opening of hostilities.

The psychological problem with cosmetic surgery is that there is something 'not real' about a body after surgery, and if the body no longer appears 'real' or 'genuine' because of artificial enhancement, then there seems something 'dishonest' about the person as well. This explains male uneasiness about cosmetic surgery, for if a woman is not 'real' in this aspect, how honest is she being about the rest of her appearance, or her life? And if a woman's looks matter so much to her that she is willing to risk the scalpel and sacrifice truth on the altar of attraction will her partner constantly have to tiptoe around this 'landmine' of her appearance? Could he ever dare to be honest about that dress? So, cosmetic surgery to a man may mean added stress, and the extra tension of constantly wondering if he has reassured her enough about her looks, given how much work she has put into them.

The truth is that men want women to look fabulous, but to achieve this effortlessly without having to labour at it. Part of the reason for this is if she had to work so hard to look good, what will she look like when the labour becomes too much effort? But perhaps the real secret anxiety for men is this: if a woman is willing to put all this effort and sacrifice in for a man, what is the man expected to do for her in return?

9

LET'S TALK ABOUT SEX

Quick and dirty

Sex is like bridge: if you don't have a good partner, you better have a good hand.

Charles Pierce

THE RESULTS OF THE LARGEST SCIENTIFIC SURVEY OF PENIS SIZE ever conducted in the world have recently been published. The penis proportions of 5,122 men were collected over twenty-five years at the famous Kinsey Institute of Sex Research at Indiana University and analysed by US psychologists Dr Anthony Bogaert and Dr Scott Hersberger. Their finding is that homosexual men have larger penises on all measures of size – from flaccid to erect, in terms of circumference and length – than heterosexual men. For example, the average heterosexual man's penis was smaller when erect by over one cubic inch in volume than the average homosexual. This finding is all the more remarkable as on average the homosexual men had slightly smaller bodies in terms of weight and height than the heterosexuals, and generally the bigger a man's body, the larger his penis.

One possible explanation for this difference in penis size is that homosexual men have been found to tend towards starting puberty earlier than heterosexuals, and puberty is the starting point of a surge of testosterone secretion in the male body which begins to decline only from the mid-thirties onwards. As testosterone is one of the hormones that determines penis proportion, longer exposure to these higher testosterone levels could explain why gay men end up with larger penises.

This testosterone theory has other implications for male body shape, for the group of genes which help to determine penis proportion are also involved in finger and toe size. In chapter 5 I introduced you to the work of Dr John Manning on the difference in length between a man's fourth finger and his second. Given that testosterone partly determines penis size, the longer a man's fourth finger is compared to his second, the larger his penis could be. The link with finger and toe size may also explain where the folk story that penis size is linked with foot length came from. As surveys repeatedly find that most men think (erroneously) that their penises are smaller than average, can we expect men to become obsessed with shoe and glove size?

Yet surveys of penis size have found a remarkable lack of variation: two-thirds of men fall within an inch smaller or longer than the average 6.14 inches at erect length Bogaert and Hersberger found. So if penis size when erect is so similar, why are men so anxious and obsessed by size? Part of the answer may be that men most often gaze upon their penises when they are in a non-erect state, and flaccid length is not a good predictor of erect length.

Smaller flaccid penises tend to 'catch up' with larger flaccid ones when they become erect; in other words, there is a convergence in size as the penis becomes erect. In fact, the bigger a flaccid penis, the less it grows in size when erect.

Many women might find the male preoccupation with the size and shape of the penis somewhat amusing, but there is in fact a key aspect of this area of the male anatomy and physiology which has a direct impact, so to speak, on them. Remarkable new research by psychologist Dr Gordon Gallup and colleagues from the State University of New York suggests that semen could have clinically significant mood-enhancing effects on women.

For the study, published in the prestigious journal *Archives of Sexual Behaviour*, 293 college females were divided into groups depending on their frequency of condom use during sex. Condom use is a measure of the presence of semen in the reproductive tracts of the sexually active, and this research has established for the first time that women having sex regularly with condoms are more depressed than those who never use condoms. Also, depressive symptoms and suicide attempts among females who used condoms were strongly associated with how often condoms were used. Less than 5 per cent of women who never used condoms had attempted suicide, yet almost 30 per cent of women who usually used condoms had. Sexually active women who never used condoms were also significantly less depressed than women who abstained from sex altogether. However, the fact that depression scores among females who were not having sex did not differ from those who were using condoms demonstrates that it is not sexual activity per se that antagonizes depression. For women who did not use condoms at all, the length of time since their last sexual encounter was strongly associated with depressive symptoms – the longer the period, the more depressed they were. This effect also held for women who reported using condoms some of the time. But for those who used condoms most or all of the time, this association was not found.

Semen is known to contain several chemicals and hormones that have mood-elevating or -altering properties and have been shown to be absorbed through the vagina. They can be measured in the bloodstream within a few hours of intercourse. Among these substances are testosterone, oestrogen, follicle-stimulating hormones, luteinizing hormones, prolactin and several different prostaglandins. Testosterone is indeed absorbed more quickly through the vagina than through the skin.

Alternative explanations for this finding were tested for by the study, but no effect on depression was found. Even if semen does antagonize depressive symptoms in women, the authors of the study point out that it is still not clear where this effect originates. They were unable to comment on whether any other method of semen application, for example oral or anal, and whether the sex was between heterosexual or homosexual couples were important factors, and indicated that their research could investigate such issues in the future.

If this finding proves to be replicated then it suggests some novel explanations for previously puzzling phenomena such as post-natal depression and mood swings through the menstrual period. These new avenues are important, as when it comes to mental and emotional problems one of the most consistent and perplexing differences between the sexes involves the prevalence of depression: women are between three to five times more prone to it than men.

For men, the key psychological and biological issue isn't usually the mood-enhancing (or otherwise) effect of their semen on women, but more the mood-enhancing (or otherwise) effect of getting an erection. If most men are stuck with the anatomy they were born with, does that mean there is nothing we can do to improve matters in the bedroom?

We are not used to thinking of the state of our sex lives as telling us anything much about our general health, or even in terms of predicting when we are going to die. It is, after all, not something about which we usually volunteer much information to our GPs. Yet it is estimated that over 153 million men around the world experience serious difficulties getting an erection. Over the age of forty the rate is one in seven men, and as many as 50 per cent in this age group have at least occasional problems.

New medical research suggests that men in particular need to start paying serious attention to their sex lives, because performance in bed has now been linked crucially to the state of your heart and your general cardiovascular system. A new study found that in 70 per cent of men, future blockage of coronary arteries leading to heart disease is pre-dated by erectile dysfunction, suggesting that impotence could be an early warning sign that arteries are beginning to block. Difficulty achieving an erection is often down to inadequate blood flow, leading to a lack of engorgement of the penis. In other words, basic plumbing is usually the main culprit – exactly the same kind of plumbing problem that is the basis of heart attacks and strokes. The arteries that lead to the penis, and which are responsible for supplying the increased blood flow that produces an erection, are significantly smaller than the vessels supplying cardiac muscle in the heart. This means a much less significant obstruction is all it takes to produce difficulty getting an erection.

This is a vital advance in helping us know the state of our arteries before blockages get so severe as to produce a heart attack. In up to 70 per cent of patients a sudden heart attack out of the blue is the very first sign of coronary artery disease with no prior warning whatsoever like chest pain or exercise difficulty. If doctors could have an early warning system for the development of blockages they could sooner introduce patients to preventive strategies such as treatment to lower blood pressure, reducing fats like cholesterol and lipids in the bloodstream, plus lifestyle changes such as healthier diets and more exercise, all of which could reduce atherosclerosis (the thickening of the arteries) before it gets to a dangerous state.

Dr Piero Montorsi and colleagues at the Institute of Cardiology at the University of Milan is the pioneering heart doctor whose research and theories have led to this revolutionary way of predicting who is going to get a heart attack years before it actually happens. Dr Montorsi argues that from data he and other researchers have collected, problems achieving an erection in men over sixty predict the development of heart disease on average three years later. However, he believes that in younger men the length of time between erection difficulties and later heart disease is likely to be much longer than this, meaning that as a predictor of the future state of your heart the condition of your wedding tackle is even more helpful the younger you are.

One advantage of going to your doctor early and getting a check if achieving an erection is becoming a problem is that strategies such as taking cholesterol-lowering drugs do seem to reduce atherosclerosis. Dr Montorsi argues that if these strategies improve the artery function in your heart, they are also likely to do the same in penile arteries, meaning that your sex life would improve dramatically. The most common physical problem that leads to erectile dysfunction appears to be diabetes, but high blood fats (hyperlipidemia), smoking and high blood pressure are all linked to atherosclerosis so it's possible that any of these significant medical problems could be detected if men went to their GPs much earlier with erection difficulties. GPs themselves should probably ask their male patients much more routinely about their sex lives as a useful screening measure for possible future heart disease.

The problem is that men tend to avoid going to the doctor much more than women do; they are also particularly loathe to confront any problems they might be having in bed. This means that practically it's going to be down to female partners all around the country to encourage or indeed insist that their male partners go to the doctor when problems in bed are beginning to develop.

This is undoubtedly going to lead to a lot of strain in relationships, but if it's a choice between that and the stress of having to call for an ambulance because your partner has suddenly developed severe chest pains . . .

Another problem is the widespread belief that the causes of not being able to 'get it up' are usually 'psychological' and down to stress or nervousness or other emotional problems like anxiety or depression. Dr Montorsi's research and other studies are all beginning to point in the direction of erectile dysfunction being a physical problem rather than a psychological one.

Case Study

Jim was a patient referred to me by his GP because, among other issues, he was suddenly having problems getting an erection. He had gone to his GP because he had assumed this was all down to getting depressed as he had recently been laid off at work; in fact he had really been dragged along reluctantly by his partner, citing symptoms of depression, difficulty sleeping, loss of weight and appetite. One classic symptom of depression is indeed loss of libido, and Jim certainly had gone off sex recently.

It would have been easy simply to put this down to his depression and prescribe an anti-depressant, but on close questioning it turned out that actually Jim was pretty keen on having sex; it was just that he had lost his confidence because of a few recent 'failures' in bed. As a result of not wanting to endure the strain and pressure of seeing whether he could 'get it up', he indicated a lack of interest in sex whenever he was asked by his partner. He would claim to be tired, or stressed, or low. It was indeed easier to own up to being depressed rather than continue to worry about his inability to produce an erection.

When I saw him, after taking a careful clinical history and finding out that it wasn't loss of desire that was the problem but recent erectile dysfunction, I wondered about his cardiovascular system. He was a smoker and didn't do much exercise; indeed, he was a bit overweight and his blood pressure was high. Again, all of this could have been the result of depression, which often leads to comfort eating and smoking. We did some counselling but I also referred him back to his GP for a full cardiac work-up.

Blood testing revealed that his fats and cholesterol were high and he was put on lipid-lowering drugs, a diet, an exercise plan and some anti-hypertensive medication. A treadmill test revealed some very early signs of cardiac artery blockage. With counselling and the eventual arrival of a new job plus a healthier lifestyle (he managed to give up smoking), Jim cheered up, lost weight, his blood pressure and treadmill test returned to normal, as did his blood fats, and lo and behold his sex life improved dramatically! He had been referred for mild depression following a job loss, but we may have ended up saving his relationship and his life by spotting the earliest warning sign of future heart disease.

ADVICE FOR A HEALTHY SEX LIFE

Finding the motivation to exercise can be difficult, so it may interest you to know that a recent spate of research has found that exercise promotes a better sex life.

Dr Carole Pinnock and colleagues from the Repatriation General Hospital in Adelaide, Australia, recently conducted a survey of impotence in the community and found that a history of vigorous exercise was protective against erectile dysfunction for men across all ages. Since an erection has a lot to do with plumbing and hydraulics, anything which narrows or diminishes the effectiveness of blood flow to the penis makes erectile dysfunction more likely, so improving your cardiovascular fitness is a direct contribution to ensuring you are less likely to suffer from impotence.

Similarly, Dr White and colleagues from the Physical Education Department at the University of California found in a diary study of men that aerobic exercise led to significantly greater sexuality enhancements in the form of frequency of various intimate activities, reliability of adequate functioning during sex, percentage of satisfying orgasms, and so on. Moreover, the degree of sexuality enhancement among exercisers was strongly associated with their individual improvement in fitness.

It would also seem that the best form of foreplay is to get a female partner to do a bit of exercise before sex. Dr Suling Li and colleagues at the Loyola University in Chicago found that relatively active and very active women had significantly fewer and less distressing sexual symptoms, such as vaginal dryness and decreased sexual desire, than inactive women. The authors concluded that physical activity may be an important alternative/adjunct to hormone therapy, particularly for sexual symptom management for women.

Dr Cindy Meston and colleagues from the Department of Psychiatry, University of Washington, Seattle, investigated the effects of acute exercise on sexual arousal in women. In two experimental sessions, thirty-six women viewed a neutral film followed by an erotic film. In one of the sessions, the women were exposed to twenty minutes of intense exercise before viewing the films. Acute exercise significantly increased vaginal blood flow responses to an erotic film among sexually functional women and those with low sexual desire. The results suggested that increased nervous system arousal achieved through exercise affects physiological sexual response in women in a positive way.

Finally, Dr Holmes and colleagues at the University of Arkansas investigated college students in terms of their exercise habits, perceived sexual desirability, and body image. Exercise level was strongly positively associated with perceived physical attractiveness, perceived sexual desirability, and perception of self as a sexual partner.

So regular exercise appears to have a direct benefit on your performance not just on the playing field, but in bed as well. This is a vitally important thing to know, because one of the greatest causes of discontent in relationships between men and women is that sexual appetites seem to be different. Women's capacity for sex is in fact greater than men's, in the sense that women can have more sex and more orgasms than men over a set period of time, yet the controversy continues to rage as to whether men and women have different sex drives.

Psychologist Professor Roy Baumeister from Case Western Reserve University in the USA appears, however, to have finally resolved this age-old dispute. His recent review of the research indicates that the average young man gets sexually aroused several times a day while the average young woman experiences the same only twice a week. However, some 45 per cent of men but only 15 per cent of women report masturbating at least once per week. Women are almost four times more likely than men to say they have never masturbated.

If men and women do have different sex drives, then the number of times they end up having sex in a relationship could be the result of a compromise and does not reflect the number of times they really want sex. To get a true picture of how often each gender actually desires sex, a good place to look is gay and lesbian relationships, as these are not constrained by what the opposite sex wants. Research into this issue has found that two years into a relationship, two-thirds of gay men are having sex at least three or more times per week, but the corresponding figure is only one-third of lesbians.

If men and women have different sex drives, then a vital aspect of maintaining a healthy relationship as a couple could be how this difference is negotiated without recrimination or blame. It would appear from the research that the only time a couple in fact coincide in terms of level of sex drive is when a relationship is starting, passion is high, and intimacy is rising. Understanding that for the rest of your life your sex drives are unlikely to coincide again like that is now a vital relationship survival skill.

Most people find talking about sex difficult, without

the added burden of talking about it to the person you are actually having sex with, and on top of all that stating what you like and what you don't like. As a result, most people spend very little time talking about their sex lives. This is a mistake, because one of the basic points about sex is that it is supposed to be enjoyable. But unless you express your views, preferences or curiosity about any subject, including sex, you will be unable to make sure it goes ahead in a way you can enjoy. Even if you do find it embarrassing to talk about, remember that the aim of the conversation is to improve your sex life, and if your partner cares about you he or she will want that as well. Remember, too, that the potential benefits make it a worthwhile enterprise.

Just as everyone has different tastes when it comes to fashion, hairstyles and the food they eat, the same applies to sex. You would not dream of going into a restaurant and simply letting other people choose your meal for you, but that is exactly how most people approach sex. There is no set way of making love which is guaranteed to please everyone, just as there is no one meal which everyone in the world likes. Also, even if you are served your favourite meal every day, the likelihood is that a change will add spice to your diet. But no changes will occur if they are not requested.

Lack of assertiveness in bed in terms of asking for what you want is the number one reason for an unsatisfactory sex life. It is amazing the desperate consequences that can arise simply because most people are too embarrassed to ask their partner about their sexual preferences. Men may even resort to using a prostitute because they are too inhibited when it comes to asking their wife or girlfriend for a particular sexual favour, when in fact she might not have minded bestowing that favour had she only been asked. Women might complain that their husbands are 'no good in bed', and go off sex altogether or have an affair, yet at no time do they actually let their partner know what they want, thus giving the partner a chance to improve their sex lives. Another problem is that many people think the other person ought to know already what they want, or that by dropping hints or using body language they have already conveyed clearly what they want, and been rebuffed. I am afraid there really is no substitute for a frank conversation about sex. It's more likely to get your message across than 'mind-reading'.

Timing is all-important when it comes to talking about sex. Asking for what you really want just after sex, for instance, may seem like a dissatisfied complaint. Instead, bring the subject up when sex is not actually on the agenda. Another important point to bear in mind is that sex is a reciprocal activity: it is best to start the conversation off by enquiring what the other partner would like before pitching in with what you want. Communication about sex works best when it is a form of trading where both partners agree to changes in equal measure. In other words, you will do something for your partner if he or she will do something for you. If you start talking about sex in a way that suggests it is only the other person who must make changes, then this is likely to result in defensiveness and hurt feelings. Many people object to talking about sex because they believe it ought to be spontaneous and natural, but sex can only be spontaneous when you and your partner can take part confidently, knowing what the other person likes. And you can only get to that stage by talking to each other.

10

DON'T TAKE YOUR LOVE TO TOWN

Sleeping around

Love is a gross exaggeration of the difference between one person and everybody else.

George Bernard Shaw

SARAH MIKACH AND MICHAEL BAILEY, PSYCHOLOGISTS AT Northwestern University in Illinois, have recently published in the prestigious academic journal *Evolution and Human Behaviour* the results of an in-depth investigation into a new breed of modern woman who has unusually high numbers of sex partners. Their research completely turns on its head the previous negative views of psychologists about the backgrounds of promiscuous women, and instead finds them to function better psychologically in many respects than the less permissive.

Twenty women were drawn from the general population who were aged between twenty-five and thirty-five and who had individually slept with a minimum of twenty-five different partners to a maximum of two hundred, with an average per woman of almost sixty sex partners. This group was compared with nineteen more typical women of a similar age whose average number of sex partners was four.

Previously it had been thought that one of the most reliable differences between the genders was that men were more interested in casual sex without emotional involvement than women were. Promiscuity for men was thought by psychologists to have fewer negative repercussions for their psychology because men were programmed by their biology to prefer indiscriminate sex, as a way of maximizing their chances of passing genes on to the next generation. In contrast, evolutionary psychologists believed, female reproductive strategy centred on investing in relationships, as a way of ensuring they had mated with someone prepared to assist in the raising of children. Previous sex research had found that promiscuous women still felt somewhat demeaned by 'one-night stands', and casual sex left them feeling vulnerable and anxious about a partner's possible lack of interest in longer-term commitment to the relationship. So before Mikach and Bailey's revolutionary new study, the overwhelming academic view was that women who were sexually indiscriminate were being driven by some kind of psychological problem.

Previously it had been theorized that permissive women were unconsciously adopting an adaptive evolutionary strategy of trading any individual male commitment for the chance of mating with men of higher genetic quality – which perhaps meant they were only 'sleeping around' because they were surrounded by men of inferior prospects. Yet Mikach and Bailey found instead that the more promiscuous women placed significantly greater value on the physical attractiveness of a potential partner than non-promiscuous women – in fact, promiscuous women were being choosier about the appearance of the men they slept with.

Research had also established that girls from father-absent and divorced-parents homes tend to sleep with more men. The theory was that they might have learned during a disturbed childhood that men were unreliable, so they never considered developing longer-term relation-ships. It was believed in academic circles, then, that a major predictor of promiscuity in women was a past history of early family stress in various guises, yet the new research from Mikach and Bailey found that promiscuous females had no greater chance of coming from dysfunctional families than non-promiscuous women.

Another theory Mikach and Bailey have forced us to re-appraise was that 'loose' women were not attractive enough in various respects to inspire emotional investment from men, so they were being forced to move from partner to partner because of continual rejection. Sexologists believed as a result that more promiscuous women would in fact be less physically attractive than those who tended to seduce men willing to stay in longer-term relationships. Yet another idea was that they suffered from low self-esteem, which they were continually trying to bolster by reassuring themselves of their desirability by 'sleeping around'. In fact, the new data reveals that promiscuous women were rated on physical appearance as more likely to have the kind of bodies most women aspire to and which men would find more attractive. They also scored higher on self-esteem than non-promiscuous women.

The key characteristic that distinguishes women who enjoy unusually high numbers of sex partners appears to be that they simply prefer casual sex. They have the same attitude to intercourse that men have always held. Indeed, these women share more masculine attitudes in other areas of life too. For example, another study by Michael Bailey also confirms that women in the top 10 per cent in terms of number of sex partners are just as likely as promiscuous men to have been sexually unfaithful to a steady partner. Also, these promiscuous women were not attracted to men because of their status or economic success; instead they emphasized more basic physical attractiveness as determining whom they slept with. This is a very male approach to sexual relationships. The more feminine attitude is to place status above physical appearance, supposedly in the search for superior future parental investment.

These more traditionally masculine attributes of assertiveness and lack of constraint perhaps also partly explain the careers chosen by these more promiscuous women. They appear to be drawn more from the artistic and creative fields, with actresses coming top followed by marketing and sales, public relations and advertising, writers, artists and editors. Occupying the bottom of the female promiscuity league are accountants, doctors and librarians, in that order.

But why should this group of women emerge right now? Previous research conducted in the early 1990s on never-married women in their twenties found that with increasing sexual experience the periods of abstinence and the time spent between sexual relationships declined, so these dynamics produced an ever-increasing rate of sex partners. As the average age at which women marry has been rising over the last few decades, an increasing number of women are seeing their pre-marital years as a time to 'play the field', rather like men have always done, before settling down. Whereas before, casual sex might have meant trying different men out to see who were the best marriage prospects, now it seems sleeping around is being done just for the pleasure of sex and not much else.

An underlying theme which recurs over and over again in the research and when talking to highly promiscuous women, as I have done in my clinics, is one of control. They clearly intend to retain autonomy in their lives and see emotional investment in relationships with men as the price women used to pay for sex. They now insist on retaining mastery of their relationships with men, even to the extent of controlling how and whether they show their emotions to their partners.

One of the women interviewed by researchers, an academic anthropologist, had had a total of sixteen one-night stands and an average of three different partners every year. She is a typical promiscuous woman, according to this research. She fantasized on average once every two weeks about someone other than her current partner, and did not believe she needed to be emotionally involved with someone before having sex with them. Before her current boyfriend, she felt intercourse was just a competition between friends to see who could get the most. Though there were occasions when she would resist sleeping with a man if she really liked him, to ensure he did not think she was easy, during this 'game' she would think 'of sex the way a man does . . . it's all about getting laid with no strings attached'. She would even keep 'safe' partners, men willing to give more commitment in a relationship, in reserve while she was looking for or actually seeing another partner. If annoyed with a boyfriend, she would arouse him as much as possible and then refuse to have intercourse.

What is emerging from this research is the arrival of a new type of modern young woman who, having gained more control than previous generations over fertility, careers and finances, is now seeking similar dominion in the arena of personal relationships. These women are now so in command of their emotional lives that they can choose to have casual sex just for the pleasure of it, without feeling guilt. They choose their partners almost exclusively on the basis of physical attraction, and can make the decision to share their bed as quickly as men have always been able to, and without any sense that the sex 'means anything'. Perhaps the emergence of this new type of woman is a sign that we are entering the final stage of the battle of the sexes.

MATE POACHING

American psychologists David Schmitt and David Buss have recently published the results of a remarkable study which for the first time illuminates a form of mating behaviour that until now has remained a secret aspect of our love lives.

'Mate poaching' is the attempt to gain a partner not from the available pool of single people, but instead from those already in relationships. It is different from adultery, as this is not about a one-night stand or a brief fling, but the attempt to gain a long-term relationship by breaking up another that already exists. Adultery is frequently about sex; mate poaching is about luring someone who was already in another relationship into a serious monogamous association.

The new research found that around 85 per cent of men and women have experienced someone else trying to attract them away from an ongoing relationship, and over 50 per cent reported making the attempt themselves. Although this figure is only for attempts at mate poaching, not for successful poaching, this astonishingly high rate indicates a lack of respect for the 'out-of-bounds' nature of ongoing relationships. The research also found that England has one of the highest rates of mate poaching, 32 per cent of men and 18 per cent of women having taken their current partner away from another relationship. For men, this is almost twice the rate of mate poaching found in the USA and three times the rate in France; for women it is twice the rate found in France (see table).

Rates of Mate Poaching Around the World

People who were already in romantic relationships were asked, 'Did this relationship result from you attracting your current partner away from someone else?' The findings are as follows, across the world. The international data seem to indicate that mate poaching is relatively common in England.

	Men	Women
Canada–Toronto	23%	12%
Canada–Quebec	6%	9%
USA	17%	15%
England	32%	18%
France	10%	11%
Portugal	17%	14%
Slovenia	15%	9%
Croatia	19%	18%
Greece	13%	16%
Israel	9%	3%
Turkey	19%	8%

And those were the figures for current relationships. When people were asked if they had ever in the past been successfully attracted away from a partner, the percentages in the US rose to 40 per cent of men and 30 per cent of women. The data on past experiences of mate poaching have not yet been collected for Britain, but if the figure for the US is used as the basis for an estimate, given that the English have much higher rates of mate poaching than the US, it is likely that many men and women in England have been poached at some time.

Exactly why England should come so high up the league table for mate poaching is still mysterious to psychologists. Schmitt and Buss suggest some possible theories, including the effect of the greater media attention given here to celebrity adultery, rendering poaching more acceptable as part of our culture. Also, our religious beliefs are less focused on the sanctity of marriage than in many other countries. Another possible contributory factor is that the availability of guns is more widespread in many other societies. A more violent sub-culture makes poaching a higher risk, as the anger of the person left behind is more likely to prove dangerous. The more easy-going English are perhaps less likely to be violent in this manner if poached from, resulting in potential poachers who are less discouraged to 'have a go'.

The other remarkable finding from this research was that women aged over thirty were eight times more likely to have tried to poach a man than women aged under thirty, which appears to be concrete evidence for the desperation induced by the infamous biological clock. Which leads us nicely to the so-called 'Bridget Jones effect'. Bridget Jones, I'm sure you'll recall, is the heroine of the famous books and films who complained that all the best men appear to be married. Professor Buss and Dr Schmitt posed the question, what do you do when indeed all the best mates are unavailable because they are already spoken for? The logical answer is mate poaching. Perhaps as women postpone marriage in favour of their careers they increasingly find themselves arriving in their thirties without the kind of partner they want to settle down with and turn more to mate poaching as a way of securing Mr Right.

Schmitt and Buss, who are both evolutionary psychologists, believe that the motivation for mate poaching lies in our genes. Indeed, they believe that most of our behaviour today can be explained by the fact that we are all descended from ancestors who were able to solve the problem of passing on their genes to future generations by finding a mate. The fact that we are around at all means they must have been rather good at finding suitable mates. So a large part of our behaviour is inherited from them, and we are driven by the desire to find a good partner with which to mix our genes. The more attractive, intelligent and resourceful that mate is – in other words, the more desirable they are in the 'market place' – the more likely it is that our offspring will inherit these appealing characteristics, and the higher the chances of our children similarly attracting future mates and continuing to pass on our genes for ever more.

If we are driven by our genes not to mate with just any old person but with someone who exhibits desirable characteristics, what do we do when we can't find them? The answer, according to Schmitt and Buss, is mate poaching. Indeed, we might query what is wrong with someone if they are available and single; if they are so desirable, how come they haven't been snapped up? It could be that simply being in a relationship is a signal to others that your desirability is assured, and this prompts more interest. Many married men report this effect. They found it difficult to attract female interest when they were single, but once a wedding ring was stuck on their finger other women began to view them in a new light.

Schmitt and Buss also probed what were the most successful mate-poaching tactics, and found a marked gender difference. The most effective ploy for men was to display generosity, which was seen by women as a good sign that the men would provide resources for them in the future. For a woman in a relationship with a mean man who doesn't buy her presents or pamper her, another man's generosity becomes particularly attractive. For women, the most effective mate-poaching strategy was displaying easy sexual availability. Here it is possible to see the basis for a lot of misunderstanding between the sexes. Many men being poached by women misinterpret their sexual availability as an indication that a brief fling is on the cards, whereas the real intention of the women is to poach. This was the basis of the plot for the successful film *Fatal Attraction*. Another tactic poaching women were found to use with some success was speaking derogatorily about the appearance of the woman already in the relationship with the target male, while making strong efforts to enhance their own appearance.

The real lesson of their findings, Schmitt and Buss warn us, is that those already in relationships need perhaps to be more vigilant and attentive, to devote more energy into making the relationship so attractive that poaching is unlikely to happen. Certainly their research revealed two points that should prove cautionary. The first is that in most women's cases the poaching was done by someone formerly regarded as a platonic male friend. Secondly, when the researchers investigated why mate poaching should be so popular, one possible reason was that successfully poaching a mate raises the self-esteem of the poacher, and the poached. Which of course raises the question of why someone in a supposedly loving relationship felt they needed a boost to their ego in the first place.

The higher rate for poaching in England suggests that we are more complacent about our relationships, and don't dedicate ourselves enough to preserving them once they have started. It would appear that most people in long-term relationships or marriages become complacent because they take for granted the permanence of the union. But Schmitt and Buss's work is a warning always to be working to ensure our partners feel loved. If you value a relationship highly you are unlikely to succumb to poaching.

THE SCANDALOUS HORMONE

Another theory about the roots of sexual promiscuity derives from research based more on male biology rather than sociology. Why does the man who has everything – not necessarily famous but with a wonderful career, a trophy wife and an adoring family – still so often risk everything for a casual affair? The worlds of sport, business and politics (the Clinton affair has not yet faded from memory) are replete with examples of sex scandals wrecking the family lives or careers of otherwise highly successful men. Now new research into the role of the male sex hormone testosterone in enhancing the competitive drive for dominance yet at the same time contributing to the destruction of family life promises to supply a biological answer for the first time.

Testosterone has long been linked with the drive for dominance over others, even when more passive compliance might be in your best interests. For example, prison inmates who test high for testosterone levels are more likely to have committed violent crimes, engaged in criminal activity at an early age, been more dominant in prison, violated prison rules more often, and been judged more severely by parole boards. As we saw in chapter 5, testosterone is related to a general sensation-seeking tendency, and that can have positive or negative effects depending on one's social background and resources. Individuals low in socio-economic status often find the most exciting things to do are illegal, while those from higher classes can find activities that are both stimulating and socially acceptable, like driving fast cars instead of stealing them, arguing instead of fighting, playing competitive sports instead of brawling.

Although men usually have testosterone levels between twenty to forty times that of women, exactly how potent testosterone can be has been demonstrated by studies which found that the hormone level increases in women in line with the status of their professions, and is higher in more aggressive women. But as testosterone is found in much higher concentrations in men, might its effect on male behaviour have been underestimated?

In the early 1990s Alan Booth and James Dabbs of Penn and Georgia State Universities published their research on 4,500 army veterans which revealed that men producing more testosterone are less likely to marry and more likely to divorce. What was particularly startling was the finding that testosterone levels did not have to be abnormally high to have a negative effect on marriage. Certainly men with mid-range levels of testosterone were more likely to report lower marital success than those with low measures. Booth and Dabbs actually found that men in the top third of the population for testosterone concentrations are 50 per cent less likely ever to get married, but of those who do, 43 per cent are more likely to get divorced, 31 per cent are more likely to have separated temporarily because of marital strife, 38 per cent are more likely to have had extramarital sex, and 12 per cent are more likely to have hit their wives.

But now Allan Mazur and Joel Michalek from Syracuse University have developed this work further. They have recently published the novel results of their investigation into 2,100 US Air Force veterans who received four medical examinations over a ten-year period. The main finding was that testosterone fell and remained low when the men got married, but rose with divorce, the rise in levels *preceding* by two years the divorce and remaining high until three years after the break-up. This work is ground-breaking because, as testosterone appears to rise before the time of the divorce, there is a strong suggestion that changes in the man's environment which cause such rises may then make marital breakdown more likely. This change might reflect the man's experience of dominance outside as well as inside the family home. Testosterone in non-human primates rises when males achieve or defend dominant positions, and falls when they are dominated.

This link between testosterone, dominance and competition could mean that men with high testosterone levels tend to carry contentious competitive behaviour into relations with the opposite sex. This would result either in difficulty finding a spouse and therefore never marrying, or once married being unable to sustain the relationship and divorcing, or if still married, having a poor-quality marriage. Aggression and dominance behaviour are well suited to gathering and amassing resources, and achieving and maintaining status, but when unchecked they are not conducive to the co-operation and mutual support essential to intimate heterosexual relations, especially those of a mutual nature. Moreover, sensation-seeking behaviour, linked to testosterone, may mean that men with high testosterone become bored with marriage more quickly than others, and seek out other partners, thus jeopardizing the relationship.

Research has found that athletes' testosterone levels rise shortly before they compete, as if in anticipation of the fray. This pre-competition boost may make the individual more willing to take risks, as well as improve co-ordination, cognitive performance and concentration – all effects produced by testosterone. For one or two hours after athletic competition testosterone levels of winners are higher compared to losers, and these results have been replicated in sports as contrasting as tennis, wrestling and chess. Similar effects occur among sports fans who are not themselves participants in the physical competition. Following the 1994 World Cup soccer tournament in the final of which Brazil beat Italy, testosterone increased significantly in Brazilian fans who had watched the match on television, and decreased in Italian fans.

It seems, therefore, that the act of competing for dominant status affects male testosterone in two ways: the hormone rises in the face of a challenge as if it were an anticipatory response to impending competition, and stays high in the victor but declines in the loser. Why this should be is not known. One possibility is that winners are soon likely to face other challengers; a high testosterone level prepares them for this eventuality. The drop in testosterone among losers may encourage withdrawal from other challenges, thus preventing injury.

But high-testosterone, aggressive behaviour is now seen by many social scientists as no longer functional in urban, industrialized cultures, and in fact may be dysfunctional in terms of optimum psychological development. Teresa Julian and Patrick McKenry at Ohio State University found in a study of thirty-seven middle-aged men that lower testosterone levels were associated with better marital satisfaction and higher-quality parent–adolescent relationships. Perhaps a low-testosterone-driven sex-role convergence is a very adaptive coping mechanism at mid-life for men, when to move towards such traditionally defined female traits as passivity, sensuality, nurturance, affiliation and expressiveness may benefit a marriage and family life. But the implication of this new research is that to achieve a content family life, many married couples may now have to reconsider seriously the role of a career which encourages competitiveness in the man, thus raising his testosterone levels and in turn endangering the marriage.

ON INFIDELITY

When US psychologists David Buss and Todd Shackelford from the University of Texas studied 107 couples who had been married for less than a year in order to assess susceptibility to infidelity within that first year and how likely the participants were to commit infidelity, they asked each participant to report on themself and their partner, who also did the same. This design enabled each person to give a self-rating and to have an intimate peer rating. The researchers found that while low

'Conscientiousness' and high 'Narcissism' generally predicted the desire to commit infidelity, these were better predictors in females. 'Openness to Experience' was a predictor of susceptibility to infidelity in men. 'Openness to Experience' is another term, perhaps, for adventurousness, and may therefore explain the prevalence of affairs in those successfully climbing career ladders. The wife of a newly elected British MP, for example, who had just discovered her husband's assistant was pregnant by him after a six-year affair, recently announced that this mistress was merely number twenty-six in a long series of dalliances.

The scale of this MP's adultery echoes some recent findings by psychologists studying infidelity – a world about which many speculate but where hard data are difficult to come by. Although infidelity remains the main reason cited when petitioning for a divorce, surprisingly little advance has been made by psychologists investigating the predicament. Unsurprisingly, those who are unfaithful tend to be extremely cautious about discussing such activities, and unlike those suffering from more obvious psychological problems do not necessarily think there is anything 'wrong' with them. But now the new science of extramarital affairs has begun to produce some surprising findings.

Psychologists Vincent Egan and Sarah Angus of Glasgow Caledonian University recently published a unique study into the mind of the adulterer – unique in that it investigated the personality structure of those who actually admitted to infidelity as opposed to merely expressing a strong desire for it, as is more usual for scientific surveys in this field. They deduced from their sample that while the number of men and women who commit adultery may not be significantly different (indeed, in their sample roughly twice as many women as men admitted to infidelity, but the sample was drawn from a workforce which was overwhelmingly female), if a man is going to have extramarital sex he tends to commit the 'offence' many more times than women do. The psychologists found that one reason for this was that women are much fussier than men when it comes to who they will choose to have an affair with.

Joanna Scheib, a psychologist at the University of California, recently looked into this phenomenon of female preference. She found women much more heavily inclined towards striking good looks and physical appearance in a prospective male for an illicit affair, compared to what men looked for when seeking a 'bit on the side'. What was particularly intriguing about her survey was that these women were much more concerned about 'good character' when it came to looking for a long-term mate. Scheib speculated that for women, 'extra-pair mateships' may serve an unconscious or evolutionary function of obtaining 'good genes', because attractiveness was more important in extra-pair mateships to the detriment of good character. The evolutionary psychology theory behind this we have encountered before: women are searching for a good-looking man with whom to produce a good-looking son who himself is more likely to pass on her genes, while she seeks a partner of good character to stay with her and help her look after the good-looking son – with the 'father' not suspecting it's not his son.

If this female strategy sounds incredibly manipulative

and psychopathic, traits more traditionally associated with the personality of the male adulterer, then it may be sobering to learn that Egan and Angus, the Glasgow psychologists, found from their sample that female adulterers were not statistically significantly less manipulative and deceitful. They argue that this is relatively straightforward to understand: irrespective of gender, the skills needed to carry out infidelity and mate-stealing, and to find a way to have sex with another person despite the other person's 'mate-guarding' strategies, require an active willingness to betray another's trust and intimacy.

If adulterers are found to score high on manipulativeness and deceit, does that mean they are actually psychologically dysfunctional in some way, and perhaps even treatment should be offered, or at least considered? Previously, psychologists speculated that perhaps the preference for a series of short-term mates was indicative of a childhood during which no proper secure attachments developed with parental figures. Perhaps unresponsive, abusive or inconsistent care-giving produces children who develop a negative sense of themselves and others. They may be unable to be comfortable with true intimacy and trust, so they avoid longer-term, more healthy relationships. But now a new theory is gaining ground in the adultery field. Maybe it's actually the other way round: maybe it's those who have high self-esteem and who are desirable who sleep around, simply because they can and it makes sense from a genetic standpoint to do so.

David Schmitt, whom we encountered earlier in this chapter, is one of the prime advocators of this new thesis.

He points out that the headlines tend to be dominated by men of 'high mate value', i.e. high status and self-esteem, who engage in promiscuous and unfaithful mating strategies. This has clear reproductive advantages to them in terms of passing on their genes to future generations, even if there is massive fall-out among current wives and girlfriends. The intriguing finding from his research is that men who are prone to infidelity tend to score much higher on self-esteem and social confidence than men who prefer longer-term monogamy. The preference for short-term mating was associated more in women with the insecure attachment personality traits that theory predicted, suggesting that actually for women extramarital affairs are a stronger indicator of 'something wrong' in their general emotional health.

The one negative personality feature that Schmitt will concede is found in those who 'sleep around' is that both men and women tend generally to trust others less. He argues, however, that this means this adult relationship strategy might now make sense, given a certain kind of childhood. If these adulterers were brought up in the kind of family environments that were unstable, or where relationships were not dependable, it would make sense to assume that this is the same kind of relationship you will experience in the future, and you become an adult who prefers not to trust.

The problem is that the unfaithful and the promiscuous may be willing to concede on the trust issue, given how many positives psychologists are now finding linked to their behaviour. For example, Dr Gillian Rhodes and a team of psychologists based at the University of Western

Australia found recently that the more facially attractive you are as a man the more short-term partners you are likely to have had, while the more facially attractive you are as a woman the more long-term partners you are likely to have had. This provides an interesting scientific confirmation of the widespread reluctance among women to consider an extremely good-looking man for a long-term relationship, because of their fear that he will be unfaithful or unable to commit. Men, in contrast, are just very grateful if they land a beautiful woman, without considering the possible downsides. It would seem that science is proving that particular female intuition completely justified.

So there you have it. Unfaithful men are good-looking, confident, and enjoy high self-esteem. But it's not just having a certain personality that is enough to predict affairs or promiscuity. Opportunity has also to be available, and the modern era now provides hitherto unparalleled chances for sexual impropriety.

One key aspect of modern life which renders affairs more likely is frequent business travel by one partner in a marriage. This factor has been found by psychologists to be one of the strongest predictors of marital infidelity. One survey found that when businessmen travel they are twice as likely as a holiday traveller to have sex with someone new while away.

The reasons are not hard to find. Business travellers tend to have the kind of disposable income needed to conduct affairs, i.e. to pay for meals, presents and hotel rooms, and the wealthy are more attractive than the married but poor. Business travel, of course, often means that the company is paying for the meals and hotel room anyway, rendering the affair even more convenient and affordable. One US survey found that over 90 per cent of men earning more than $75,000 a year were unfaithful. In addition, travel for commerce is often scheduled in advance so illicit encounters can be pre-planned, unlike more conventional infidelities when the absence of a spouse cannot be anticipated so far ahead. Any place where business travellers congregate, such as hotels, or bars near hotels, will have developed escort and other services to meet this demand. Moreover, frequent business travel can be stressful, boring and lonely, and these are all emotional states that enhance the drive for affiliation during such trips. Such a lifestyle will also probably have introduced strains to the marriage, creating a double whammy of preparing the background and providing the opportunity.

And there are other contributory factors. Another problem is that conducting important business abroad is replete with its own triumphs and successes, all of which we need to share with someone close by, not thousands of miles away down a phone line. So emotional closeness can develop rapidly with anyone around to listen to us talk about our day, potentially leading to an affair, even if it was unlooked for. Airline travel also necessitates much waiting around in lounges, bars and lobbies, all of which are areas where social interaction between apparently single people can develop easily. The very fact that strangers who meet in these circumstances are unlikely to encounter each other again or be in a position to cause embarrassing complications at work or near home renders the 'quickie affair' even more tempting.

Of course, it is not just the person doing the travelling who is prone to affairs, though statistically they are more likely to transgress than the person left behind. But temptation is also more likely to befall anyone left alone at home often, particularly if the person back home has a job which gets them out of the house and meeting others regularly.

Warning Signs

Some studies suggest that when a spouse is suspicious that their partner is having an affair, they are right 90 per cent of the time. But how to tell the difference between jealousy, possessiveness, paranoia and the harsh truth: your partner *is* 'playing away'?

Although some business travel is inevitable in many jobs, it is also the case that those using these trips to conduct affairs will be disinclined to limit the number or length of trips taken. So if a partner retains their equanimity remarkably well despite receiving news of having to go away again, this should raise suspicions that the business trip is being relished for reasons other than that they love their job.

Other signs that a partner is highly likely to be indulging in business travel affairs include the absence of any invitation or interest in combining a business trip with a mutual holiday, or to use the air miles accumulated to bring a partner along. A tendency to avoid talking about the details of a trip, like what sightseeing or business was done – because this causes uncomfortable feelings of guilt to rise to the surface, and/or increases the risk that some indiscretion will give them away – is also a subtle but ominous sign. In addition, a failure to make the quickest arrangements to travel there and back should also start ringing alarm bells.

How to Catch a Cheat

Often when an affair is finally revealed the jilted partner kicks themselves for having suspected for a long time but never acted on those suspicions. This is partly because they didn't want to appear to be checking up on their partner, thus casting themselves in the role of the possessive, jealous or frankly unstable spouse. The problem is, if this puts you off any form of checking, you will certainly miss the affair going on under your nose.

The most obvious and simple check is to ring the partner who is away or at home earlier or later than usual. Those who are not in when they should be or who appear reluctant to talk for long might be relying on the routine you've both got into in your relationship to slip an affair into the schedule. Another basic check is credit-card statements or receipts. Do they record more expensive meals than just one person would eat, or at more glamorous night spots than a single person needs for a quick bite? Some, of course, get so careless as to buy presents or flowers. You would be surprised how often the false sense of security of a seemingly trusting partner engenders bizarre risk-taking in the unfaithful. Of course, unconsciously many want the affair to be discovered as a way of finally bringing to a head issues they are unable to confront themselves. In this situation they are really involved in what psychologists term an 'exit' affair: they are trying out different relationships to see which will give them the confidence to survive a marital breakdown.

Unexpectedly turning up at the office can sometimes unveil a romantic situation. A worrying sign is if whenever you ring the office, colleagues seem uncomfortable talking to you. A good way of getting to know your spouse's real work movements is to ring a colleague and pretend to be planning a surprise birthday or celebration party, and tell them you need to know when is the best time to spring it on them. You may be amazed to discover that your partner has had a regular early afternoon off on the very day they usually come home latest from work. An old but reliable trick is to give a time you are returning from a business trip which is purposely half a day later than the time you really get back, in order to see what happens when you turn up unexpectedly early home. Alternatively, turn up suddenly at the airport to give your spouse a surprise lift home.

Checking your phone bill, your partner's mobile phone records or even the call memory facility can be a revelation too. Even more devious but sometimes necessary to unmask the unfaithful is to announce a new business trip and then say you need to pop out to the shops for an hour. On your return, press redial on your phone to find out if your spouse rang anyone while you were out, to let them know when they were now available for a tryst.

The most extreme means of establishing the truth behind any suspicions, of course, is to hire a private detective. But however you set out to uncover what your partner is really up to, the key issue to resolve first is this: what would you actually do if you found out your partner *was* betraying you? In fact many spouses, for a variety of reasons, would not choose to do anything about an affair anyway. In particular, they do not feel in a position to leave a partner on whom they might depend financially or emotionally. They may fear being alone again or have nowhere else to go anyway. The inability to introduce a consequence or ultimatum that your partner will heed renders it unlikely that you can stop them having future affairs. In such a situation, trying to find out whether your partner is having an affair is usually pointless. Indeed, the inability to do anything definite about an affair makes it unlikely you will be trying to detect adultery in the first place, as you are consequently unmotivated to discover the uncomfortable truth.

The best of all solutions, as I've said before, is to work to make an affair an impossibility in your partnership. We'll discuss this subject further in chapter 12.

HOW LIKELY ARE YOU TO COMMIT ADULTERY?

Adultery Scale

Each statement is followed by two possible responses: agree or disagree. Read each statement carefully and decide which response best describes how you feel. Then tick the corresponding box. Please reply to every statement. If you are not completely sure which answer is more accurate, tick the one you feel is most appropriate. Do not read the scoring explanation before filling out the questionnaire. Do not spend too long on each statement. It is important that you answer each question as honestly as possible.

		AGREE	DISAGREE
1	My partner does not usually get me the gift I really want	A	B
2	I can confide absolutely anything to my partner	B	A
3	Life used to be a lot more exciting	A	B
4	If we should ever break up, getting over it would take ages	B	A
5	I do not usually get jealous if my partner looks at another	A	B
6	I have had a happier childhood than most people	B	A
7	If my partner and I argue, I am right almost always	A	B
8	Many, if not most, parts of me are not easy to live with	B	A
9	There are aspects of sex I wish we could talk about	A	B

		AGREE	DISAGREE
10	Adultery is wrong for religious reasons	B	A
11	I do not care that much what others think about me	A	B
12	I very rarely meet very sexually attractive people	B	A
13	Compliments are deeply flattering	A	B
14	Only a few people are attracted to me on a first meeting	B	A
15	My duty is to myself before my partner	A	B
16	It is easy to ignore my partner's faults	B	A
17	I used to be too idealistic about love	A	B
18	The relationship influences my moods a lot	B	A
19	On average, per week, the number of arguments we have exceeds the number of times we have sex	A	B
20	No-one else could give me what I get from my partner	B	A

Score

Add up your score by totalling the number of As and Bs in each box you have ticked.

16 or more As: You have probably felt more committed to the relationship in the past than you do now, and you may be beginning to reappraise whether this really is 'the big one' you had rather hoped it might be. You would have regrets if it ended, but you are not prepared to devote yourself to making significant long-term personal sacrifices for your partner. Hence you are scoring high on the likelihood of committing adultery. Either you have already been unfaithful, in which case your motivation for completing the questionnaire suggests a certain concern as to whether your partner can guess the awful truth, or you are seriously considering it. If this high score comes as a shock to you, it may be you do not fully appreciate how vulnerable you are to meeting someone deeply attractive on that boozy weekend conference in Paris, who charms you relentlessly just a few days after a major row with your spouse. A particularly dangerous time for you would be just after your partner highlights some unforgivable fault or commits an indiscretion. Besides these situational crises, another reason you are more predisposed to adultery than lower scorers is your more playful attitude to love, characterized by psychologists as a ludic lovestyle. This basically means you believe relationships are there for you to gain something positive from them, and if they become problematic for any reason you have a low threshold for deciding that the work a relationship might need is just too much aggravation compared to the excitement and possibility of a new relationship. Compared to lower scorers in this quiz you tend to be more confident with members of the opposite sex, so you believe that if the worst comes to the worst you deserve a new and perhaps better partner rather than attempting to flog a dead horse.

Between 11 and 15 As: While not scoring as highly on the likelihood of committing adultery, you are actually quite vulnerable to doing so if you found yourself in the wrong place at the wrong time with the right person. This is because while your commitment to your marriage is quite good, something is lowering it at times, and this, combined with a certain frustration that the relationship and perhaps even your life in general has not lived up to all you had hoped for yourself, is making you more restless than you may realize. Your longing to relive the excitement at the beginning of your current relationship, and your dissatisfaction with the prospect of longer-term serenity in your marriage, means your boredom could be quite dangerous. One crude measure of whether as time goes by the chances of adultery will increase, but which has also been found to be startlingly accurate, is to calculate on average, per week, whether the number of arguments you have exceeds the number of times you have sex.

Between 6 and 10 As: You are scoring below average on the likelihood of committing adultery, which means, unlike more unstable relationships, you can communicate emotionally as well as factually with your partner. However, it may be you are still in the stage of a relationship where there are many rewards for closeness – such as giving each other a lot of pleasure – and few costs – such as in-laws or children. Close relationships endure times of pressure only if you feel your complaints about your partner will be heeded. While your marriage is good, the chances of adultery can only be calculated to be near zero if you have managed to get past the key danger points in married life. The first five years of marriage with no affair is an excellent sign for the future; early child-rearing years are also a dangerous period for marriages as the added stress plus the presence of someone who may steal attention you normally reserved for each other makes this a common time for a first adulterous liaison. A widespread misconception is the idea that children bring a couple closer together; in fact, the decreased time they have alone together is corrosive to a high-quality relationship. A particularly worrying sign for your current relationship is if you are going out for romantic dates together much less now than in the early years of your relationship. Problems over arranging baby-sitting is a frequent excuse given by couples for deciding not to take the romantic side of their relationship seriously any more. Be wary of this short-sighted approach. How good will it be for your children if the long-term consequence of this is a poor-quality marital relationship or, even worse, divorce following adultery?

Between 1 and 5 As: The reason you are very unlikely indeed to commit adultery is that you feel close, or are endeavouring to feel close, on many different levels to your partner, from sexual closeness to what is known among psychologists as 'operational closeness' – a measure of how much daily tasks are shared and life is organized together. However, it is possible to be close in all these different ways yet not really be emotionally close.

The ability to understand and appreciate the feelings and experiences of your partner is crucial. Often the longer a relationship goes on, the less impact both partners' thoughts and feelings may have on each other – a sure sign of growing distance and increasing likelihood of adultery. However, in your relationship that impact is frequent and strong over many diverse areas of life – or if this is not yet the case, it is certainly your aim to make it so. Perhaps a rather more traditional attitude to marriage accompanies a set of values which make you unlikely to philander. Still, one danger of your total commitment to your partner is that they may have begun to take your affections a little too much for granted. There is no reason why the emotional side of your relationship cannot continue to be nurtured by romantic gestures. For example, when was the last time your partner complimented you on your appearance? These little niggles aside, the only thing you have to worry about in your marriage now is your partner's score!

I I

LOVE IS A STRANGER IN AN OPEN BAR

How to know who is right for you

You come to love not by finding the perfect person, but by
seeing an imperfect person perfectly.

Sam Keen

THE LIST IS GROWING AND GROWING. SADIE FROST, GWYNETH
Paltrow, Demi Moore, Madonna, Lulu and Joan Collins
are just a few of the female celebrities who are raising eyebrows because they dare to challenge the convention that
older women don't date younger men. Celebrity men are
not immune from the trend either: at twenty-five Justin
Timberlake dated Cameron Diaz, thirty-four; actor Ralph
Fiennes, forty-three, met his former partner Francesca
Annis, sixty-two, when she played his mother in a London
stage production of *Hamlet*.

It doesn't take a Sigmund Freud to raise an immediate
question: is the unconscious issue here that the man is
looking for a mother, not a proper partner, and the
woman is similarly, at heart, seeking someone to

infantilize? The very phrase 'toy boy' conveys the widespread prejudice at the heart of the phenomenon, which is that being a 'toy' means that this cannot be a serious or adult relationship.

But now new research recently published by the Office for National Statistics confirms that these celebrity women are just part of a much wider movement. Data investigating marriage trends in the UK finds that the proportion of women marrying men younger than them has almost doubled in the last twenty-five years: now, in over a quarter of all new marriages the husband is younger than his wife.

Psychologists speculate that there are many reasons for this significant shift in marriage patterns, but perhaps most intriguingly this new trend could be telling us something about the changing psychology of women, but in a much more positive way than the old Freudian theories centring on a surrogate for a mother/son relationship. Historically, women worried that they might be traded in for a younger model if they didn't look after themselves and their partners adequately; there was a sense of competition from the younger generation in the 1960s that led feminists to voice concerns about a major threat to female solidarity or sisterhood. Maybe these statistics are telling us that modern women now feel they can offer younger men quite a lot over younger women in terms of confidence, experience, and perhaps even economic power. Before, women went for older men because being older they were in a more secure and stable part of their career life cycle compared to younger men, whose prospects were more uncertain. Today, with more financial independence, women are less concerned about the prospects of their potential mates, and indeed are becoming more masculine in the way they think about partners: they are focusing more on appearance, how pleasing the other person is going to prove to be with, and how good they are going to be in bed.

A lot of the attraction to younger men is perhaps about sex, because traditionally women reach their sexual peak about a decade or two after men do, so in fact from a sexual standpoint it makes sense for women to date men younger than them. There is also the point that because women traditionally look after themselves better than men do, they have a more prolonged 'shelf life' in terms of appearance. As looks seem to be becoming more of a premium for women in their men, women are tending to look for men as appendages, trophies or accessories to adorn them.

Another trend is that as women advance in years they often seem to remain more fun-loving and youthful than many men do. Here is a quote from an older female client of mine from my marital therapy clinic who later married a younger man after giving up on older men. 'The older men didn't seem to share my desires,' she said. 'I wanted to get out and have fun and go to clubs and go dancing and be out and about, but they just wanted to settle down into a rut. I definitely didn't want a rut. That's what I had just got out of, and I wasn't keen to step back into one.'

If women are spreading the net wider into previously forbidden areas, does this mean they are getting better at choosing who is right for them in the longer term?

THE RIGHTS AND THE WRONGS

Everyone gets wedding-day nerves, and one of the main causes is the enormity of the decision you are taking: have you found Mr Right, or are you making a huge mistake? (I shall use the terms Mr Wrong and Mr Right here for convenience. If you are a man, you can easily substitute a 'Mrs'.) What would make a big difference to most people's wedding days in terms of alleviating these nerves – indeed, it's pretty helpful for the marriage as well – is to feel more confidence that you are making the right decision, and I hope to be able to show you how. And I don't mean along the lines of the confusing advice you get given by your mum, who usually disagrees with your best friend. I mean *really* know. But in solving the conundrum of how to know whether in fact the man you intend to marry really is Mr Right, I have some good news and some bad news.

First the bad news: there is, in fact, no surefire way to know whether the man you are planning to walk up the aisle with is not going to be someone you run away from later in your life. Most people who divorce were just as convinced they had met the man of their dreams as you might be now. But just before you quickly turn the page wondering what, then, is the point of reading on, here's the good news: there are ways of being pretty sure you are not marrying a Mr Wrong. This may sound paradoxical, but in fact as long as you are not marrying a Mr Wrong, most relationships will survive the rocky patches and can grow and indeed bloom into something wonderful.

So the first mistake people make which later leads to

the lawyers is asking the wrong question. Don't focus on whether you have met the right person – the unknowability of the answer will just make you nervous as your wedding day approaches. Instead, ask yourself, am I sure I am not marrying a Mr Wrong? Mr Wrong may possess many desirable and dizzyingly attractive qualities, you could even fancy him like crazy, but none of this has any bearing on whether he is really Mr Right. Attractive qualities explain why you like him; they do not have much to do with whether you can live with him for fifty years. Instead, the key question is whether or not you are compatible. Marriages that survive occur between two compatible people, not necessarily between people who were crazily in love when they first met.

To determine what you're incompatible with, simply ask yourself what are the qualities in a partner you simply could not tolerate. Which characteristics would be so awful that there could be no compensations? For some people this might be fidelity. In other words, he may be good-looking and a millionaire, but if he broke his marriage vows and persistently slept around, could you live with that? If not, this immediately becomes an incompatibility and you cannot go down the aisle with someone whose loyalty you doubt. In this case, before you decide to marry you would have to check carefully on this man's track record. What do his ex-girlfriends say? Does he indeed have a lot of ex-girlfriends? A man who has had many short relationships is unlikely to take to monogamy like a duck to water.

For other women, it could be financial hardship which is the incompatibility – they feel more able to tolerate infidelity than no second holiday every year. But whatever you do, don't fall for the common trap of falling in love with a man's potential rather than what he really is. If poverty is an incompatibility and your fiancé is pretty poor right now, don't marry him because you have fallen for his sales patter that he is going to be a millionaire in the future. If he never makes it then you are still stuck with your incompatibility and you will probably eventually separate, or you will stay married and be miserable. Fall in love with your partner for what they already are, not what they might become. Rarely do things work out as planned.

Listing your incompatibilities and checking if your partner has any of them is not a popular or easy activity, though if people did it more the divorce rate would dwindle. This is because it changes the focus from all that you find wonderful in your partner to what you might not be able to stand. No-one likes to dwell on the negatives in the run-up to a wedding, but remember, it is what you find irritating or exasperating that will eventually drive you apart, no matter how much you were attracted to the person in the first place. Strong attraction tends to wane with the passing years, so the passion that helped you overlook those annoying traits or habits will ebb away.

One way of recognizing your incompatibilities is to recall when you have experienced most distress or anger in previous relationships, romantic or otherwise. A source of incompatibility that affects practically everyone, though they may not be fully aware of it, is if in crisis or suffering great personal misfortune they do not receive adequate emotional support from those close to them. So a key characteristic your future husband must have for the marriage to last is the ability to provide you with psychological assistance when you are in distress. The problem is, how are you going to find this out? When we are out attempting to woo or seduce others, the last thing we want to do is beset them with our crises or problems. Instead, we like to present ourselves in as good a light as possible.

But this point goes to the heart of when you finally know that you have met Mr Right, or at least that you are not with Mr Wrong. You can go a long way towards confirming this after experiencing a crisis together and assessing how he reacts to stress, and how supportive he is when you are not at your best. Indeed, this is so important that I often advise couples not to marry until they have been through at least one crisis together. Most people whose marriages last first knew they had found Mr Right after surviving some form of trauma together. 'But what if there is no crisis on the horizon?' some lucky people complain to me. 'We could wait for ever!' In that situation, you should go out of your way to do something stressful together, perhaps by taking a holiday that would put you both under pressure, like hiking or camping. For it is only under strain that many people's true characters really emerge. After all, you don't want the first real stress you both experience to be your wedding preparations. By then it could be too late to realize that you have indeed met Mr Wrong.

The Incompatibility Time Bombs

Marital therapy professionals can spot couples who at first glance appear to be deeply in love and vow they will be together for ever, but who are doomed to break up eventually. How do they detect those relationships living on borrowed time, even though the couple believe it will last for ever? The answer lies in the six key incompatibility time bombs.

Incompatibility time bomb number one is based on social status. Your social standing determines much of your character, your tastes, your values and who your friends are, so differences in social status are often a fundamental incompatibility. For example, how many of your friends come from a different social class from you? Choosing someone of a different social status usually ensures you end up having too little in common to make the relationship work. Also, your fundamental values, in terms of attitudes to money and long-term goals, will be too far apart for the gap to be bridgeable.

Incompatibility time bomb number two is based on your background. Your background is determined by your family and includes your religion and your ethnic status. If your partner's family finds it difficult to accept you, which is more likely if you are very different from them, then they will consciously or unconsciously be working away at driving a wedge between you and your partner because they don't feel you are right for their family. You don't just live with another person when you choose someone, you partly enter another family, and that is less threatening if the new family atmosphere feels similar to your own background. This time bomb often only explodes after you have children, when gaping differences about the 'proper' way to bring them up become apparent.

Incompatibility time bomb number three is based on your lifestyle. Your lifestyle includes your leisure interests and the balance between work and home life. If you do not participate in each other's leisure interests then you will not be sharing your most enjoyable and relaxing times together, which means you end up not associating your partner with having fun, only with problems, such as the mortgage and sorting out the kids. If you have widely different attitudes to the balance between home and work then one of you will be spending much time alone resentfully waiting for the other, and this will drive you apart eventually.

Incompatibility time bomb number four is based on your looks. Research has found that most people tend to end up choosing lifelong partners who are similar in terms of physical attractiveness to themselves. It seems, although we may not be aware of it consciously, that we are very precise in knowing where we stand in the appearance desirability league tables. A more magnetic partner may often wonder if the 'grass is greener' outside the relationship; meanwhile, the less attractive partner may feel less able to be assertive when their 'trophy' partner behaves unacceptably, for fear of losing them, thus ensuring that the relationship gradually stops serving their needs.

Incompatibility time bomb number five is based on your age. The older partner over time becomes impatient with the lack of maturity and life experience of the younger one, eventually leading to the older partner beginning to act like a parent to the younger. The markedly more youthful member of a couple may place the older member on a pedestal, and feel less important in the relationship because of the age gap. They will find it more difficult to stand up for their own point of view because of internal pressure to put the older one's preferences first.

Incompatibility time bomb number six is based on your track record. If one partner has had very few relationships while the other was busy sowing their wild oats, or one had relationships that were long and deep while the other partner's were quick and superficial, these two people are unlikely to last together. This is because the kind of relationships you had in the past reveal volumes about your attitudes to making life as a couple work. For example, men who have had a large number of brief relationships in the past are highly likely to end up having an affair if they try to settle down with someone who cannot understand and meet their craving for novelty and excitement.

If you follow the incompatibility model of predicting which relationships will last, the number of couples in the media spotlight who are clearly sitting on time bombs such as these is, at least at first glance, astonishing. Most people go about choosing their lifetime partners in completely the wrong way. The classic error they make is to put commitment before compatibility: they commit to someone before checking for the key incompatibility time bombs. Sometimes a couple can defuse one or more of them, but only if they do the bomb disposal work before they settle down together. Otherwise, shhh, can you hear the ticking?

IS THIS THE REAL THING? IS THIS LOVE?

Many relationships end despite the fact that at the beginning both parties felt that this was the 'real thing' for both of them. Sometimes it is difficult to judge whether we have met the person who is going to be our life partner because strong and confusing emotions cloud our judgement. Even when we feel they could be the right one, we are often left with nagging doubts about what would happen if someone better came along, or whether there is someone out there even more compatible.

But psychological research into love has found that it is possible to predict which relationships are on firmer foundations from the answers partners give to the kinds of questions printed below. Results of tests similar to this have been found to be surprisingly strongly predictive of the future course of a relationship. Also, if a major change occurs in your relationship, or you simply want to see how things are progressing, you may revisit the questionnaire to gauge whether your relationship is stable, improving or deteriorating over time.

Love Scale

Each statement is followed by two possible responses: agree or disagree. Read each statement carefully and decide which response best describes how you feel. Then tick the corresponding box. Please reply to every statement. If you are not completely sure which answer is more accurate, tick the one you feel is most appropriate. Do not read the scoring explanation before filling out the questionnaire. Do not spend too long on each statement. It is important that you answer each question as honestly as possible.

		AGREE	DISAGREE
1	My partner influences my opinions of others	A	B
2	I find being close to people is a risky business	B	A
3	My partner influences greatly how I spend my free time	A	B
4	What I watch on TV is not affected by my partner	B	A
5	My partner seeks out my opinions during important decisions	A	B
6	In any relationship the vital consideration is whether or not I will be hurt	B	A

		AGREE	DISAGREE
7	It is easy to agree about the division of our roles	A	B
8	I often wonder if others would have made me happier	B	A
9	My partner often seeks my opinion	A	B
10	My self-confidence is the same as before I met my partner	B	A
11	Discussions of problems rarely lead to big fights	A	B
12	I often have to persist a lot to get my partner to talk	B	A
13	What we do in the relationship should make me as happy as my partner	A	B
14	I usually agree with my partner's wishes just to get on	B	A
15	We do an equal number of romantic things for each other	A	B
16	Recently I have discussed relationship problems with others close to me	B	A
17	No friendships are used for confidences more than this relationship	A	B

	AGREE	DISAGREE
18 I bury my feelings if they will cause trouble in the relationship	B	A
19 There is no-one more supportive during stressful times than my partner	A	B
20 It is easier to be myself alone than in this relationship	B	A

Score

Add up your score by totalling the number of As and Bs in each box you have ticked.

16 or more As: You are scoring well above average on having found the relationship which is likely to be the one in which you are going to spend the rest of your life. However, the result could be skewed if you are doing this questionnaire within only a few months of having met your partner as the first flush of passion could be biasing your answers a little too much in a positive direction. It might be worthwhile revisiting the questions in a year's time to check on how things are progressing. The latest psychological research suggests that the true indicator of the best long-term relationships is when both parties feel their affiliation is getting stronger year after year.

Between 11 and 15 As: You are scoring around average to above average for the likelihood that this relationship could be the right one for you in the long term, but there are clearly still some teething problems. It might be that while you feel strongly attracted to your partner you have placed love and commitment above compatibility, which means you have neglected to consider whether the two of you are really compatible in terms of personality and lifestyle. Remember, many couples separate because although they were in love they were not compatible. You only need one deep incompatibility for an otherwise strong relationship to founder. Make a list of the things you could never live with and then check that your partner does not possess any of these. If they do, it may be time to consider whether you could make a big change and learn to live with this, or whether your partner could change, or whether this might not be the right long-term relationship for you after all.

Between 6 and 10 As: You are what psychologists call a pursuer when it comes to your relationship, which means that you often take the role of seeking emotional contact with your partner, which in turn means that they do not spontaneously provide the emotional support you need and often have to be encouraged to do this. The problem is, this also means that you are often having to expend great effort to get your needs met in this relationship, which suggests that there may come a time in the near future when you could become too exhausted or disillusioned to continue to make the relationship work. Alternatively, at a time of great stress, when you most need support from your partner and you don't have the emotional resources to invest in them to get them to provide the support, it is likely your inability to make it work will finally become clearer to you. If you want to make this relationship better you may need to consider how to get your partner to give more without your expending energy, and this may require a frank discussion with them. Or you may have to begin considering that this might not be the best relationship for you in the long run. **Between 0 and 5 As:** You are scoring very low on this being the right long-term relationship for you, and this begs the question of why you are still in it. It is likely that your pessimistic view of the alternatives to this relationship is what is keeping you there. This pessimism could be based on your financial insecurity outside the relationship, or your low self-esteem which tells you that you could not cope alone, or your ability to find another person willing to care for you. The best relationships are the ones in which people feel very optimistic about their alternatives outside the relationship, but choose to remain in the current relationship because they feel this is the right person for them. It might be helpful to consider tackling your negative view of alternatives by enhancing your own financial security, changing your employment situation, or boosting your self-esteem by taking a more proactive approach to your appearance and socializing.

THE LOVE MAP

But some people, even after assessing themselves against the time bomb criteria above, remain unaware of their incompatibilities or how potent they may eventually prove to be, and this is because they don't know themselves very well. In that situation it is vital to get to know yourself a bit better before marrying.

Psychologist Professor John Gottman, the world's leading expert on why some marriages work and others fail, has developed a radical new theory on the secret to a successful union, based on the concept of the Love Map. The Love Map is Gottman's term for the part of your brain where you store all the relevant information about your partner's life.

Gottman's research at the University of Washington into thousands of married couples led him to an astonishing discovery: many people who had lived with each other for years, and even appeared on the surface to be deeply in love, actually knew shockingly few details about each other's lives. Gottman discovered that a powerful predictor of how long a relationship would last was how many apparently trivial minutiae you knew about your partner – for example, a wife knowing that her husband preferred his salad dressing on the side, or a husband knowing what his wife's favourite TV show was. It was trifling details such as these that seemed to be the best measure of the relationship's health. Without a detailed Love Map, you can't really know your spouse. And if you don't really know someone, argues Gottman, how can you properly love them?

Love Maps are important because they protect a couple from dramatic upheavals. If you know such seemingly petty things as which brand of coffee your partner prefers, you are more likely to be able to appreciate each other's goals in life, worries and hopes, and it is this sort of knowledge, as revealed by your Love Map of the other person, that predicts how well couples will cope with stress. If husband and wife are already in the habit of keeping up to date with each other's lives and are aware of what each other is thinking and feeling, they can more easily be sensitive to the other person's changing needs.

Of course the main criticism of Gottman's research is that it is difficult to know whether he is putting the cart before the horse. Maybe the very fact that you have a detailed Love Map of each other's lives means you are already deeply interested and fascinated in each other, i.e. the Love Map is a sign of your affection for each other, rather than a cause of it. It could be that as your partner starts to irritate or exasperate you, you stop caring how they take their salad dressing. Even if this is the case, a poorly detailed Love Map would still be an ominous sign for a marriage, at the very least an indicator that things need to improve for the relationship to prosper in the future.

It is also true that couples underestimate how upsetting it can be for the other party when small details are unknown. This is usually perceived as more deeply uncaring than the trivial information would appear to warrant. This is because there are few gifts a couple can give each other greater than the joy that comes from feeling known and understood. In my clinical experience it is astonishing how much partners can be oblivious to the hurt caused by the lack of a Love Map with which to negotiate the relationship.

I'll give you an example using a couple I once worked with. The wife told the husband from the start of the relationship that she was allergic to flowers, yet he continued to bring her flowers every birthday for the next two decades. This lack of Love Map information on his part was partly caused by her failure to be brutally honest about how hurt she felt at his lack of consideration. She held herself back because she felt sorry for him and how busy he was, working hard to pay back their steep mortgage. But if you don't have an accurately functioning Love Map, any relationship will be in danger of foundering. Just as the other person has to ask for information to fill out their Love Map of you, similarly there is responsibility on you to provide much of that detail without having to be prompted. Many couples often feel they shouldn't have to pass on this kind of information; the other person should already know it. However the Love Map is built up, the key thing is to have it.

Another couple who had been in a long-term relationship that had ended and restarted on numerous occasions revealed, on filling out a version of the Love Map questionnaire below, that the male partner thought the woman's favourite meal was pasta, when in fact it was Thai food. When asked what his female partner's two most important aspirations were, he responded with 'Getting married to me . . .' and stopped there because he simply couldn't come up with another answer. This revealed another key reason for a tattered or incomplete Love Map – self-centredness in the other party. If one partner is too wrapped up in themselves, their ability to generate Love Maps for anyone other than themselves will be grossly impaired. This is why the Love Map questionnaire can be very revealing about your relationship: it can illuminate how much the other person is really thinking about you.

HOW GOOD IS YOUR LOVE MAP OF YOUR PARTNER?

Each statement is followed by two possible responses: agree or disagree. Read each statement carefully and decide which response best describes how you feel. Then tick the corresponding box. Please reply to every statement. If you are not completely sure which answer is more accurate, tick the one you feel is most appropriate. Do not read the scoring explanation before filling out the questionnaire. Do not spend too long on each statement. It is important that you answer each question as honestly as possible. And you should check with your partner that you have indeed got the answers correct before scoring this questionnaire.

		AGREE	DISAGREE
1	I am good at choosing films my partner will enjoy	A	B
2	I can correctly name my partner's two best friends	B	A
3	I know my partner's favourite way of relaxing	A	B
4	I can list my partner's three favourite books	B	A
5	I know the most stressful things that happened to my partner during their childhood	A	B
6	I know what my partner would want to do first if they suddenly won the lottery	B	A

		AGREE	DISAGREE
7	I know who my partner finds most supportive other than myself	A	B
8	I know the three happiest times of my partner's life	B	A
9	I know my partner's ideal holiday	A	B
10	I know the three of their relatives my partner likes the least	B	A

Score

Add up your score by totalling the number of As and Bs in each box you have ticked.

8 or more As: You possess an extremely detailed Love Map of your partner's everyday life, including their hopes, dreams and fears. This is probably because you keep in touch with each other by spending a certain amount of time every week or every day enquiring about what is happening in each other's life.

Between 6 and 7 As: Your Love Map is more detailed than average but there are significant gaps where fairly large parts of your partner's life remain uncharted territory. This is probably because you might be mistaken in thinking you already know all there is to know when in fact you should realize that it is impossible ever to have a complete Love Map. As your partner changes over time you need to update your map more regularly by keeping more in touch with them.

Between 3 and 5 As: Your Love Map is showing some

gaping holes. Your partner could be becoming a stranger to you more than you realize. A key issue is whether you believe you still probably know more about them than anyone else, in which case you need to encourage them to be more forthcoming about themselves. It could be you do not show enough interest, which leads them to find it difficult to share with you what is going on in their life. Beware if others have a better Love Map of your partner than you do; then it would appear your disconnection from each other is partly because of an increasing connection between your partner and others.

Between 0 and 2 As: You are more or less strangers to each other. If this comes as a complete shock you could have entered the groove of what marital therapists call a 'parallel relationship' without realizing it. This means that although you live together and appear to be compatible, in fact you are living more or less separate lives, perhaps because you are too busy with projects you do not share. You need to rediscover each other by spending more time together, in particular with shared goals.

12

WILL YOU STILL NEED ME WHEN I'M SIXTY-FOUR?

Making it last

Love is what happens to men and women who don't know each other.

W. Somerset Maugham

MOST CURRENT ADVICE ABOUT HOW TO IMPROVE YOUR marriage or relationship is based on psychological research conducted on younger couples. In fact, very little research has ever been conducted on enduring relationships. This is odd, as surely the true secrets of marital success can be learned only from those triumphant couples who make it into old age with their relationship intact.

Perhaps one reason older couples have been relatively ignored by marital therapists is that their marriages tend to be more influenced by a pre-1960s attitude to relationships. The 1960s was the start of a new approach which emphasized always talking to your partner about how you felt, and that it was better for couples to openly express problems rather than suppress them. Prior to that, successful marriages were founded on a high respect for tact and discretion when talking intimately, and distaste for direct expression of conflict. In other words, you often kept your feelings to yourself and only obliquely referred to things you wanted changing.

But the latest research is now taking marital therapy and theory full circle and suggesting that the more old-fashioned approach might indeed be more suited to maintaining a relationship. For the first time, marital therapists have been studying long-married couples to see whether they have something to teach younger couples struggling to be happy together.

A spate of recent studies has discovered that elderly couples report less expression of affection and self-disclosure than younger couples, but higher marital satisfaction. Older couples also appear less interested in what the other is saying during a marital conflict discussion than younger couples, yet still seem to end up being more affectionate to each other.

For example, Dr Monisha Pasupathi of the Centre for Lifespan Psychology at the Max Planck Institute of Human Development in Germany has recently published the results of a unique study into couples who had been married for an average of forty years. The startling result was that long-married happy couples displayed much less of the usual kind of deeply interested listening behaviour when a partner was talking than younger couples. These 'interested' listening behaviours are supposed to encourage the other partner to disclose what they are really feeling, and include maintaining eye contact and nodding reassurance. This was indeed a puzzling finding, and it prompted the researchers to ask why it was that older married couples could be so happy together when in fact they appeared so disinterested when the other was talking about a conflict issue.

One answer could be that not getting too involved when your partner is talking about something negative which they want to get off their chest allows them to ventilate their emotions with a degree of safety. Remaining relatively unengaged allows the listener to avoid being drawn into responding with an opinion or suggestion that might then escalate the situation into one of conflict. It may be a useful safety valve in a marriage simply to provide the space to allow your partner to sound off about a problem. They will inevitably feel better having had their say.

Communication experts Paul Zietlow and Alan Sillars from Ohio State University recently also found that the approach of older couples has something to teach the young. Their research revealed that younger couples tended to engage intensely with each other by alternating between a heavy analysis of their problems and confronting each other about their difficulties. Since the likelihood is that few people are going to agree completely with each other in terms of their innermost feelings, the more they talk about them the more likely they are to encounter sticking-points. Meanwhile, much older, retired couples, when they did make remarks to each other, tended to be 'non-committal' – this means they tended to make statements which were in fact largely irrelevant to the conflict issue. This is described by marriage experts as a 'low risk, low disclosure' style of communication, which is much like casual conversation or small talk. It may be that the more modern approach of younger couples of always engaging in an in-depth analysis of a marital difficulty will tend to ensure that all problems appear deep and large. The ability not always to get into an intense dissection of an issue helps to keep more trivial difficulties in perspective, and also keeps your powder dry for really important predicaments.

Another recent study recorded the problem-solving discussions of sixteen young couples with an average age of twenty-four, and sixteen retired couples with an average age of sixty-eight. The elderly couples used fewer responses when asked to describe how they felt about what their partner had just said, and perhaps as a result were much less likely to disagree than the younger couples. It seems there could be some important advantages in terms of reducing longer-term conflict in not always saying what is immediately on your mind about what your partner has just said.

Such results indicate that much of the received wisdom of modern marital therapy may need to be thrown out. We might in fact learn more about the true secrets of a successful marriage from our parents and grandparents than the trendy outpourings of so-called marriage experts.

Tips from the Latest Research on the Secrets of Success of Older Marriages

(1) Listen without feeling you have to respond all the

time with your own reaction to what your partner is saying.

(2) Don't always analyse what is wrong with the relationship whenever a difficulty arises. Some problems go away with time and don't need to be solved immediately.

(3) Don't feel you need to tell your partner everything you are feeling all the time. Learn to share only the most important emotions.

(4) Don't always talk about conflicts in ways that demand your entire energy and concentration.

(5) Don't see the solution to all your problems as lying in your partner. Some issues are for you to solve for yourself.

THE POWER OF ILLUSION

'Whatever does she see in him?' is a common refrain from the mouths of friends mystified by yet another example of bizarre partner choice by someone who could clearly do 'so much better'. But new psychological research suggests the last laugh could be on the friends. They may have failed to grasp that the real secret at the heart of all long-running stable marriages could be the ability to harbour positive illusions about your partner and not see past the illusion to the awful reality.

Widespread positive illusions were the subject of a

flurry of psychological research interest when a series of experiments established that in some respects it's the clinically depressed who hold a more accurate view of reality, while the rest of us appear to retain our more upbeat mood because we suffer from positive illusions. These illusions include not noticing so much when others are lying to us – the depressed are actually more perceptive in this area – and holding unrealistically positive views of our own talents (the depressed are more level-headed and less prone to self-deception). Then again, it's precisely because they are more likely to see the world as it really is, warts and all, and not through the rose-tinted spectacles the rest of us are loath to remove, that may explain why they get depressed in the first place.

Now the latest psychological research is suggesting that a similar self-deception mechanism may explain the success of long-standing marriages characterized by high marital satisfaction scores. It seems the secret at the heart of the best unions is to perceive your partner as a lot nicer than they really are. Several different studies converged on this startling conclusion from a variety of contrasting perspectives. Recent research published in the prestigious academic journal *Social Behaviour and Personality* measured a phenomenon referred to as 'marital aggrandizement'.

Marital aggrandizement entails an idealized appraisal of one's spouse and marriage to the exclusion of any negative beliefs and perceptions. Those who aggrandize their marriages tend to endorse items on personality tests which are extremely unlikely to be true, e.g. 'My spouse has never made me angry', or 'I do not recall a single argument with my spouse'. The theme that emerges is a strongly selective memory which ignores the occurrence of negative events over the course of one's marital history.

Marital aggrandizement was previously thought by psychologists to be most prevalent among newlyweds, reflecting the novelty of married life and an incomplete knowledge of one's spouse. Early on in a relationship, for instance, one may feel confident about endorsing statements such as 'I have never known a moment of sexual frustration during my marriage', because the experience has yet to occur. Objective endorsement, however, theoretically becomes increasingly unlikely with the passage of time. Yet psychologists Norm O'Rourke and Philippe Cappeliez at the University of Ottawa have now uncovered surprisingly high levels of marital aggrandizement in a sample of 400 couples who had been married an average of almost forty years. Those who appeared most happy with life in general and with their marriages in particular tended to be the couples who aggrandized their marriages, which led to their being labelled 'Pollyannas' by the researchers. Pollyannas are those who firmly believe, often with little evidence, that what they have is the best of all possible worlds. They are not the 'grass is greener' types who wonder if they could have done better. This group accounted for 52 per cent of the sample. The rest, who appraised their relationship history more realistically and were honest about past negative events, tended to score significantly lower on marital satisfaction.

The fact that what underpins the successful marriage is a delusionally positive perception of a partner has recently been confirmed by other evidence, including another group of psychologists' finding that the members of more satisfied marriages perceived more virtue in their partners than did their friends or other close acquaintances, more even than their partners themselves. Dr Sandra Murray and colleagues at the State University of New York have published a series of studies over recent years which comprise an attempt to get to the bottom of whether we stay with the person we are married to because we tend to perceive them in a more positive light than strict reality warrants. The theory is that being relatively blind to their faults and vices helps us to live with them, and keeps the marriage going for much longer than if we were more dispassionately aware of their flaws.

To answer this question, the psychologists compared what spouses thought of each other with the opinions of very close friends and others who knew the spouse well. The key finding, that highly satisfied spouses tend to see more virtue in their partners than their partners perceive in themselves, becomes more impressive when we consider that most of us tend to regard ourselves in a more positive way than is strictly objective. For example, husbands in this study rated themselves much more positively on various personality features than their own friends did. Despite the already generous nature of these self-assessments, the more maritally satisfied wives still perceived even greater virtue in their husbands. Dr Murray concluded that the reason these delusions about partners are so common in sturdy marriages is that to be happy we strongly need to believe we are in the right relationship with the right person, someone who will be there for us come what may. This perceptual bias acts as a protective buffer, allowing satisfied, secure intimates to dispel potential doubts or reservations almost in advance of their occurrence.

Another example of delusional thinking at the heart of good marriages was highlighted by another recent study published by Sandra Murray's group, which examined the issue of our preference for marrying a 'kindred spirit'. A kindred spirit is someone who appears specially to understand us and share our experiences, probably because they see the world the way we do, and are therefore in important respects just like us. Murray's group measured marital partners' personalities, values and day-to-day feelings and compared these to ratings for marital satisfaction, and sure enough, those in the happiest, most stable marriages were those most likely to believe that their partners were like them, even when an objective comparison of personalities found that actually the similarity was much more imagined than real.

This plethora of new psychological studies suggests that the real issues in your marriage are not the faults you notice in your spouse and try to point out to them. Instead, therapists may now need to encourage more deluded thinking in their patients.

ON IMPROVING RELATIONSHIP CONTENTMENT

When scientists measure the happiness of couples during their relationships and plot the results, they discover what is known as a U-shaped curve – a kind of law of relationship happiness. Basically, happiness seems to drop off after a couple have committed to each other. Then the happiness level bumps along on the ground for a while – kids don't help, incidentally – but as the children grow up and leave home, the happiness seems to return to the heady heights of those early days when they had just met.

The problem for marital therapists and couples themselves is how to avoid such a deep and plummeting U shape. Couples who plumb the grim depths are likely to break up and will therefore never get to experience the uplift the research tells us will arrive eventually. The gambit most couples seem to adopt to prevent the fall to the bottom of the curve is to try and spend more time together: they surmise that perhaps it is the brief time they now spend together compared to when they first met which is the cause of their growing slowly apart. And it is certainly true that in our busy times and work-obsessed culture the competing demands of children and careers mean that couples find themselves hardly spending any quality time together.

'Quality time' was a term coined to highlight the point that any relationship's most productive period is that spent when the other person is the subject of your un-divided attention. So watching the TV together doesn't in fact count. A recurrent theme in my marital therapy clinics is that when I ask a couple about the last time they went out together on a 'date', just the kind they used to look forward to when they first met, they greet the question with blank looks. I frequently discover that the last time they were at the cinema together was when *The Sound of Music* was first released! But now new research on the secret of how to improve relationship contentment, recently published by psychologist Dr Arthur Aron and colleagues from the University of New York, suggests that the key issue is no longer just spending quality time together. It now turns out that it is a specific kind of quality time that will influence whether you stay together in the long run. The intriguing implications of this research is that though many couples may be spending a lot of time together, if they are not doing the *right* things during that time to keep the relationship going, then the relationship could be just as doomed as if they hardly saw each other.

Aron's advice to couples is based on his novel theory of relationship quality, which focuses on boredom as being the central problem in most couples' unhappiness. He points out that the key aspect about the start of any relationship is that it is an extremely exciting time for both parties. But then boredom seems to set in, and it is the monotony of the couples' longer-term life together which in the end kills the relationship. His argument is that it is therefore vital to keep up a certain level of thrill in the relationship otherwise one or both parties will start looking elsewhere to replace the excitement they have now lost.

What this theory means practically is that if your quality time together comprises going out for a meal or seeing a film, as it does for most couples, then this may not be enough. Instead, the new research suggests that you should both participate in activities that contain a certain key characteristic: excitement. Merely pleasant pastimes are not potent enough to enhance relationship quality;

instead, the activities must be emotionally arousing. Pleasant activities, according to Aron's research, include things like visiting friends, going to the cinema, going to church or eating out; exciting activities include going to music concerts, seeing plays, skiing, hiking and dancing.

One explanation of why doing exciting things together leads to a much bigger boost in terms of relationship quality comes from a famous psychological experiment. Men were asked to cross a narrow, swaying 450-foot suspension bridge made of wooden planks attached to wire cables. Frequent gusts of wind caused the bridge, which spanned a deep canyon, to sway in a precarious manner allowing anyone crossing it glimpses of jagged rocks and swirling water a few hundred feet below. When the men crossing this dangerous-looking bridge met a woman on the other side, it seems the excitement caused by the crossing made them feel more attracted to her – at least more so than when men crossed a lower, safer bridge. The physical and emotional arousal caused by the dangerous or 'exciting' bridge seems to lie at the root of this.

The theory suggests that the emotional arousal resulting from one source may become linked to another. Let's say, for example, that you have a row with your partner every time you go to a particular restaurant. The theory predicts that after a while you will associate the restaurant with bad times. Even if you went there without your irritating partner, you still wouldn't enjoy the meal because of the strong association. The emotion produced by one experience – the nasty partner – has become associated with another – the restaurant itself. Similarly, if you do enough exciting things with your partner, then after a while you will associate them with excitement. This means that they don't have to work hard to be exciting all the time, as they probably did when you first met them. Specifically, the theory proposes that such associative arousal will lead to greater attraction.

The problem is that given the stress most couples face during an average week, they often want to relax and not do anything too challenging by the time the weekend arrives. But beware, this could be dangerous, and in the long run lead to the kind of boredom that spells the death knell of the relationship. So, finally, here are a few tips for finding those rickety bridges that should keep your relationship pepped up:

(1) When you are out together on a date, ban the discussion of the kind of everyday problems, such as the mortgage and the children's school reports, that usually dominate your conversation at home. On a date no problems will be discussed; only good times and sentiments will be shared.

(2) Do things that make your heart beat faster. Dancing and sports are good because they involve emotional arousal.

(3) Do things that involve interaction. Watching films is fine as long as you discuss the film at length afterwards.

(4) Explore new interests. Trying new things is scary, but the research suggests that being a bit scared in fact helps people to bond.

(5) Don't be afraid of stress on a date. You need to relax together as well, but not everything you do together in your leisure time should be calming. Consider amateur dramatics, or anything that puts some social pressure on you as a couple.

CAN YOU LOVE?

To conclude this chapter, a brief word on the importance of loving well to the longevity of a relationship. Alongside Denmark, Britain has the highest divorce rate in the European Union, and over 50,000 couples seek help with marriage guidance every year. But our problems with loving each other do not end there. Many of the difficulties of our children, like youth crime and drugs, can be attributed to the breakdown in parent–child relationships, which means, in other words, that we seem to have trouble loving our children, and they have difficulty loving us.

While the media seems obsessed with the idea of romantic love, described by Freud as a 'temporary psychosis', the more important issue of how to love someone deeply over a long period of time, which will give a relationship a greatly improved chance of lasting the distance, has received much less attention. Psychotherapists have developed the idea that there are in fact many different ways of loving others; some are more likely to result in good long-term relationships, while others are predictive of short-term relationships. While many therapists believe everyone has the innate capacity to love, not everyone has had life experiences that have made it clear to them how to love in the deepest sense. The relationship from which we learn most about love is that with our parents, primarily from observing how they behave towards each other. However, even if we have witnessed what we believe to have been a loving relationship between our parents, or between themselves and ourselves, it is often difficult to put into words how this form of love is different from others.

If you want to examine your own ability to love, try the questionnaire below.

ABILITY TO LOVE SCALE

Each statement is followed by two possible responses: agree or disagree. Read each statement carefully and decide which response best describes how you feel. Then tick the corresponding box. Please reply to every statement. If you are not completely sure which answer is more accurate, tick the one you feel is most appropriate. Do not read the scoring explanation before filling out the questionnaire. Do not spend too long on each statement. It is important that you answer each question as honestly as possible.

AGREE DISAGREE

1   I have a clear idea of the kind of
    person I fall for   A   B

		AGREE	DISAGREE
2	Relationships going wrong usually mean I am being betrayed	B	A
3	I could thrive outside a relationship	A	B
4	I fancy people equal in attractiveness to myself	B	A
5	My relationships do not demand too much attention	A	B
6	In relationships, I either feel too distant or too close	B	A
7	I notice others' moods before they speak about them	A	B
8	The more I know about others, the more I get disappointed	B	A
9	I get on better with the opposite sex than my own	A	B
10	I am often surprised by the strength of others' feelings	B	A

Score

Add up your score by totalling the number of As and Bs in each box you have ticked.

8 or more Bs: You are most likely to exhibit the form of love known by therapists as 'infantile love'. You have never grown out of the love an infant has for itself, and a very young child always puts its own needs first; those of others barely reach their consciousness. In other words, you love yourself most of all, and this makes it difficult for you to love others deeply. Your long-term relationships are dominated by the feelings of your partner that you are basically too selfish. You need to learn to make more personal sacrifices for others in order to develop the side of you capable of deep love.

Between 5 and 7 Bs: You can love others more than yourself, unlike higher scorers, but you only love those who have some obvious connection with you. In other words, you deeply love only close family or people who are very similar to you. This means you love the 'you' in them, which is only a slightly more developed form of loving yourself. Your long-term relationships are dominated by the feelings of your partners that they dare not change or develop too much, as this will risk alienating you. Your love is stifling. Only when you can love others because of their differences to you can you begin to love deeply.

Between 3 and 4 Bs: You are capable of deeper forms of love than higher scorers, but this is still mostly of the type therapists call 'adolescent love'. What this means is that you love others because they please you. They have things you like, or qualities you respect; particularly impressive to you in others are qualities or things you do not have yourself. Your love is of the greedy type, and once your partners stop having what you covet you will lose interest. You need to learn to love others even when they may have nothing more than you, or even a lot less.

Between 0 and 2 Bs: Congratulations! Your answers suggest that you are capable of the deepest form of love, what therapists call the 'adult stage of love'. You love others simply because their happiness makes you happy. The happier they are, the happier you are. Hence, your happiness is of the most selfless variety and is likely to be the foundation for the most lasting of relationships. However, for your love to be appreciated and nurtured, you need to ensure your lover is able to love you in the same way. The best love is mutual.

To summarize, at the heart of all great marriages is 'Shock and Awe' – to coin a phrase used by the US military to describe its tactics in invading Iraq. Military terms are, surprisingly, often invoked to explain married life. 'Shock' refers to the fact that you should be a little afraid of your spouse – afraid of upsetting them or getting on the wrong side of them. It's that fear which keeps you on the straight and narrow. 'Awe' refers to the fact that you should fundamentally respect your partner and hold them in some awe. 'Shock and Awe' – remember that, next time you consider a pre-emptive strike.

13

IF YOU CAN'T GIVE ME LOVE, HONEY, THAT AIN'T ENOUGH

Breakdown, divorce and separation

The big difference between sex for money and sex for free is that sex for money usually costs a lot less.

Brendan Behan

SCIENTISTS ARE ABLE TO PREDICT WHICH NEWLYWEDS ARE going to divorce in six years' time after observing just three minutes of a couple attempting to resolve a major area of marital disagreement.

This is the conclusion of researchers from the Gottman Institute, a famous couples therapy centre in Seattle, Washington, after studying 124 couples, average age in the mid-twenties, who had been married for just six months. The couples were observed closely in a laboratory so that the researchers could note the precise way in which they interacted during a fifteen-minute discussion of an ongoing disagreement in their marriage. The couples were then contacted six years later to find out how the marriages had fared, and during that period there had been seventeen divorces.

Professor Gottman and his team found that marital disagreements can be divided into three distinct phases: the first is called agenda building, where both sides present their views and feelings on a problem; then comes the arguing phase, in which each tries to persuade the other; followed by the negotiation phase, where compromise is the apparent goal. What happened in just the first three minutes of this process, otherwise known as the 'start-up phase', predicted who would get a divorce six years later. Couples in marriages that proved to be stable in the longer term displayed less negative and more positive emotions at the very beginning of a marital conflict discussion.

The typical pattern of a marital dispute uncovered by this research is that the wife usually starts the conversation, and does this by delivering an overview of the problem. Often this is presented as a global defect she has identified in the husband's character, and which is termed by marriage experts as a 'criticism'. A 'criticism' differs from a 'complaint' in that a 'complaint' is more specific and does not suggest that the problem is such an overwhelming one as a defective personality characteristic. Critical statements would be of the type 'you always' or 'you never', and the marriage researchers term a start-up by the wife that is immediately globally critical of the husband as 'harsh'. This is a predictor of divorce, as opposed to a 'softened' start-up, which is not an attack on the husband's entire character but more on a specific problem that is acknowledged to be only a part of his behaviour. The husband's initial reaction to the wife's opening is then either defensive, in marriages destined for divorce, or in marriages which will survive he will tend not to escalate her negativity by being more open to her influence. A particularly ominous start-up phase is one in which the husband immediately rejects the wife's opening comments. The Seattle team concluded from this that marriages work to the extent that men accept influence from women.

Professor Gottman has termed these crucial processes at the beginning of a marital argument 'The Four Horsemen of the Apocalypse', as they herald the beginning of the end for a marriage. The Four Horsemen are criticism, defensiveness, contempt and stonewalling (listener withdrawal). If any of these factors are present at the very beginning of a marital dispute the discussion enters a downward spiral of negativity on 96 per cent of occasions. As in only 4 per cent of interactions between couples does the conflict avoid this slippery slope, it seems that saving marriages depends hugely on driving these Four Horsemen out.

Listener or emotional withdrawal at the very beginning of an argument was a particular characteristic of men in the face of criticism from their wives. Gottman's theory to explain this is that men find marital disagreements initiated by their spouses more emotionally exhausting and stressful than women do. This could explain why so many men prefer to take withdrawal to its extreme conclusion, and retreat altogether from their families, often leaving home as a response to marital conflict. This could also account for why marriages that survive arguments in the longer term usually feature a wife who is able to initiate discussion of a problem but at the same time use humour to soothe her partner, so that he does not get emotionally overwrought during the conflict. Soothing is the process of keeping a partner calm while getting them to address the problem.

The same scientists also found in another study that they can predict with over 90 per cent accuracy which married couple is going to get a divorce in future by observing how a couple handles what scientists call 'post-conflict conversation'. In their laboratory, the scientists again asked couples to discuss a subject which was contentious in the relationship, then observed what happened when the couple were asked to follow the conflict discussion with a subject they usually enjoyed talking about. This is called a 'rebound' conversation by the scientists, and what predicted who would get a divorce was how much husbands continued to display disgust and contempt of their wives during the more 'pleasant' chat. It seems, then, that the degree of 'overspill' from a row – what might also be termed sulky feelings, or bearing a grudge – also predicts future break-up.

Intriguingly, the researchers also found that if a wife continued to show affection in the face of negative emotions from her husband, this in fact predicted a much higher likelihood of future relationship collapse than if she responded with anger. Gottman points out that his research in this area contradicted the widely held view that anger is destructive to marriage. It could be that the wife displaying affection in the face of her husband's contempt and disgust represents fear, compliance and subservience due to over-domination by the husband. The ability to withhold affection when a husband spits venom is, it seems, a healthier sign.

The other surprising finding from Gottman's latest research is that the technique of 'active listening', so beloved of marital therapists, was found to be utterly irrelevant in determining which marriages survive and which don't, and was not the crucial factor in helping to resolve marital conflict. 'Active listening' involves summarizing a partner's feelings (e.g. 'sounds like this makes you pretty angry') and validating feelings (e.g. 'I can understand why this would make you upset'). Instead, the team's findings led to the suggestion that increased softening and gentleness during start-up by the wife, soothing by her of the husband during the argument, plus increased acceptance by him of her influence, are the most important factors that prevent future divorce.

Perhaps the most interesting discovery the Gottman team made is that it is not whether you argue that determines the future of your marriage – indeed, it is healthier to argue than resentfully to put up with something you do not like – but rather *how* you argue. In particular, how you start your arguments determines how your marriage will end.

COUPLES ARGUING

Couples, even those who stay together successfully, spend more time arguing than doing practically anything else. Indeed, arguing could be described as the favourite activity of couples, and it is inevitable because:

(1) When two individuals live together or share some aspect of their lives, neither can expect to get only their own way all the time. Having to sacrifice your independence in order to share your life with someone else is likely to produce disagreements.

(2) Your partner is the person who is most accessible when you are disgruntled, so they will tend to be aware of your bad moods more than anyone else. This creates more opportunity for argument.

(3) Because you are tied together to some extent, even if you offend your partner they are unlikely to storm out of the house never to be seen again. Hence arguing with a partner can sometimes seem safe – no terrible consequences will flow immediately from it. Interestingly, we do not usually treat others in our lives, such as people at work, in quite such a cavalier way; we are usually more worried about offending them so we hold back from arguing with them.

(4) Often we feel our partner is not listening to us carefully enough so we think we are being taken for granted. Having a row, or at least raising your voice, sometimes becomes a way of ensuring you get their attention.

More productive ways of arguing include the following:

(1) Turn a complaint into a wish. Instead of focusing on what your partner does which annoys you and complaining about it, concentrate on what you would like them to do instead of the thing they are doing which irritates you so much.

(2) The more concrete, practical and concise you are when it comes to telling your partner about the things you wish would change, the better. It is difficult for your partner to know exactly what you want if your wish is for them to be 'a better husband'. It becomes clearer if you want them to 'take out the rubbish and occupy the kids while I make dinner'.

(3) Instead of listing all the things they do which are bad and using 'you' in your sentences, use 'I' and talk more about how what they are doing is affecting you. So, instead of complaining that your husband is late home from work again, say that it upsets you because you are worried about where he is and you think it shows his lack of consideration for your feelings.

(4) Choose the time when you have a discussion carefully. Arguments between couples tend to happen at particular times – when they've just returned from work, for example, or when they're in a car driving somewhere. Observe these

patterns and point them out to your partner. Make a special effort to avoid issues likely to inflame the other at those flashpoint times.

(5) When your partner does something annoying, mention it immediately; don't just put up with it and let your resentment fester. This will strain your relationship and lower its general quality. It also makes it difficult for your partner to address the problem when you eventually bring it up long after he or she was actually doing the thing that was wrong.

(6) When you are having an argument, stick to the issue. Do not indulge in what is known as 'kitchen-sinking', throwing everything else that annoys you into the argument at the same time.

(7) Try to ensure that the argument does not get out of hand, especially that it does not become deeply personal and attacking. The point of an argument is to introduce change, not to entrench positions. Couples who are not good at arguing do not possess strategies for de-escalating arguments once they heat up.

(8) Focus on the behaviour of the other person, not on personal aspects. If you attack the actual person rather than what they are doing they will get defensive and find it difficult to respond.

That's a lot to absorb, so here, by way of conclusion, are four points that are worth reiterating:

(1) All couples argue. What differentiates the healthy relationship from the unhealthy one is the intensity, destructiveness and frequency of arguments.

(2) It is better to discuss what is bothering you than to hide it for fear of having an argument.

(3) Learn to have arguments which do not sour the relationship. In other words, have productive arguments, not destructive ones.

(4) Choose the time of the discussion carefully so that you have time, privacy and little likelihood of interruption.

ON CONFRONTATION

Our culture expects people to behave reasonably, and as most of us believe we do behave reasonably we are outraged when it seems to us that others are not 'playing by the rules'. The problem is, once the emotional temperature has been raised in a confrontation, we are in danger of losing our temper, and this makes it even more difficult to negotiate a settlement. This is because:

(1) Once we get angry we stop listening carefully to the other person.

(2) When angry, we become impatient for a resolution when often a little patience is what is needed.

(3) The other person, confronted by our anger, also becomes angry, or defensive or afraid. Given these emotional states, a successful resolution of a confrontation is even more unlikely.

(4) When angry, we see everything in simplistic terms, in black and white. But life is rarely that simple.

Given that the vast majority of us would concede that getting angry during an argument is not helpful, why do we do it so often?

(1) After we have let off steam, we usually feel better for having got the issue out of our system. But what we are often doing is taking out our frustrations with other aspects of our lives on whoever is annoying us at that time. The over-reaction is rarely helpful.

(2) Sometimes anger does appear to work and we may sometimes get our way. However, what we do not realize is that we may have got an even better resolution had we not got angry.

(3) We think we are powerfully standing our ground and standing up for ourselves. In fact, it is perfectly possible to be assertive but not aggressive.

Remember, anger doesn't solve anything. Indeed, by getting angry we often make enemies, which means in the future others will not be so willing to help us out, or to see our side during another confrontation. This is one of the long-term negative effects of getting angry during disputes of which we are usually not aware. So stop getting angry, and instead follow these golden rules for resolving contentious issues:

(1) Stay calm. If you find yourself getting angry, take some time to reset your equilibrium. If getting angry, count to ten; if very angry, count to a hundred.

(2) If you are setting out to confront someone and find it difficult not to be in a bad temper, talk the problem over with a neutral party or a friend first to get your anger out of your system or to get some perspective on it before you meet your adversary.

(3) Try to see the problem from the perspective of your adversary. Maybe you do not know everything about the situation from their standpoint. The more you understand their motivation the better you will be able to negotiate with them.

(4) State as calmly and as objectively as possible how the issue looks from your standpoint, then state how the situation makes you feel, then suggest a solution and say why you think it's a good one.

Point out the advantages for the other party of your solution – in other words, go for a win-win solution rather than a win-lose solution (one in which the confrontation is seen as having a victor and a loser).

(5) Try to stay as solution-oriented as possible and keep the discussion focused on solutions rather than complaining about the problem.

(6) If you are up against someone who is being unreasonable, examine the balance of power between you. You are more likely to win situations where the other person is dependent on you and you are not dependent on them. If this is not the case, seek to increase gradually their dependence on you and reduce your dependence on them as a way of preparing yourself for the confrontation.

(7) Persistence and tenacity are the watchwords of successful negotiation through a confrontation. The reason why anger sometimes seems to work is that it makes us less likely to persist with someone who appears threatening. While it may be wise to beat a hasty retreat, if every time the other person repeats the action you want them to stop you do something, no matter how small, to remind them you are unhappy with the situation, they are more likely to stop. Calm persistence is better than the occasional angry outburst.

EQUITY THEORY

There are other clues from research into marriages that a relationship is going to end other than analysing the nature of arguments.

Sometimes a relationship ends many months, perhaps even years, before the people in the relationship actually realize it. Men in particular are prone to this as they can more easily compartmentalize their lives. They may not be aware that the relationship has died because they are too busy at work to notice, for example. The first inkling something has changed for the workaholic might be noticing an accumulation of unresponded-to messages for the girlfriend on the answer machine; a quick scouting trip confirms she doesn't appear to have been at the flat for a few weeks.

One of the earliest signs that a relationship is terminally ill centres on what psychologists call 'equity theory'. The idea behind equity theory is that we tend to like to be in equal relationships. So, if we notice that we are giving to the relationship much more than we are receiving, this will irritate us. Alternatively, if we are not psychopaths, should we find we are receiving much more from the other person than we give them, this will make us feel guilty. Again, one of the earliest signs that a relationship might be on its last legs in terms of our commitment to it is our increasing unhappiness when a partner puts themselves out for us. It might be that they cook us an extra special meal, or give us a particularly expensive present on our birthday. If we find ourselves strangely unsettled by their generosity or affection for us, this is because at the back of our minds we realize it is unlikely we can drum up the enthusiasm required to reciprocate in the future.

Equity theory does not demand that you reciprocate in precisely the same way for whatever your partner gives you, of course; rather, it predicts that you will feel a need to balance things in terms of fairness by returning in some way the rough equivalent of what you have been given, even if it is on your terms. But if you do find yourself discouraging your partner from elaborate acts of affection, while the cover might be because you find all that lovey-dovey stuff too sentimental, in fact it suggests that you should do the decent thing and withdraw your deposit before too much interest has accumulated on it.

ARE YOU EMOTIONALLY DIVORCED?

Couples I see in therapy at my clinic are often surprised at how accurate it is possible to be in terms of predicting who will eventually separate and whose relationship will recover from rocky periods, even after meeting them for only a short period. This is because all relationships which eventually end in divorce or separation do not just suddenly arrive at termination; instead they go through phases of deterioration.

The first phase of a divorce is what marital therapists call the 'emotional divorce'. This can occur many years before the legal separation, but once it has happened, unless both parties recognize it and work to reverse it, then physical separation, or an extramarital affair, is an absolute certainty. The emotional divorce is often completely overlooked by a couple for this reason: they think it is natural that they no longer feel the kind of romantic infatuation that characterized the early days of their courtship; the relationship is 'bedding down', they think, into the more companionable, less passionate phase all couples go through. In fact, something much more serious could be on the cards. Although you appear to be far from physical separation or even rowing, you are already emotionally disentangling from each other, separating in terms of feelings. To the outside world you appear very much together, but inside the relationship the real connection has died.

There are three key early warning signs that emotional divorce has begun:

(1) You can't see the obvious problems

One early sign of an emotional divorce is when you believe your partner is not communicating with you, and you put this down to a problem in them. It could be that they appear to be too busy, or under stress, or too tired to spend time relating. In fact, the issue isn't what they are not doing; they *are* communicating something, only you are unable to hear it, partly, perhaps, because the thought that there is a serious problem is so awful a prospect you prefer to go into denial over it.

Relationship experts believe it is impossible not to communicate as everything you do sends a kind of message in a relationship. If your partner starts coming home late from work but refuses to answer properly your enquiries about why, that in itself is a communication.

The real question is, why is your sensitivity to what

your partner is trying to tell you so much reduced now compared to when you first met. When someone hasn't got the time to listen to you and snaps back whenever you try to speak to them, in fact they are communicating something pretty loud and clear about the state of the relationship. So one of the first signs of emotional divorce is when you are no longer as sensitive to what they are feeling. This problem arises for numerous reasons, for example because you are no longer relaxed in the relationship, or able to concentrate fully on your partner, or too scared of what is actually obviously happening to see it clearly.

(2) You become the score keeper in the relationship

Another early sign that the emotional divorce has begun is becoming resentful of doing things for your partner, perhaps tidying up after them or giving them a lift to the station. What is really happening here is that because you feel the relationship is already draining you or taking advantage of you, you have become wary of giving more.

Relationship therapists call this phase of the emotional divorce 'score keeping'. This refers to the tendency to mentally tally up who is getting what from the relationship in order to check that the imbalance in benefits is not getting so great as to cause the relationship to topple over. In a good affiliation you feel so much benefit from being with your partner that you don't get into a state of permanent resentment about doing favours for them. Obviously in any relationship from time to time it is inevitable that you will feel the other person should pull their weight more. 'Score keeping' only kicks in when you believe that they are persistently not responding to imbalances you point out.

(3) You never say exactly what you think

A third sign that emotional divorce has begun is when you know there is something you want your partner to change in their behaviour, or their attitude and you don't directly bring the issue up. Instead you hint or criticize a related problem, but you don't tackle the real question straight-forwardly. For example, instead of directly addressing your fears that your partner is attracted to his new secretary and this is why he is now late home so regularly, you persistently ask what kind of day he had in the office, and get no nearer the real predicament.

The reason you do this is that you don't want to stir up too much upset or strong emotion in the relationship. Yet, as we discussed earlier in this chapter, research into relationships that last into the long term has in fact found that they are slightly stormier than those that fail. They are not quite as turbulent as others that tend to founder, of course, but the point is that couples who last do have times when their emotional temperature is raised. By confronting a problem rather than ignoring it, they give themselves an opportunity to produce change and help preserve the relationship. It is the couples in the throes of emotional divorce who trundle along apparently smoothly when beneath the surface the relationship has died because no-one had the courage to administer mouth-to-mouth for fear of causing too much upset.

It is true that all relationships subside as time goes on

into less intense experiences, but relationship research has also found that a key predictor of who stays together and who doesn't is whether you are able to say that as each year goes by your relationship is getting better and better. The emotionally divorced don't feel things are on the rocks, but they cannot acknowledge the kind of year-on-year improvement that those in truly good relationships can. Instead, the problem with the emotionally divorced is that they have come to accept a plateauing out of the relationship when in fact they should be more ambitious and want more from their relationship than it is delivering. They have come to accept that routine and going through the motions is what a relationship is all about, when in fact there's a whole lot more to it.

ARE YOU EMOTIONALLY DIVORCED?

Emotional Divorce Scale

Each statement is followed by two possible responses: agree or disagree. Read each statement carefully and decide which response best describes how you feel. Then tick the corresponding box. Please reply to every statement. If you are not completely sure which answer is most accurate, tick the one you feel is most appropriate. Do not read the scoring explanation before filling out the questionnaire. Do not spend too long on each statement. It is important that you answer each question as honestly as possible.

	AGREE	DISAGREE
1 My partner can successfully hide from me what they really think	A	B
2 My opinion matters to my partner even if they don't agree with it	B	A
3 I have friends whose relationships I envy	A	B
4 My partner fears me not approving of something they do	B	A
5 My partner's features that I fell in love with have now changed	A	B
6 My partner feels proud about introducing me as their partner to anyone	B	A
7 In a crisis my partner is not necessarily the best person to turn to for support	A	B
8 Outsiders observing our relationship are envious of what we have together	B	A
9 The balance of power in the relationship can slip away from me too often	A	B
10 My partner could not be genuinely happy without me	B	A

Score

Add up your score by totalling the number of As and Bs in each box you have ticked.

8 or more As: You are scoring so high on emotional divorce that the probability is that one of you has already seriously begun to consider actual divorce or separation, and only a very strong external reason is keeping you together, such as children, financial insecurity or fear of being alone.

Between 6 and 7 As: You are scoring above average on emotional divorce which means your relationship does have compensations but serious drifting apart is occurring which neither of you seem motivated enough at the moment to act upon. It could be that pride over having to admit that something you are involved in is no longer working so well is preventing both of you from confronting the need for change, or to work at your relationship.

Between 3 and 5 As: You are scoring around average to below average for emotional divorce, which means it is extremely unlikely your relationship will go through a full emotional divorce. However, there are still problems from time to time, which means you feel your partner does not give you their full attention or take the relationship seriously enough. They and you need to give more time to the relationship for a larger part of the week than is the case at the moment.

Between 0 and 2 As: You are scoring very low on getting an emotional divorce, which means you could only have just met! However, if you have known each other for a while then it appears your relationship is going from strength to strength, so that unlike higher scorers the only real issue for you is to ensure that things continue to improve in the future. Smug complacency is your biggest enemy.

14

CONCLUSION: SIMPLY THE BEST?

Love does not consist in gazing at each other, but in looking together in the same direction.

Antoine de Saint-Exupéry

WHILE IT SEEMS INTUITIVELY OBVIOUS THAT BEING WITH A partner you feel close to and from whom you obtain emotional support is good for your mental health, it may be less apparent that who you choose to marry also determines how long you will live. A new study by Dr Roni Tower and colleagues from Columbia and Yale Universities has found that the style of marriage you are in alters your chances of dying early from a variety of medical conditions by a factor of up to five.

Previous research had established that just being married as opposed to single was generally good for your health in a number of ways, although positive effects were usually significantly greater for husbands compared to wives. For example, evidence has suggested that if you are married or happily cohabiting in the long term you will suffer from less depression and will live significantly longer compared to the single, divorced or widowed. Now Dr Tower and his team have added to this knowledge: it is vital to get the choice of partner right if you are to get the full health benefits from marriage.

This new study asked married partners separately (when out of earshot of each other) who they relied on most for emotional support and who they felt most close to and intimate with. The first startling finding was that only 51 per cent of husbands named their wives when asked this question, while even fewer wives (46 per cent) named their husbands. Generally speaking, for both husbands and wives the worst mortality rate was found in partners neither of whom named the other as the special person on whom they relied for emotional support and closeness. These were couples who were married but not happily so; perhaps they were in what marital therapists call 'parallel marriages', where both partners are living together but really their lives run like parallel lines, rarely if ever intersecting.

Interestingly, the lowest mortality rates were found in those who were named by their partner as a key source of emotional support and closeness, but who themselves actually named *someone else* as the one special person in their life. This result applied to both husbands and wives. One obvious immediate speculation is that having an extramarital affair may be good for your health! But this is an unlikely interpretation of the data, because those who have affairs are not usually perceived to be good sources of emotional support by their partners. Indeed, the results suggest an opposite conclusion: it would seem that the secret to a long, healthy life is to provide such good emotional support to your partner that you are named by them as the rock on which they rely. Perhaps as a result of being such a wonderful partner and human being you attract other sources of emotional support from friends and relatives, which means you don't have just your own partner as your sole source of psychological bracing.

But perhaps the most intriguing result of all from this study was the finding that in less than a third of instances was there reciprocation between married partners in terms of naming each other as key sources of emotional support. It seems that when you think your partner is the key person in your emotional life, the chances of this being a mutual feeling are fairly slim.

Then again, perhaps we tend to underplay the extent to which we rely emotionally on our partners. The Population Research Unit at the University of Helsinki, in one of the largest scientific studies of its kind, recently investigated the lifespans of more than 1.5 million Finns and confirmed that there is significantly excessive mortality shortly after spousal bereavement. Moreover, this mortality rate was found to be more than three times higher for men compared to women, though for both genders it is highest during the first week after the death of the spouse, and then drops slowly but steadily during the following six months. I'm sure we can all produce examples to back up this observation. Former British Prime Minister James Callaghan died just eleven days after his wife Audrey; in 1998, Tom Cookson, husband of famous novelist Catherine, died just three weeks after his wife; in June 1994, playwright Dennis Potter departed a week after his wife Margaret; Country and Western superstar Johnny Cash died in September 2003, less than four months after his wife June.

The Population Research Unit also found from other studies that although the mortality rate goes up for all causes of death following a spousal bereavement, death due to ischemic heart disease appears to rise most dramatically. So it appears that the hearts of men (predominantly) often cannot cope with the grief of losing a life partner. These men are literally dying from a broken heart. One theory is that the grief of losing someone as close to you as a marriage partner is one of the greatest strains it is possible to face, and this enormous stress has a direct and deleterious effect on your physical health, in particular the cardiovascular system. Women perhaps cope with the stress of grief better than men because expressing emotional turmoil, venting distress, confiding in others and using formal resources such as psychotherapy are all more feminine strategies. Men tend to remain silent and keep feelings of distress and anxiety to themselves.

But when the single are compared in general to the married, men appear to benefit much more from marriage than women in health and mortality terms. So perhaps it's not so much the strain of grief that explains the dramatically high chances of following your spouse shortly after their death, but more the medical advantages of marriage which are suddenly removed. This benefit of marriage to male mortality is explained as follows: the institution provides emotional support, constrains risk-taking behaviour (men tend to be more risk taking compared to women; guess who more often gets who to slow down on the motorway, for example), stimulates a healthy lifestyle, buffers stressful experiences, and partly replaces professional healthcare (men, after all, are much more reluctant to go to the doctor than women). It is interesting that women don't appear to receive many of these benefits from marriage compared to men. Marital therapists speculate that women might encounter more stress within a marriage than men do because, traditionally, they have less bargaining power and higher expectations. For women, a divorce or widowhood might even turn out to be a relief more than a burden.

Some of the researchers who specialize in this area wonder if this strong 'bereavement spousal mortality effect' might be peculiar to wealthy Western societies which don't benefit from the extended family networks found in poorer countries. They argue that because families in the West today are expected to be socially and economically autonomous, older spouses may become more highly dependent on each other, and may have few alternative sources of emotional and instrumental support once a partner passes away. Newly bereaved spouses must adjust to the loss of an enduring emotional relationship while managing the daily decisions and responsibilities that were once shared by the couple. There is even speculation that it might be possible to predict which kind of man is most vulnerable to an early death following the loss of his female partner. Spouses who maintained a more rigid gender-based division of labour in the household might experience more profound psychological readjustment upon loss. Those who relied most heavily on their late spouses may be ill prepared for their new responsibilities, and may become distressed or feel urgently in need of a spousal substitute to fill the void left by the death.

But just before all the single men reading this rush off to get married in order to live longer, there is some further evidence that for both genders a small but significant rise occurs in the mortality rate in the period after your wedding day. This surprising finding comes from one of the most comprehensive recent surveys of the mortality impact of marital status, involving the annual follow-up of a sample of over 12,000 German adults by Dr Hilke Brockmann and Dr Thomas Klein from Bremen University and the University of Heidelberg. This study found that basically it's the key *transitions* that are potentially dangerous to your health – those into as well as out of wedlock. This instantaneous shift in the mortality rate after the wedding may be explained by the stress of the new situation and by the profound change in living circumstances. For example, marriage is often associated with a geographic move for at least one partner. The spouse who moved may have had to cut emotional networks and change social interaction patterns and daily routines. However, after two years, the research suggests, married partners adapt to their new life and the mortality rate starts to improve compared to unmarried people.

But if moving into and out of a marriage is stressful and can be injurious to your health, and more so for men compared to women of course, is there anything men can learn from what women are doing in terms of coping better? Wives have been identified generally as their husband's main and sometimes only confidants, whereas women are more likely to have someone in addition to their husband to whom to turn – most often, another woman. Women are more likely to have close relationships outside their marriage and are thus the ones most likely to nurture and sustain the couple's social relationships. These different social and relationship patterns could be the key when it comes to adjusting to bereavement. It has been suggested that widows generally receive more social support than widowers, and that this higher level of social support protects or buffers them against the deleterious effects of partner loss. So it seems that if you want to live long, get some key relationship support in addition to your marriage partner. In other words, make friends and cultivate your friendships, and work hard not to alienate members of your family. Or more prosaically and rather unromantically, don't put all your emotional eggs in one basket.

How two personalities may be best combined in a relationship is one of the most intriguing and complex questions that psychologists have attempted to answer. In considering a myth by Aristophanes, Plato speculated in his dialogue *The Symposium* that men and women were once a unified entity until the god Zeus, in a temper, separated them. Since then, it is said, everyone has searched for his or her ideal mate. This yearning for our severed ideal half is what the ancient Greeks believed leads to love.

Certainly, that intense emotional state which accompanies the sense that one has finally met one's ideal life partner seems to underpin an enormous amount of our behaviour, thoughts and passions. Scientific psychology is the attempt to dispense with wishful thinking and passion and instead use cold reason and rational critical analysis to help us understand this, ourselves and others. I think it is possible that we can learn useful things from psychology to assist us in finding the perfect mate.

Remember, the more alike in some key personality terms a couple is, the more likely it is that such a partnership will survive in the longer term. However, the other intriguing point research has made is that the more we enjoy another's company when we first meet them, for whatever reason, the more likely we are to *believe* we are similar to them, much more than we really are. Enjoying being with someone for a short while is not the same thing as rationally calculating how alike the two of you really are, and many mistakes are made about compatibility and similarity because emotion often triumphs over reason. The main take-home message, therefore, is to become more aware of the strong emotions that can grip us in the arena of love, and to try to keep our intellect functioning at its highest level when it comes to choosing and maintaining the key relationship in our lives.

Your psychiatrist's advice on the emotionally fraught day of 14 February, indeed in terms of the whole emotionally fraught world of attraction, is to take a break from the pressure to be perfectly romantic and focus instead on some neglected but possibly more important values such as friendship and genuine concern for others, beyond immediate self-interest.

Instead of focusing on the idea that you need to find the right person for you straight away, devote your energies to fully engaging with life and developing an appetite for all that it has to offer. The more you are enjoying yourself – the more fun you are having – the more attractive you become to others. This is because, ultimately, we all want to share our lives with someone who will bring something to a relationship, rather than someone who will only take.

Engaging with life in its totality naturally means interacting more with others, because all that life has to offer is the product of other human involvement. If you develop your interest and enthusiasm in, say, geology or classic cars, this inevitably means you will become involved with others who share your passions. And the more your relationships with others improve and multiply, the more likely you are finally to meet the right kind of person for you. In fact, the best way to meet the right one for you is through your connection with those you already know and trust. The shared values and interests of friends is the best selection strategy; no dating agency can hope to replicate this strong connection. This 'search strategy' is not about targeting that particular person right away, but more about developing your appetite for life in general. You really need to be having the kind of life that others will want to share.

The big mistake most people make is to believe that life begins after they meet Mr or Mrs Right. It's important to recognize that your life needs to be one of fulfilment *before* you can meet the kind of person who will be drawn to you in a healthy and positive way, rather than someone who gets enmeshed with you simply because of your own neediness – someone who you feel is going to fix things for you or rescue you from yourself.

This brings us back to my preferred bottom-line advice in the arena of seduction and love. Stop trying to find the right person, and instead try to be the right person. You will then find that the right person comes along sooner or later, having been drawn to the qualities in you that have now made you simply irresistible.

NOTES

INTRODUCTION

Maestripieri, Dario; Roney, James R.; DeBias, Nicole; Durante, Kristina M.; Spaepen, Geertrui M., 'Father Absence, Menarche and Interest in Infants Among Adolescent Girls', *Developmental Science*, 7(5), 560–66, November 2004.

Manning, J. T.; Trivers, R. L.; Singh, D.; Thornhill, R., 'The Mystery of Female Beauty', *Nature*, 399(6733), 214–15, 20 May 1999.

CHAPTER I

Biddle, Jeff E.; Hamermesh, Daniel S., 'Lawyers Looks and Lucre', *Journal of Labor Economics*, 16, 172–201, 1 January 1998.

Buss, David M., 'Desires in Human Mating', *Annals of the New York Academy of Science*, 907, 39–49, 2000.

Hamermesh, Daniel S.; Biddle, Jeff E., 'Beauty and the Labor Market', *American Economic Review*, 84(5), 1174–94, December 2004.

Kanazawa, Satoshi, 'General Intelligence as a Domain-Specific Adaptation', *Psychological Review*, 111(2), 512–13, April 2004.

Kanazawa, Satoshi; Kovar, Jody L., 'Why Beautiful People Are More Intelligent', *Intelligence*, 32(3), 227–43, 2004.

Kanazawa, Satoshi; Still, Mary C., 'Teaching May Be Hazardous to Your Marriage', *Evolution and Human Behavior*, 21(3), 185–90, May 2000.

Miller, Geoffrey, *The Mating Mind: How Sexual Choice Shaped the Evolution of Human Nature*, 503ff, 2000 (New York, NY, US, Doubleday & Co.).

Miller, Geoffrey, 'Mental Traits as Fitness Indicators: Expanding Evolutionary Psychology's Adaptationism', *Annals of the New York Academy of Sciences*, 907: 62–74, 2000.

Previti, Denise; Amato, Paul R., 'Is Infidelity a Cause or a Consequence of Poor Marital Quality?', *Journal of Social and Personal Relationships*, 21(2), 217–230, April 2004.

Previti, Denise; Amato, Paul R., 'Why Stay Married? Rewards, Barriers, and Marital Stability', *Journal of Marriage and Family*, Vol. 65(3), 561–73, August 2003.

Singh, Devendra, 'Female Judgment of Male Attractiveness and Desirability for Relationships: Role of Waist-to-Hip Ratio and Financial Status', *Journal of Personality & Social Psychology*, 69(6), 1089–1101, December 1995.

CHAPTER 2

Bartels, Andreas; Zeki, Semir, 'The Neural Basis of Romantic Love', *Neuroreport*, 11(17), 3829–34, 27 November 2000.

Chen, Denise; Haviland-Jones, Jeannette, 'Human Olfactory

Communication of Emotion', *Perceptual and Motor Skills*, 91(3, Pt. 1), 771–81, December 2000.

Chen, Denise; Haviland-Jones, Jeannette, 'Rapid Mood Change and Human Odors', *Physiology & Behavior*, 68(1–2), 241–50, December 1999.

Jones, John T.; Pelham, Brett W.; Carvallo, Mauricio; Mirenberg, Matthew C., 'How Do I Love Thee? Let Me Count the Js: Implicit Egotism and Interpersonal Attraction', *Journal of Personality & Social Psychology*, 87(5), 683–85, November 2004.

Kanazawa, Satoshi; Kovar, Jody L., 'Why Beautiful People Are More Intelligent', *Intelligence*, 32(3), 227–43, 2004.

Lewis, Michael (ed.); Haviland-Jones, Jeannette (ed.), *Handbook of Emotions* (2nd edition), xvi, 720ff, 2000 (New York, NY, US, Guilford Press).

Madan, Anmol; Caneel, Ron; Pentland, Alex, 'Voices of Attraction', September 2004, submitted to AugCog Symposium of HCI, 2005.

Meston, Cindy M., Ph.D.; Frohlich, Penny F. M. A., 'Love at First Fright: Partner Salience Moderates Roller-Coaster-Induced Excitation Transfer', *Archives of Sexual Behavior*, 32(6), 537–44, December 2003.

Murrell, Audrey J.; Frieze, Irene Hanson; Olsen, Josephine E., 'Mobility Strategies and Career Outcomes: A Longitudinal Study of MBAs', *Journal of Vocational Behavior*, 49(3), 324–35, December 1996.

Pelham, Brett W.; Carvallo, Mauricio; DeHart, Tracy; Jones, John T., 'Assessing the Validity of Implicit Egotism: A Reply to Gallucci (2003)', *Journal of Personality & Social Psychology*, 85(5), 800–7, November 2003.

Sinclair, H. Colleen; Frieze, Irene Hanson, 'When Courtship

Persistence Becomes Intrusive Pursuit: Comparing Rejecter and Pursuer Perspectives of Unrequited Attraction', *Sex Roles*, 52(11–12), 839–52, June 2005.

Stapert, John C.; Clore, Gerald L., 'Attraction and Disagreement-produced Arousal', *Journal of Personality and Social Psychology*, 13(1), 64–9, 1969.

Tombs, Selina; Silverman, Irwin, 'Pupillometry: A Sexual Selection Approach', *Evolution and Human Behavior*, 25(4), 221–28, July 2004.

CHAPTER 3

Campbell, W. K.; Foster, C. A.; Finkel, E. J., 'Does Self-love Lead to Love for Others? A Story of Narcissistic Game Playing', *Journal of Personality and Social Psychology*, 83, 340–54, 2002.

Campbell, W. K.; Foster, C. A., 'Narcissism and Commitment in Romantic Relationships: An Investment Model Analysis', *Personality and Social Psychology Bulletin*, 28, 484–95, 2002.

Epley, Nicholas; Savitsky, Kenneth; Gilovich, Thomas, 'Empathy Neglect: Reconciling the Spotlight Effect and the Correspondence Bias', *Journal of Personality & Social Psychology*, 83(2), 300–12, August 2002.

Gilovich, Thomas; Medvec, Victoria Husted; Savitsky, Kenneth, 'The Spotlight Effect in Social Judgment: An Egocentric Bias in Estimates of the Salience of One's Own Actions and Appearance', *Journal of Personality & Social Psychology*, 78(2), 211–22, February 2000.

Masterson, James F. (ed.); Klein, Ralph (ed.), *Disorders of the Self: New Therapeutic Horizons: The Masterson Approach*, x, 435ff, 1995 (Philadelphia, PA, US, Brunner/Mazel, Inc.).

Mueller, Claudia M.; Dweck, Carol S., 'Praise for Intelligence Can Undermine Children's Motivation and Performance', *Journal of Personality & Social Psychology*, 75(1), 33–52, July 1998.

Savitsky, Kenneth; Epley, Nicholas; Gilovich, Thomas, 'Do Others Judge Us As Harshly As We Think? Overestimating the Impact of Our Failures, Shortcomings, and Mishaps', *Journal of Personality & Social Psychology*, 81(1), 44–56, July 2001.

CHAPTER 4

Campbell, W. K., 'Narcissism and Romantic Attraction', *Journal of Personality and Social Psychology*, 77, 1254–70, 1999.

Campbell, W. K.; Baumeister, R. F.; Dhavale, D.; Tice, D. M., 'Responding to Major Threats to Self-esteem: A Preliminary, Narrative Study of Ego-shock', *Journal of Social and Clinical Psychology*, 22, 79–96, 2003.

Campbell, W. K.; Bonacci, A. M.; Shelton, J.; Exline, J. J.; Bushman, B. J., 'Psychological Entitlement: Interpersonal Consequences and Validation of a New Self-report Measure', *Journal of Personality Assessment*, 83, 29–45, 2004.

Campbell, W. K.; Bush, C. P.; Brunell, A. B.; Shelton, J., 'Understanding the Social Costs of Narcissism: The Case of Tragedy of the Commons', *Personality and Social Psychology Bulletin* (in press).

Campbell, W. K.; Foster, C. A., 'Narcissism and Commitment in Romantic Relationships: An Investment Model Analysis', *Personality and Social Psychology*, 28, 484–95, 2002.

Campbell, W. K.; Foster, C. A.; Finkel, E. J., 'Does Self-love Lead to Love for Others? A Story of Narcissistic Game Playing', *Journal of Personality and Social Psychology*, 83, 340–54, 2002.

Campbell, W. K.; Goodie, A. S.; Foster, J. D., 'Narcissism, Confidence, and Risk Attitude', *Journal of Behavioral Decision Making*, 17, 297–311, 2004.

Campbell, W. K.; Rudich, E.; Sedikides, C., 'Narcissism, Self-esteem, and the Positivity of Self-views: Two Portraits of Self-love', *Personality and Social Psychology Bulletin*, 28, 358–68, 2002.

Finkel, E.; Campbell, W. K., 'Self-control and Accommodation in Close Relationships: An Interdependence Analysis', *Journal of Personality and Social Psychology*, 81, 263–77, 2001.

Twenge, J. M.; Campbell, W. K., 'Age and Birth Cohort Differences in Self-esteem: A Cross-temporal Meta-analysis', *Personality and Social Psychology Review*, 5, 321–44, 2001.

Twenge, J. M.; Campbell, W. K., '"Isn't it fun to get the respect that we're going to deserve?" Narcissism, Social Rejection and Aggression', *Personality and Social Psychology Bulletin*, 29, 261–72, 2003.

CHAPTER 5

Hönekopp, Johannes; Voracek, Martin; Manning, John T., '2nd to 4th Digit Ratio (2D:4D) and Number of Sex Partners: Evidence for Effects of Prenatal Testosterone in Men', *Psychoneuroendocrinology* (in press, corrected proof).

Kelly, S., Dunbar, R., 'Who Dares Wins: Heroism Versus

Altruism in Female Mate Choice', *Human Nature*, 12: 89–105, 2001.

Nyhus, Ellen, K.; Pons, Empar, 'The Effects of Personality on Earnings', *Journal of Economic Psychology* (forthcoming; published online at http://dx.doi.org doi:10.1016/j.joep. 2004.07.001).

Roney, James R., 'Effects of Visual Exposure to the Opposite Sex: Cognitive Aspects of Mate Attraction in Human Males', *Personality and Social Psychology Bulletin*, 29(3), 393–404, March 2003.

Roney, James Richard Jr, 'Psychological and Hormonal Responses of Men to Sensory Cues from Women', *Dissertation Abstracts International: Section B: The Sciences and Engineering*, 63(7–B), 3518, February 2002.

Roney, James R.; Maestripieri, Dario, 'Relative Digit Lengths Predict Men's Behavior and Attractiveness During Social Interactions with Women', *Human Nature*, 15(3), 271–82, 2004.

Roney, James R.; Mahler, Stephen V.; Maestripieri, Dario, 'Behavioral and Hormonal Responses of Men to Brief Interactions with Women', *Evolution and Human Behavior*, 24(6), 365–75, November 2003.

Waynforth, David, 'Mate Choice Trade-offs and Women's Preference for Physically Attractive Men', *Human Nature*, 12(3), 207–219, 2001.

Waynforth, David; Delwadia, Sonia; Camm, Miriam, 'The Influence of Women's Mating Strategies on Preference for Masculine Facial Architecture', *Evolution and Human Behavior*, 26(5), 409–16, September 2005.

CHAPTER 6

Andrews, Paul W., 'The Psychology of Social Chess and the Evolution of Attribution Mechanisms: Explaining the Fundamental Attribution Error', *Evolution and Human Behavior*, 22(1), 11–29, January 2001.

Barrett, Louise; Dunbar, Robin; Lycett, John, *Human Evolutionary Psychology*, xiv, 434ff, 2002, (Princeton, NJ, US, Princeton University Press).

Bond, Charles F. Jr; Omar, Adnan; Pitre, Urvashi; Lashley, Brian R.; Skaggs, Lynn M.; Kirk, C. T., 'Fishy-Looking Liars: Deception Judgment from Expectancy Violation', *Journal of Personality & Social Psychology*, 63(6), 969–77, December 1992.

Bond, Charles F. Jr; Thomas, B. Jason; Paulson, Rene M., 'Maintaining Lies: The Multiple-audience Problem . . .', *Journal of Experimental Social Psychology*, 40(1), 29–40, January 2004.

DePaulo, Bella M.; Lindsay, James J.; Malone, Brian E.; Muhlenbruck, Laura; Charlton, Kelly; Cooper, Harris, 'Cues to Deception', *Psychological Bulletin*, 129(1), 74–118, January 2003.

DePaulo, Bella M.; Kashy, Deborah A., 'Everyday Lies in Close and Casual Relationships', *Journal of Personality & Social Psychology*, 74(1), 63–79, January 1998.

Dunbar, Robin, 'Not by Genes Alone: How Culture Transformed Human Evolution', *Nature*, 432(7020), 951–2, 23 December 2004.

Ekman, Paul, 'Emotional and Conversational Facial Signals', *Otology & Neurotology. Abstracts from the 9th International Facial Nerve Symposium*, 23, Supplement 1:S106, 2002.

Ekman, Paul; Magee, John J.; Frank, Mark G., 'Psychology: Lie Detection and Language Comprehension', *Nature. Insight: Biodiversity*, 405(6783), 139, 11 May 2000.

Ekman, Paul; O'Sullivan, Maureen, 'Who Can Catch a Liar?', *American Psychologist*, 46(9), 913–20, September 1991.

Ekman, Paul; O'Sullivan, Maureen, 'Who Is Misleading Whom? A Reply to Nickerson and Hammond', *American Psychologist*, 48(9), 989–90, September 1993.

Frank, Mark G.; Ekman, Paul, 'Appearing Truthful Generalizes Across Different Deception Situations', *Journal of Personality & Social Psychology*, 86(3), 486–95, March 2004.

Hartwig, Maria; Granhag, Par Anders; Stromwall, Leif A.; Vrij, Aldert, 'Detecting Deception Via Strategic Disclosure of Evidence', *Law & Human Behavior*, 29(4), 469–84, August 2005.

Haselton, Martie G.; Nettle, Daniel; Andrews, Paul W., 'The Evolution of Cognitive Bias' in Buss, David M. (ed.), *The Handbook of Evolutionary Psychology*, 724–46, 2005 (Hoboken, NJ, US, John Wiley & Sons, Inc.), xxv, p. 1028.

Johnson, Amanda K.; Barnacz, Allyson; Yokkaichi, Toko; Rubio, Jennifer; Racioppi, Connie; Shackelford, Todd K.; Fisher, Maryanne L.; Keenan, Julian Paul, 'Me, Myself, and Lie: The Role of Self-Awareness in Deception', *Personality and Individual Differences*, 38(8), 1847–53, June 2005.

Sternglanz, R. Weylin; DePaulo, Bella M., 'Reading Nonverbal Cues to Emotions: The Advantages and Liabilities of Relationship Closeness', *Journal of Nonverbal Behavior*, 28(4), 245–66, 2004.

Vrij, Aldert, 'Why Professionals Fail to Catch Liars and How They Can Improve', *Legal & Criminological Psychology*, 9(2), 159–181, September 2004.

Vrij, Aldert; Mann, Samantha, 'Detecting Deception: The Benefit of Looking at a Combination of Behavioral, Auditory and Speech Content Related Cues in a Systematic Manner', *Group Decision & Negotiation*, 13(1), 61–79, January 2004.

CHAPTER 7

Fink, B.; Penton-Voak, I. S., 'Evolutionary Psychology of Facial Attractiveness', *Current Directions in Psychological Science*, 11, 154–58, 2002.

Hennessy, Robin J.; McLearie, Stephen; Kinsella, Anthony; Waddington, John L., 'Facial Surface Analysis by 3D Laser Scanning and Geometric Morphometrics in Relation to Sexual Dimorphism in Cerebral-craniofacial Morphogenesis and Cognitive Function', *Journal of Anatomy*, 207(3), 283–95, September 2005.

Hinsz, V. B., 'Facial Resemblance in Engaged and Married Couples', *Journal of Social and Personal Relationships*, 6, 223–29, 1989.

Keating, Caroline F.; Doyle, James, 'The Faces of Desirable Mates and Dates Contain Mixed Social Status Cues', *Journal of Experimental Social Psychology*, 38(4), 414–24, July 2002.

Keating, Caroline F.; Randall, David W.; Kendrick, Timothy; Gutshall, Katharine A., 'Do Babyfaced Adults Receive More Help? The (Cross-cultural) Case of the Lost Resume', *Journal of Nonverbal Behavior*, 27(2), 89–109, Summer 2003.

Mazur, Allan; Booth, Alan, 'Testosterone and Dominance in Men', *Behavioral and Brain Sciences*, 21(3), 353–97, June 1998.

Mazur, Allan; Mueller, Ulrich, 'Facial Dominance' in Somit, A.

and Peterson, S. (eds), *Research in Biopolitics*, Vol. 4, 99–111, 1996 (London, JAI Press).

Penton-Voak, Ian S.; Chen, Jennie Y., 'High Salivary Testosterone is Linked to Masculine Male Facial Appearance in Humans', *Evolution and Human Behavior*, 25(4), 229–41, July 2004.

Perrett, David I.; Burt, D. Michael; Penton-Voak, Ian S.; Lee, Kieran J.; Rowland, Duncan A.; Edwards, Rachel, 'Symmetry and Human Facial Attractiveness', *Evolution and Human Behavior*, 20(5), 295–307, September 1999.

Pettijohn, Terry F. II, 'Relationships Between U.S. Social and Economic Hard Times and Popular Motion Picture Actor Gender, Actor Age, and Movie Genre Preferences', *North American Journal of Psychology*, 5(1), 61–66, 2003.

Pettijohn, Terry F. II; Tesser, Abraham, 'History and Facial Features: The Eyes Have It for Actresses but not for Actors', *North American Journal of Psychology*, 5(3), 335–43, 2003.

Pettijohn, Terry F. II; Tesser, Abraham, 'Threat and Social Choice: When Eye Size Matters', *Journal of Social Psychology*, 145(5), 547–70, October 2005.

Slater, Alan, 'Visual Perception in the Newborn Infant: Issues and Debates', *Intellectica*, 34, 57–76, 2002.

Zebrowitz, Leslie A.; Montepare, Joann M., 'Appearance DOES Matter', *Science*, 308(5728), 1565–66, 10 June 2005.

Zebrowitz, Leslie A.; Olson, Karen; Hoffman, Karen, 'Stability of Babyfaceness and Attractiveness Across the Life Span', *Journal of Personality & Social Psychology*, 64(3), 453–66, March 1993.

Zebrowitz, Leslie A.; Rhodes, Gillian, 'Sensitivity to "Bad Genes" and the Anomalous Face Overgeneralization Effect: Cue Validity, Cue Utilization, and Accuracy in Judging

Intelligence and Health', *Journal of Nonverbal Behavior*, 28(3), 167–85, 2004.

CHAPTER 8

Braun, Devra L.; Sunday, Suzanne R.; Huang, Amy; Halmi, Katherine A., 'More Males Seek Treatment for Eating Disorders', *International Journal of Eating Disorders*, 25(4), 415–24, May 1999.

Brewis, Alexandra A., 'The Accuracy of Attractive Body-size Judgement', *Current Anthropology*, 40(4), 548–53, August–October 1999.

Lynch, Shawn M.; Zellner, Debra A., 'Figure Preferences in Two Generations of Men: The Use of Figure Drawings Illustrating Differences in Muscle Mass 1', *Sex Roles*, 40(9–10), 833–43, 10 May 1999.

Manson, J. E.; Willett, W. C.; Stampfer, M. J., 'Body Weight and Mortality Among Women', *New England Journal of Medicine*, 333(11), 677–85, 1995.

Mishkind, Marc E.; Rodin, Judith; Silberstein, Lisa R.; Striegel-Moore, Ruth H., 'The Embodiment of Masculinity: Cultural, Psychological, and Behavioral Dimensions' in Kimmel, Michael S. (ed.), *Changing Men: New Directions in Research on Men and Masculinity*, 37–52, 1987 (Thousand Oaks, CA, US, Sage Publications, Inc.), 320ff.

Singh, Devendra, 'Body Shape and Women's Attractiveness: The Critical Role of Waist-to-hip Ratio', *Human Nature*, 4(3), 297–321, 1993.

Singh, Devendra, 'Is Thin Really Beautiful and Good? Relationship Between Waist-to-hip Ratio (WHR) and Female Attractiveness', *Personality and Individual*

Differences, 16(1), 123–32, January 1994.

Spitzer, Brenda L.; Henderson, Katherine A.; Zivian, Marilyn T., 'Gender Differences in Population Versus Media Body Sizes: A Comparison Over Four Decades', *Sex Roles,* 40, 7–8, 1999.

Stice, E., 'Risk and Maintenance Factors for Eating Pathology: A Meta-analytic Review', *Psychological Bulletin,* 128, 825–48, 2002; ibid, 40(7–8), 545-65, 20 April 1999.

Tovée, Martin J.; Mason, Suzanne M.; Emery, Joanne L.; McCluskey, Sara E.; Cohen-Tovée, Esther M., 'Supermodels: Stick Insects or Hourglasses?', *Lancet,* 350(9089), 1474–75, 15 November 1997.

Tovée, Martin J.; Hancock, Peter J. B.; Sasan Mahmoodi, Sasan; Singleton, Ben, R. R.; Cornelissen, Piers, L., 'Human Female Attractiveness: Waveform Analysis of Body Shape', *Proceedings of the Royal Society B: Biological Sciences,* 269: 1506, November 7, 2002, 2205–13.

Vaughan, Kimberley K.; Fouts, Gregory T., 'Changes in Television and Magazine Exposure and Eating Disorder Symptomatology', *Sex Roles,* 49(7–8), 313–20, October 2003.

Yu, D. W.; Shepard, G. H. Jr, 'Is Beauty in the Eye of the Beholder?', *Nature,* 396, 321–22, 1998.

CHAPTER 9

Baumeister, Roy F., 'Gender Differences in Erotic Plasticity: The Female Sex Drive as Socially Flexible and Responsive', *Psychological Bulletin,* 126(3), 347–74, May 2000.

Baumeister, Roy F.; Sommer, Kristin L., 'What Do Men Want? Gender Differences and Two Spheres of Belongingness:

Comment on Cross and Madson (1997)', *Psychological Bulletin,* 122(1), 38–44, July 1997.

Bogaert, Anthony F., Ph.D., 'Sibling Sex Ratio and Sexual Orientation in Men and Women: New Tests in Two National Probability Samples', *Archives of Sexual Behavior,* 34(1), 111–16, February 2005.

Bogaert, A. F.; Hershberger S., 'The Relation Between Sexual Orientation and Penile Size', *Archives of Sexual Behavior,* 213–21, June 1999.

Gallup, Gordon G. Jr, Ph.D.; Burch, Rebecca L., BS; Platek, Steven, MBA, 'Does Semen Have Antidepressant Properties?', *Archives of Sexual Behavior,* 31(3), 289–93, June 2002.

Holmes T.; Chamberlin P.; Young M., 'Relations of Exercise to Body Image and Sexual Desirability Among a Sample of University Students', *Psychol Rep.,* 74, (3:1), 920–22, June 1994.

Manning, J. T.; Trivers, R. L.; Singh, D.; Thornhill, R., 'The Mystery of Female Beauty', *Nature,* 399(6733), 214–15, 20 May 1999.

Montorsi, Piero; Ravagnani, Paolo M.; Galli, Stefano; Rotatori, Francesco; Briganti, Alberto; Salonia, Andrea; Deho, Federico; Montorsi, Francesco, 'Common Grounds for Erectile Dysfunction and Coronary Artery Disease', *Current Opinion in Urology,* 14(6), 361–5, November 2004.

Pinnock, Carol B.; Stapleton, Alan M. F.; Marshall, Villis R., 'Erectile Dysfunction in the Community: A Prevalence Study', *Medical Journal of Australia,* 171, 353–57, 1999.

Rellini, A.; McCall, K. M.; Randall, P. K.; Meston, C. M., 'The Relationship Between Self-reported and Physiological Measures of Female Sexual Arousal', *Psychophysiology,* 42, 116–124, 2005.

CHAPTER 10

Allen, Elizabeth S.; Atkins, David C.; Baucom, Donald H.; Snyder, Douglas K.; Gordon, Kristina Coop; Glass, Shirley P., 'Intrapersonal, Interpersonal, and Contextual Factors in Engaging in and Responding to Extramarital Involvement', *Clinical Psychology: Science & Practice*, 12(2), 101–30, Summer 2005.

Benedict, Jeffrey R., *Athletes and Acquaintance Rape*, xiii, 105ff, 1998 (Thousand Oaks, CA, US, Sage Publications, Inc.).

Benedict, Jeffrey; Klein, Alan, 'Arrest and Conviction Rates for Athletes Accused of Sexual Assault' in Bergen, Raquel Kennedy (ed.), *Issues in Intimate Violence*, 69–175, 1998 (Thousand Oaks, CA, US, Sage Publications, Inc.), xiii, p. 314.

Booth, A.; Dabbs, J., 'Testosterone and Men's Marriages', *Social Forces*, 72, 463–77, 1993.

Burack, Richard D., 'Relationships Between Temperament and Levels of Social and Nonsocial Cognitive Development in Children', *Dissertation Abstracts International*, 39(8–B), 4003, February 1979.

Buss, D. M.; Shackelford, T. K., 'Susceptibility to Infidelity in the First Year of Marriage', *Journal of Research in Personality*, 31, 193–221, 1997.

Charles, Kathy E.; Egan, Vincent, 'Mating Effort Correlates with Self-reported Delinquency in a Normal Adolescent Sample', *Personality and Individual Differences*, 38(5), 1035–45, April 2005.

Egan, Vincent; Angus, Sarah, 'Is Social Dominance a Sex-specific Strategy for Infidelity?', *Personality and Individual Differences*, 36(3), 575–86, February 2004.

Egan, Vincent; Figueredo, Aurelio Jose; Wolf, Pedro; McBride, Kara; Sefcek, Jon; Vasquez, Geneva; Charles, Kathy, 'Sensational Interests, Mating Effort, and Personality: Evidence for Cross-Cultural Validity', *Journal of Individual Differences*, 26(1), 11–19, 2005.

Foss, Jeffrey, *Science and the Riddle of Consciousness: A Solution*, xiii, 225ff, 2000 (New York, NY, US, Kluwer Academic/Plenum Publishers).

Gordon, Kristina Coop; Baucom, Donald H., 'Forgiveness and Marriage: Preliminary Support for a Measure Based on a Model of Recovery from a Marital Betrayal', *American Journal of Family Therapy*, 31(3), 179–99, May–June 2003.

Julian, Teresa; McKenry, Patrick C., 'Relationship of Testosterone to Men's Family Functioning in Mid-Life', *Aggressive Behavior*, 15, 281–89, 1989.

Mazur, Allan; Booth, Alan, 'The Biosociology of Testosterone in Men' in Franks, David D. and Smith, Thomas S. (eds), *Mind, Brain, and Society: Toward a Neurosociology of Emotion*, Vol. 5., 311–38, 1999 (US, Elsevier Science/JAI Press), viii, 358.

Mazur, Allan; Booth, Alan, 'Testosterone and Dominance in Men', *Behavioral and Brain Sciences*, 21(3), 353–97, June 1998.

Mazur, Allan; Michalek, Joel, 'Marriage, Divorce, and Male Testosterone', *Social Forces*, 77(1), 315–30, September 1998.

Mikach, Sarah M.; Bailey, J. Michael, 'What Distinguishes Women with Unusually High Numbers of Sex Partners?', *Evolution and Human Behavior*, 20(3), 141–50, May 1999.

Rhodes, G.; Simmons, L. W.; Peters, M., 'Attractiveness and Sexual Behavior: Does Attractiveness Enhance Mating

Success?', *Evolution and Human Behavior*, 26, 186–201, 2005.

Scheib, Joanna E., 'Context-specific Mate Choice Criteria: Women's Trade-offs in the Contexts of Long-term and Extra-pair Mateships', *Personal Relationships*, 8(4), 371–89, December 2001.

Scheib, Joanna E., 'The Psychology of Female Choice in the Context of Donor Insemination', *Dissertation Abstracts International: Section B: The Sciences and Engineering*, 58(6–B), 3306, December 1997.

Schmitt, David P.; Buss, David M., 'Human Mate Poaching: Tactics and Temptations for Infiltrating Existing Mateships', *Journal of Personality & Social Psychology*, 80(6), 894–17, June 2001.

Seldin, Daniel R.; Friedman, Howard S.; Martin, Leslie R., 'Sexual Activity as a Predictor of Life-span Mortality Risk', *Personality and Individual Differences*, 33(3), 409–26, August 2002.

Zentner, Marcel R., 'Ideal Mate Personality Concepts and Compatibility in Close Relationships: A Longitudinal Analysis', *Journal of Personality & Social Psychology*, 89(2), 242–56, August 2005.

Zweigenhaft, Richard L., 'Birth Order Effects and Rebelliousness: Political Activism and Involvement with Marijuana', *Political Psychology*, 23(2), 219–33, June 2002.

Zweigenhaft, Richard L.; Von Ammon, Jessica, 'Birth Order and Civil Disobedience: A Test of Sulloway's "Born to Rebel" Hypothesis', *Journal of Social Psychology*, 140(5), 624–27, October 2000.

CHAPTER 11

Cherlin, A. J., *Marriage, Divorce, Remarriage*, 1981 (Cambridge, MA, Harvard University Press).

Constantine, J. A.; Bahr, S. J., 'Locus of Control and Marital Stability: A Longitudinal Study', *Journal of Divorce*, 4, 11–22, 1980.

Emery, R. E., *Marriage, Divorce, and Children's Adjustment*, 1988 (Newbury Park, California, Sage).

Gottman, J. M., *Marital Interaction: Experimental Investigations*, 1979 (San Diego, California, Academic Press).

Gottman, John M.; Driver, Janice L., 'Dysfunctional Marital Conflict and Everyday Marital Interaction', *Journal of Divorce & Remarriage*, Vol. 43: 3–4, 63–78, 2005.

Gottman, J. M.; Krokoff, L. J., 'The Relationship Between Marital Interaction and Marital Satisfaction: A Longitudinal View', *Journal of Consulting and Clinical Psychology*, 57, 47–52, 1989.

CHAPTER 12

Aron, Arthur; Norman, Christina C.; Aron, Elaine N.; McKenna, Colin; Heyman, Richard E., 'Couples' Shared Participation in Novel and Arousing Activities and Experienced Relationship Quality', *Journal of Personality & Social Psychology*, 78(2), 273–84, February 2000.

Cappeliez, Philippe, 'Presentation of Depression and Response to Group Cognitive Therapy with Older Patients', *Journal of Clinical Geropsychology*, 6(3), 165–74, July 2000.

Duindam, Vincent; Spruijt, Ed, 'Father's Health in Relation to Spousal Employment', *Patient Education and Counseling*, 57(1), 46–52, April 2005.

Fisher, Helen E., Ph.D.; Aron, Arthur, Ph.D.; Mashek, Debra, MA; Li, Haifang, Ph.D.; Brown, Lucy L., Ph.D., 'Defining the Brain Systems of Lust, Romantic Attraction, and Attachment', *Archives of Sexual Behavior*, 31(5), 413–19, October 2002.

Fraley, Barbara; Aron, Arthur, 'The Effect of a Shared Humorous Experience on Closeness in Initial Encounters', *Personal Relationships*, 11(1), 61–78, March 2004.

Levenson, Robert W.; Carstensen, Laura L.; Gottman, John M., 'Long-Term Marriage: Age, Gender, and Satisfaction', *Psychology & Aging*, 8(2), 301–13, June 1993.

Murray, Sandra L.; Holmes, John G., 'The (Mental) Ties That Bind: Cognitive Structures That Predict Relationship Resilience', *Journal of Personality & Social Psychology*, 77(6), 1228–44, December 1999.

Murray, Sandra L.; Holmes, John G.; Bellavia, Gina; Griffin, Dale W.; Dolderman, Dan, 'Kindred Spirits? The Benefits of Egocentrism in Close Relationships', *Journal of Personality & Social Psychology*, 82(4), 563–81, April 2002.

O'Rourke, Norm; Cappeliez, Philippe, 'Marital Satisfaction and Self-deception: Reconstruction of Relationship Histories Among Older Adults', *Social Behavior and Personality*, 33(3), 273–82, 2005.

Pasupathi, Monisha; Carstensen, Laura L.; Levenson, Robert W.; Gottman, John M., 'Responsive Listening in Long-Married Couples: A Psycholinguistic Perspective', *Journal of Nonverbal Behavior*, 23(2), 173–93, 1999.

Sillars, Alan L.; Burggraf, Cynthia S.; Yost, Susan; Zietlow, Paul H., 'Conversational Themes and Marital Relationship Definitions: Quantitative and Qualitative Investigations',

Human Communication Research, 19(1), 124–54, September 1992.

Zietlow, Paul H.; Sillars, Alan L., 'Life-stage Differences in Communication During Marital Conflicts', *Journal of Social and Personal Relationships*, 5(2), 223–45, May 1988.

CHAPTER 13

Carrere, Sybil; Buehlman, Kim T.; Gottman, John M.; Coan, James A.; Ruckstuhl, Lionel, 'Predicting Marital Stability and Divorce in Newlywed Couples', *Journal of Family Psychology*, 14(1), 42–58, March 2000.

Carstensen, Laura L.; Gottman, John M.; Levenson, Robert W., 'Emotional Behavior in Long-term Marriage', *Psychology & Aging*, 10(1), 140–9, March 1995.

Cook, Julian; Tyson, Rebecca; White, Jane; Rushe, Regina; Gottman, John; Murray, James, 'Mathematics of Marital Conflict: Qualitative Dynamic Mathematical Modeling of Marital Interaction', *Journal of Family Psychology*, 9(2), 110–30, June 1995.

Gottman, John Mordechai, 'Psychology and the Study of Marital Processes', *Annual Review of Psychology*, 49(1998), 169–97, Annual 1998.

Pasupathi, Monisha; Carstensen, Laura L.; Levenson, Robert W.; Gottman, John M., 'Responsive Listening in Long-Married Couples: A Psycholinguistic Perspective', *Journal of Nonverbal Behavior*, 23(2), 173–93, 1999.

CHAPTER 14

Brockman, Hilke; Klein, Thomas, 'Familienbiographie und Mortalität in Ost-und Westdeutschland', *Zeitschrift für Gerontologie und Geriatrie*, 35, 430–40, 2002.

Cialdini, Robert B.; Goldstein, Noah J., 'Social Influence: Compliance and Conformity', *Annual Review of Psychology*, 55, 591–621, 2004.

Cialdini, Robert B.; Sagarin, Brad J., 'Principles of Interpersonal Influence' in Brock, Timothy C. and Green, Melanie C. (eds), *Persuasion: Psychological Insights and Perspectives*, 2nd ed., 143–169, 2005 (Thousand Oaks, CA, US, Sage Publications, Inc.), xi, 353ff.

Jones, John T.; Pelham, Brett W.; Carvallo, Mauricio; Mirenberg, Matthew C., 'How Do I Love Thee? Let Me Count the Js: Implicit Egotism and Interpersonal Attraction', *Journal of Personality & Social Psychology*, 87(5), 665–83, November 2004.

Koyama, N. F.; McGain, A.; Hill, R. A., 'Self-reported Mate Preferences and "Feminist" Attitudes Regarding Marital Relations', *Evolution and Human Behavior*, 25(5), 327–35, September 2004.

Martikainen, P.; Martelin, T.; Nihtilä, E.; Majamaa, K.; Koskinen, S., 'Differences in Mortality by Marital Status in Finland from 1976 to 2000: Analyses of Changes in Marital-status Distributions, Socio-demographic and Household Composition, and Cause of Death', *Population Studies*, 59:1, 99–115, 2005.

Modin, Bitte, 'Born Out of Wedlock and Never Married – It Breaks a Man's Heart', *Social Science & Medicine*, 57(3), 487–501, August 2003.

Pelham, Brett W.; Carvallo, Mauricio; DeHart, Tracy; Jones, John T., 'Assessing the Validity of Implicit Egotism: A Reply to Gallucci (2003)', *Journal of Personality & Social Psychology*, 85(5), 800–7, November 2003.

Tower, Roni Beth, Ph.D.; Kasl, Stanislav V., Ph.D.; Darefsky, Amy S., MPH, Ph.D., 'Types of Marital Closeness and Mortality Risk in Older Couples', *Psychosomatic Medicine*, 64(4), 644–59, July/ August 2002.

INDEX

Ache of Paraguay 39
activities, exciting 276–9
adultery *see* infidelity
adultery scale 237–43
age
    and incompatibility 253
    younger partners 244–6
agenda building 285
agreement/disagreement 67–8
Ali, Muhammad 195
Alias, Aikarakudy 194–5
alternative scenarios 160
amenorrhoea 191
American Economic Review
    40
Andrews, Paul 156–7
anger, in marriage 287–8,
    292–4, 260–61
Aniston, Jennifer 33
Annis, Francesca 244
anorexia nervosa 181, 188–9
anxiety 92, 97, 124

*Archives of Sexual
    Behaviour* 69, 199
arguing phase 285
arguments, productive
    288–92
Aristophanes 311
Arizona State University
    183
Arkansas, University of
    207
Aron, Arthur 276–7
Asperger's Syndrome 157
Association of European
    Psychiatrists, Eighth
    Congress 194
atherosclerosis 202–3
attraction, theory of 129–30,
    132–3
attractiveness scale 44–9
Auckland, New Zealand
    184
autism 152

avoidance, anxious 124
avoidant personality 95–7

babies 167–8, 171–2
baby-faced features 169–71
    in men 193
background, of partners
    251–2
'bad hair day' 71–2
Balzac, Honoré de, The
    Human Comedy 169
Bartels, Andreas, and Zeki,
    Semir 50–4
Baumeister, Roy 208
BBC 18–20, 42–4
beauty 33–44
    associated with
        intelligence and
        goodness 37–43, 173
    comparative 34–5
    and earnings 40–1
    and health 39, 168
    and number of sexual
        partners 232
    and shape of jaw 173–5
    symmetry as factor in
        perception of 39, 41–2,
        167
    universal standard of
        168–77
    valued by men 38, 232
    valued by women 214,
        217, 229, 232
blind dates 164
blonde women, preference
    for 169
body building 180
body hair, and intelligence
    194–5
body image 44–9, 179
body language 111, 210
    and deception 150, 156,
        160
body mass index (BMI)
    189–92
    and mortality 191
body shape and appearance
    169–96
    female 180–3
    and incompatibility 252
    male 21–2, 178–2, 192
    portrayed in media 182–4
    preferences in 169,
        178–96
    statistics 179–82, 188–9,
        191–2
    stereotyped views of 193
body weight 181–2
Bogaert, Anthony, and
    Hersberger, Scott 197–8
Booth, Alan, and Dabbs,
    James 224–5
boredom 276–7, 278
brain, affected by love 52–5
Brandeis University, USA
    173
Braun, Devra 179
bravery 134–40
breast feeding 154
Bremen University 310
Brewis, Alexandra 184
British Medical Association
    183
Brockmann, Hilke, and
    Klein, Thomas 310
'broken record' technique 117

brush-off 114–18
bulimia 188–9
Burton, Richard 33
Buss, David, and
    Shackelford, Todd 144–5,
    227–8

Calgary University, Canada
    182
California, University of 185
    Physical Education
        Department 206
Callaghan, James and
    Audrey 307
Campbell, Keith 98
career satisfaction 126
Carnegie Mellon University
    104
Carvallo, Mauricio 65–6, 68
Case Western Reserve
    University, USA 208
Cash, Johnny and June 308
Central Lancashire,
    University of 128
Chamberlain, Neville 151
charm 111–14
charm scale 111–14
Chicago, University of 129
childhood, unstable, and
    promiscuity 214, 230, 231
children
    and marital relationship
        241, 242
    parents' praise of 99–100
    perspective of 73
Chinese 39
Churchill, Winston 196
Claremont Graduate

University, California,
    Centre for
    Neuroeconomic Studies
    154
Clinton, Bill 34, 223
Clinton, Hillary 34
cocooning 80–1
Collins, Joan 244
Columbia University 99, 305
comfort zone 91–7
commitment 26–30
    to marriage 241, 243
communication
    'low risk, low disclosure'
        269
    perceived breakdown of
        298–9
comparison, material 119–20
compatibility 311–14
    see also incompatibility
compliments 109, 112, 114,
    143, 243
condom use, and depression
    in women 199–201
confidence, social 76–85
    scale 81–5
confrontations 292–5, 300
control, in sexual
    relationships 216–17
conversation 63–4, 76–7,
    79–80
    gambits in 102–3
    timing in 77
Cookson, Tom and
    Catherine 307–8
Corey, Irwin 70
Cornell University Hospital,
    New York 179

cosmetics 64–5
Crawford, Cindy 33
crisis, and compatibility 250
critical statements 285

Darwin, Charles 195
dating programmes, TV 97, 98
Davis, Bette 171
deception in relationships
    146–53, 156–63
delusional thinking 270–4
denial
    of marital problems 297–8
    of partner's deception 147
dependency 29, 59
depression
    and marriage 305–6
    in men, and loss of libido
        204–5
    in women, and condom
        use 199–201
diabetes 203
Diaz, Cameron 244
dieting 48, 49
disaster voyeurism 120–1
divorce 34, 246, 279, 284–8
    emotional 297–304
doctors
    and hairy chests 194
    seductiveness of 133–4
    as whipping boys of
        media 183
Durham, University of 130
Dressler, Marie 171

eating disorders 188–9
    media and 183–4
    in men 179

Egan, Vincent, and Angus,
    Sarah 228–30
egotism, implicit 65–9
Einstein, Albert 195
embarrassment
    over medical
        examinations 125–6
    social 71–6, 93–4
emotional divorce scale
    301–4
emotional support 249–50,
    258, 306–7
equity theory 296–7
erectile dysfunction 201–5
    as physical problem 204
evolution 175
    theory of 130, 176
Evolution and Human
    Behaviour 130, 212
exercise
    excessive 179
    and sex life 206–7
Exeter, University of 167
'exit' affair 236
expectations, raised 23
eye contact 150
eyes, large 169–70

faces
    attraction to 164–77
    and brain structure 172–3
    resemblances 165–7
facial characteristics
    dominant 173–4
    familiar 166
    measurements 130–1
    and testosterone levels
        129–31

facial expressions, recognition
    of 54
fantasies, sexual 216
Fatal Attraction 222
FBI 149
fertility
    and body shape 184–6,
        187–8, 191–2
    declining 21
Fiennes, Ralph 244
finger length
    and penis size 198
    and testosterone level
        128–9
flattery 102–3
flirting 35, 101–6, 111,
    113–14, 114–15
Foster, Craig, and Finkel, Eli
    104
Fouts, Gregory, and
    Burggraf, Kimberley 182
Frasier 182
Freud, Sigmund 139, 245,
    279
Friends 182
friends
    interdependence of 89
    number of 87
friendship 85–90
    of convenience 123–4
    maintenance of 90, 311
    opposite-sex 86
Frieze, Irene 40
Frost, Sadie 244
Furnham, Adrian 186

Gallup, Gordon 199
gambles, taking 124–5

game playing (ludus) 104–5
Garland, Judy 171
Gaynor, Janet 171
gaze aversion 149–50
gender differences 20–1
Georgia State University
    224
Georgia, University of 98,
    104, 170, 184
Gere, Richard 33
Gilovich, Thomas, Medvec,
    Victoria, and Savitsky,
    Kenneth 70–6
Gottman, John 285–8
Gottman Institute 284–8
group living, and trust 154,
    155

hairy chests 194–5
Hamermesh, Daniel, and
    Biddle, Jeff
    'Beauty and the Labor
        Market' 40
    'Beauty, Productivity, and
        Discrimination:
        Lawyers' Looks and
        Lucre' 41
happiness level 275
Hayworth, Rita 171
heart disease
    and erectile dysfunction
        201–3
    and spousal bereavement
        308
Heidelberg, University of
    310
height, male 192
help, asking for 103–4

Helsinki, University of,
Population Research Unit
307–8
Hennessy, Robin, and
Waddington, John 172–3
heroism 134–40
Hinsz, Verlin 165, 167
Hitler, Adolf 151, 193
Holmes, Dr 207
homosexuals
and penis size 197–8
and sex drive 208
honesty 195–6
hormones 54,128–31,
154–5, 173–4, 198, 223–7
in semen 200
see also testosterone
humour, sense of 109
hunting, among primitive
tribes 139
hypothalamus 54

Illinois, University of 67
illusions, positive 270–4
impact, in relationships 144
Imperial College London 185
incompatibility 248–59
time bombs 251–3
independence 89
in women 144
India 194
Indiana University 197
inferiority, feelings of 83–4
infidelity 98, 105, 141,
144–5, 146–7, 151,
227–43, 248, 249
in business travellers 146,
232–5

detection of 234–7
suspicion of 234–5
intelligence, valued by
women 38
intimacy, physical 59

Johnson, Amanda, and
Keenan, Julian Paul 147
Jones, Bridget, effect 220
Jones, John 66
*Journal of Labour
Economics* 41
*Journal of Personality and
Social Psychology* 66, 97
Journal of Sex Research 35
Julian, Teresa, and McKenry,
Patrick 227

Kanazawa, Satoshi 34, 37
and Kovar, Jody, 'Why
Beautiful People Are More
Intelligent' 38, 39–41, 42,
43
Kasparov, Garry 195
Keating, Caroline, and
Doyle, James 175
Kelly, Susan, and Dunbar,
Robin 135–40
Khan, Jemima and Imran
33
kindness, in sexual
relationships 136, 141
kindred spirits 274
Kinsey Institute of Sex
Research 197
kitchen-sinking 291

The Lancet 188

league table, in marriage
    market 36–7
Leeds University 142
Leeson, Nick 125
Li, Suling 206–7
liars 147–52
libido, loss of 204
lie detection 146–53
lifestyle, of partners 252
lighting, low 62
likeability, and deception
    162
Lincoln, Abraham 76
listening
    active 288
    behaviour 267–9, 288
Liverpool University 135
London School of Economics
    34, 37
longevity, in marriage 34
love
    adolescent 282
    adult stage 283
    capacity for 280–3
    companionate and
        passionate 56–62
    and compatibility 257–8
    effect on brain 52–5
    and familiarity 167
    forms of 50–1, 56
    infantile 282
    neurological basis 51–5
    psychological studies of
        32–3
    symptoms of 31
    as temporary psychosis 279
love map 259–65
love scale 255–9, 279–83

Loyola University, Chicago
    206
ludic lovestyle 240
Lulu 244
Lynch, Shawn, and Zellner,
    Debra 178–9

Madonna 244
magnetic resonance imaging
    (MRI) techniques 52
Manilow, Barry 71
Manning, John T. 128, 198
Marburg, University of 173
marital aggrandizement
    271–2
marital disagreements
    284–304
marital therapy 266–7, 275,
    297
marriage 305–11
    parallel 306
    patterns 245, 259–60
masculinity
    archetypes of 180
    in women 215
Massachusetts Institute of
    Technology, Affective
    Computing Lab 63
Massachusetts, University of
    168
Masterson, James 100
masturbation, in men and
    women 208
matching hypothesis 166–7
mate poaching 217–23
Mate Value Discrepancy
    (MVD) 144–5
materialism 120

Maudsley Hospital 145
Max Planck Institute of
    Human Development,
    Centre for Lifespan
    Psychology 267
Mazur, Allan, and Michalek,
    Joel 225
media, portrayal of body
    shapes 182–4
menopause 21
Mensa 195
menstrual cycle, and facial
    features 176
Meston, Cindy, et al 207
    'Love at First Fright' 69
Michigan State University 40
Mikach, Sarah, and Bailey,
    Michael 212–15
Milan, University of,
    Institute of Cardiology
    202
Miller, Geoffrey 41–2
Mills and Boon 133
Mind, Theory of 20–1, 54,
    151–3
Mishkind, Marc 179–81
Miss America pageant 181
mistakes, learning from
    162–3
models, fashion and glamour
    181, 188–90
moderation, in male arousal
    63–4
Monroe, Marilyn 171
Montclair University, New
    Jersey, Cognitive
    Neuroimaging Laboratory
    147–8, 152

Montorsi, Pietro 202–4
Moore, Demi 244
mortality rate, and spousal
    bereavement 307–11
Mr Right, recognizing
    247–59, 311–14
Mueller, Claudia, and Dweck,
    Carol 99
Mueller, Ulrich, and Mazur,
    Allan 173
Murray, Sandra 273–4
muscularity 179–81

Napoleon I, Emperor 193
Napoleon Syndrome
    192–3
narcissism 99–100
    and flirting 104–5
natural selection 63
Nature 185
negotiation phase 285
neighbours, friendship with
    123–4
network theory 86–7
neuroeconomics 153–4
Neuroreport 52
neuroscience 50–5
New Mexico, University of,
    Albuquerque 41, 156
New York Times 100
Newcastle City Eating
    Disorder Service 189
Newcastle University,
    Department of Psychology
    187
newlyweds 272
Nietzsche, Friedrich 31
no, saying 116

North Dakota State
    University 165
Northwestern University,
    Illinois 212

obesity 186
Office for National Statistics
    245
Ohio State University 227,
    268
older couples 259–283
    secrets of success 269–70
one-night stands 213, 216
operational closeness 242
O'Rourke, Norm, and
    Cappeliez, Philippe 272
Ottawa, University of 272
ovulation 64–5
oxytocin, and trust 154–5

Paltrow, Gwyneth 244
parallel relationship 265
parent–child relationships
    279
Pasupathi, Monisha 267
penis size 196–9
Pennsylvania State University
    35, 37, 195
Pentland, Sandy 63
Penton-Voak, Ian 164–5,
    176
Perfect Match 97
Perrett, David 176
personalities, in marriage
    312–14
Personality and Individual
    Differences 147, 152
personality profiles, male 137

personality test 26–30
Peru 185
pessimism, over relationships
    259
Pettijohn, Terri, and Tesser,
    Abraham 170–1
photographic images 165,
    168, 173
    manipulated 164–5,
    176–7
Pinnock, Carole 206
Pitt, Brad 33
Pittsburgh, University of 40
plastic surgeons,
    seductiveness of 132–3
Plato, The Symposium 311
Playboy 181–2, 188
Playgirl 181
polarization hypothesis
    181
Pollyannas 273
Portsmouth, University of
    149
post-conflict conversation
    287
Potter, Dennis and Margaret
    308
praise 109, 143
preconceptions, awareness of
    161
pregnancy, risk of 63
Previti, Denise, and Amato,
    Paul 35
problem-solving discussions
    269
promiscuity
    in men 213–43
    in women 212–43

psychiatrists, seducing 25
psychological tips 24–5
puberty, male 198
pupils, dilated 62

quality time 275–6
questions
    open-ended 108
    unexpected 161–2

Reagan, Ronald 156
rebound conversation
    287
regrets of omission 75
rejection, social
    avoidance of 95–7
    fear of 92, 93–5
relationships
    hierarchy of 124
    and high testosterone
        levels 130
    quality of 276–9
relaxation 106
Repatriation General
    Hospital, Adelaide 206
repeated exposure hypothesis
    166
reproductive strategy 131,
    213, 220–1, 229, 231
Rhodes, Gillian 231–2
risk-taking 135–40, 140–2,
    153, 308–9
romance novels 133
Roney, James 129
Roseanne 182
Royal College of Surgeons,
    Dublin, Research Unit
    172

St Andrews University,
    Scotland 176
Samoa 184
satisfaction, marital 272–4
Scheib, Joanna 229
schizophrenia 151–2, 173
Schmitt, David, and Buss,
    David 217, 219–33
Schwarzenegger, Arnold
    180
score keeping, emotional
    299–300
scripts 93–5
Secret Service (US) 149
Seinfeld 182
selectivity, sexual, in women
    214, 217, 229
self-awareness, in deception
    152
self-centredness 262
self-concept threat 67–9
self-consciousness 70–6
self-criticism 117
self-deception mechanism
    271
self-disclosure 108
    to friends 89–90
self-esteem 44–9, 62
    and fear of rejection
        92–3
    friendship as aid to 88
    and infidelity 98–9,
        230–1
    and mate poaching 222
    negative views of
        97–100
    and promiscuity in
    women 214

self-help books 97–8
Sellers, Peter 195
semen, mood-altering
    hormones in 200
Seneca 156
sensitivity 118
Seven Deadly Emotions
    118–27
sexuality
    hormones and 54,
        128–31, 155
    number of partners 128,
        212–43, 232, 253
    peaks, male and female
        246
    response, exercise-related
        206–7
    sex life discussed between
        partners 208–11
    tension 86, 92–3
    women's preferences
        129–32, 215, 217,
        229
Shepard, Glenn 185
Sheridan, Ann 171
short-cuts 159
shyness
    combating 75–81
    cynical 79
Singh, Devendra 35
Slater, Alan 167
sleeping around 212–43
small talk skills 106–10
Social Behaviour and
    Personality 271
solutions, focusing on 295
speed-dating 18–20, 63–4
spotlight effect 70–6

reverse 74
Stallone, Sylvester 180
Stapert, John, and Clore,
    Gerald 67–8
start-up phase (in dispute)
    285–6
State University of New York
    66, 199, 273
statistics
    body shape and
        appearance 179–82,
        188–9, 191–2
    marriage patterns 245
    mate poaching rates
        218–9
status
    and incompatibility 251
    valued by women 21,
        140
Stendhal, Le Rouge et le
    Noir 169–70
Stice, Eric 183
Stirling, University of,
    Scotland 164
stonewalling (listener
    withdrawal) 286
stress, men's approach to
    142–3
suicide, female 199
surgery, cosmetic 195–6
symmetry, as factor in
    perception of beauty 39,
    41–2
Syracuse University 225

tact 118
Taylor, Bayard 128
Taylor, Elizabeth 33

techniques, seduction 20
technology, new 78
testosterone
    in athletes 226
    and dominance over
        others 223–7
    high levels of 128–31,
        173–4, 198
    and marriage and divorce
        224–6
    and penis size 198
    in prison inmates 223–4
    in semen 200
Texas, University of 40, 69,
    227
therapy
    as confrontation 96
    narcissists and 100
    undergone by clinicians
        126
Timberlake, Justin 244
Tombs, Selina, and
    Silverman, Irwin 62–3
Tomorrow's World, Mega
    Lab experiment 42
Tovée, Martin 187–92
Tower, Roni 305–6
toy boys 244–6
track record, and
    incompatibility 253
trust 153–7, 230, 231
    games 154, 157
TV dramas, medical
    133
Twin Towers attack 135
two-person-exchange
    environments 153
Tyson, Mike 195

Ugandans 186
United States Air Force
    Academy 104
United States Military
    Academy, West Point
    173
University College, London,
    Wellcome Department of
    Neuroimaging 50
unselfishness 136–8, 141

vocal pitch 64
Vrij, Aldert 149
vulnerabilities 158

waist-to-hip ratio (WHR)
    184–5
Washington, University of,
    Seattle, Department of
    Psychiatry 207
Waynforth, David 130
wedding-day nerves
    247–8
Western Australia, University
    of 231–2
'what if' questions 122
White, Dr 206
'Who Dares Wins' study
    135–40
    advice from 141–2
widowhood 309, 311
Williams College, USA 71
Williams, Robin 195
win-win solutions 294–5
withdrawal, emotional
    286
Would Like To Meet 97

Yale University 179, 305
Yomybato tribe 185
York University, Toronto 62, 181
younger partners 244–6
Yu, Douglas 185

Zak, Paul 153–4
Zebrowitz, Leslie 173–4
Zietlow, Paul, and Sillars, Alan 268
Zivian, Marilyn 181

THE MOTIVATED MIND
How to get what you want from life
by Dr Raj Persaud

- *Do you make New Year resolutions? . . .* Almost all of us do, because we want to achieve positive personal change. But did you know that most resolutions are repeated five years in a row?

- *Have you ever dieted? . . .* If diets work, why do we need so many? The answer lies in our belief that the latest approach will be the one that finally works – although we may be suffering from what psychologist term 'False Hope Syndrome'.

- *Do you constantly strive to fulfil your dreams? . . .* We seem to be obsessed with advantage and disadvantage, fairness and the level playing field, without realizing that it's our inner drive, motivation and the ability to overcome obstacles that are central to any success strategy.

In *The Motivated Mind*, award-winning author and psychiatrist Dr Raj Persaud investigates the latest scientific research on this fascinating subject, and he comes to some surprising conclusions. As he shows how most incentive schemes actually demotivate, and why the brain pursues happiness, he also reveals how, ultimately, it is an intriguing mind strategy that will help you get what you want from life.

'The proof of the pudding is in the eating, and Raj's direct application of his motivational theories to three case-studies on our programme was an unqualified success. The plan works!'
Richard & Judy, Channel 4

9780553813456

BANTAM BOOKS

THE MIND: A USER'S GUIDE
Consultant editor Dr Raj Persaud

We are supposed to be living in enlightened times, yet more people than ever are suffering from mental health problems. In fact statistics show . . .

One in four of us will experience some kind of mental health disorder in the course of our life
One in six will suffer from depression – most commonly between the ages of 25 and 44
One in ten people are likely to suffer from disabling anxiety at some stage in their life

The Mind: A User's Guide aims to inform and empower anyone who has experience of a mental health problem, or who has an interest in safeguarding or improving their own emotional well-being. Edited by Dr Raj Persaud, with contributions from distinguished experts, this invaluable guide has been published in collaboration with the Royal Collage of Psychiatrists. It provides accessible, jargon-free information on the latest research into brain and mind sciences, and gives distinctive descriptions of behaviour, feelings and thoughts relating to a wide variety of conditions.

In addition to clarifying and helping us to understand symptoms, treatments and therapies, *The Mind* also challenges the stigma so often associated with mental health issues, and the damaging myths and misconceptions that may prevent people from seeking professional help.

Given how common mental health problems are throughout our lifespan, *The Mind: A User's Guide* could prove to be the most valuable reference book you own

9780593056356

NOW AVAILABLE FROM BANTAM PRESS

BANTAM PRESS